By the same author

Manpower Policies for Youth
(co-editor, with Eli E. Cohen)

THE

WHITE

MAJORITY

Between Poverty and
Affluence

THE
WHITE
MAJORITY

Between Poverty and

Affluence

EDITED BY

LOUISE KAPP HOWE

Random House  *New York*

Acknowledgment is gratefully extended to the following for permission to reprint from their works:

American Jewish Committee, for *Why Can't They Be Like Us?* by Andrew M. Greeley. Copyright © 1969, by Institute of Human Relations Press, the American Jewish Committee. All rights reserved.

The American Scholar, for "Respectable Bigotry," by Michael Lerner, Volume XXXVIII, Number 4, Autumn, 1969. Copyright © 1969 by the United Chapters of Phi Beta Kappa. Originally published in *The New Journal,* a student publication at Yale University.

Columbia University Forum, for "Blue-Collar Families," by Mirra Komarovsky, Fall, 1964.

Commentary, for "Is There a New Republican Majority?" by Andrew Hacker. Copyright © 1969 by the American Jewish Committee.

Dissent, for "Middle Class Workers and the New Politics," by Brendan Sexton, May-June, 1969.

Marvin Josephson Associates, for "Revolt of the White Lower-Middle Class," by Pete Hamill, Copyright © 1969, by New York Magazine Co.

The Macmillan Company, for *Political Ideology,* by Robert E. Lane, Copyright © 1962 by The Free Press of Glencoe, a Division of The Macmillan Company.

Kim Moody, for "The American Working Class in Transition." Reprinted by permission of the author; originally published in complete form by International Socialists, 874 Broadway, New York, 1969.

New Generation, for "The Exploitation of Working Women," by Joan Jordan; "Sharing the Burden of Change," by S. M. Miller; "A Black View of the White Worker," by James Boggs; "Working-Class Youth: Alienation Without an Image," by William Simon, John H. Gagnon and Donald Carns; and "Labor: The Anti-Youth Establishment," by Lewis Carliner, Copyright © 1969 by National Committee on Employment of Youth.

Newsday, Inc., for "Life With Cappelli on $101 a Week," by Harvey Aronson, May 24, 1969, issue of *Newsday;* "How They Get Away From It All," by Gurney Williams and Jerry Parker, May 24, 1969, issue of *Newsday.*

Political Science Quarterly, for "Work Life and Political Attitudes," by Lewis Lipsitz, Copyright © 1966 by the Academy of Political Science.

Trans-action, for "Why Men Fight," by Charles C. Moskos, Jr., November, 1969, and "The Wallace Whitelash" by Seymour Martin Lipset and Earl Raab, December, 1969. Copyright © 1969 by *Trans*-action Magazine, New Brunswick, N.J.

Library of Congress Catalog Card Number: 70–117683

MANUFACTURED IN THE UNITED STATES OF AMERICA

BY THE H. WOLFF BOOK CO.

3 5 7 9 8 6 4 2

FIRST EDITION

FOR *Charlie*

ACKNOWLEDGMENTS

At last a chance to thank in print S. M. Miller, who for years has given me so many fine ideas; this book is one of them and I am indebted to him for urging me to do it. I am also enormously grateful to a number of people for their encouragement, advice and criticism: among them, Eli E. Cohen, Georgia Griggs, Joseph Kolman, Patricia Simon, Dan DeWees, Pamela Roby, William Simon, Charles Howe, Judy Herman and Anita Gross. And thanks to Alice Mayhew for her enthusiasm and expert editing. And to Theresa Massi for her typing labors. And most of all to the authors whose contributions form the body of this book.

Contents

PART 1

A MAN AND
A PHENOMENON

INTRODUCTION

Not so long ago—it only seems so long ago—in 1967 when black power was a new and startling phrase, a strange series of public rituals were held in New York. They generally took place on weekend evenings and they were officially termed debates. For four or more hours wounded white liberals would plead on stage with bitter black militants to be allowed to remain in the movement. Not only would the militants not budge, they would grow colder and angrier with each appeal for friendship, and before the evening had ended they would often storm out—to return to the real world where the roles of blacks and whites were naturally quite a bit different.

But I remember one evening when the script changed. A very tall, very young black man, whose name I never caught, went to the mike and quietly addressed the panel and the largely white audience: "Look," he said, "if you whites are really our friends and are so anxious to help us, why haven't you ever done anything to change the minds of all of your people who want us stopped? Instead of always telling us what strategy is right or wrong for blacks, isn't it time you worked out a way to keep the whites of this nation from pushing us into a police state? Pretty soon it may be too late."

The audience hardly reacted. And the panel immediately returned to yet another volley over whether the dangers of black separation were more numerous than the obstacles to integration. For myself, I remember being quite moved by what he had said but at a loss to know what could be done. It wasn't until the next year, after watching democracy at work at the Chicago convention and learning that the majority of whites had supported the police, that it became clear that if there were no answers now, they had better be found. It wasn't necessary to have the added proof in November of Wallace's strength and Nixon's victory to see that the young black man's fears were being confirmed. If the majority of whites had not yet moved to the far right, many were obviously on the way. And as the majority would go, so would go the nation.

This book stems from an issue of *New Generation* I edited at the time. The goal is the same: to learn more about the people who comprise the majority of the country, how they live, what forces are compelling them to the right and what, if anything, can be done to turn them around.

Certain facts are clear. Despite the focus in the media on the affluent and the poor, the average man is neither. Despite the concentration on TV commercials on the blond, blue-eyed WASP, the real American prototype is of Italian or Irish or Polish or Greek or Lithuanian or German or Hungarian or Russian or any one of the still amazing number of national origins represented in this country—a "white ethnic," sociologists soberly call him.

"He is the ordinary employee in the factory and in the office," says Robert C. Wood. Comprising half the nation's families, "he forms the bulk of the nation's working force. He makes five to ten thousand dollars a year; has a wife and two children; owns a house in town—between the ghetto and the suburbs or perhaps in a low-cost subdivision on the urban fringe; and he owes plenty in installment debts on his car and appliances. He finds his tax burden heavy, his neighborhood services poor . . ."

And, during the 1960's, says Richard Nixon, he was "forgotten." But, stop here: Is that really the case? Rather it seems closer to the facts to say he was ignored—consciously, carefully and, many believed, necessarily ignored. With pressures from civil rights groups mounting in the sixties, and the old reliable liberal coalition apparently intact, officials of the Kennedy and Johnson administrations considered it politically possible and, what's more, crucial to move at last on behalf of those most in need, the black and the poor, without waiting any longer to assuage the fears and prejudices of those one notch higher on the economic ladder. Attitudes would change, civil rights supporters argued, only when the objective conditions of segregation and discrimination had ended. In the meantime, they counseled, and to a limited extent the officials complied, meet fear with fear. Force integration of schools and housing and employment opportunities under threat of punishment.

The fact that it was not the middle- and upper-income groups who were asked to bear the major burden of change did not at the time seem, as they say, relevant. It just happened to be the schools and neighborhoods and jobs and autonomy of the white lower-middle class and working class that were most affected. And later when many of the same groups of affluent white liberals and radicals denouncing discrimination began to also denounce the Vietnam war, it just happened to be the sons of the lower-middle class and working class who—along with blacks—were doing the bulk of the American fighting, the "murdering" and the dying. It did not seem relevant to those of us protesting, but to

George Wallace and his close observer Richard Nixon, the consequent resentment and anger of the white majority were supremely important issues. They were as supreme as the first Tuesday after the first Monday in November.

None of this is to imply that the policies and protests against discrimination, poverty and the Vietnam war should have been relaxed in the slightest in the sixties. The tragedy is that they were not strong and persuasive enough to be more effective. At the same time, if many of those pushing for change had not been so out of touch with the needs and fears of the working class, it is possible that the protests could have been framed more carefully to show it was not the white individual who was under personal attack and that policies could have been shaped to give the white majority a reward for social change. As it was, with a policy of all stick and no carrot, it was natural that whites would resist change that appeared to be coming at their total expense. It would have been against their apparent self-interest to do anything else.

And out of touch with the working class most intellectuals and professionals have truly become. More than that, many have become too contemptuous to care. For example, in discussing this book with a number of people—intellectuals of genuine compassion who would be the first to avoid any easy generalization about blacks or youth—I found many telling me the the same thing about the average American: He's simply a boor and a bigot, a racist and fascist. Later of course came the new view from the Potomac: He's the forgotten American, the silent member of the silent majority, the common man. I'm not sure which of these two attitudes is really more offensive: the open contempt of the first or the condescension of the second. Both would seem to make understanding impossible in any case. Amid all the epithets and bromides, it is difficult to hear the breath of a living workingman.

. . .

To be sure, if one had wanted to know more about the day-by-day life of the average workingman only a year ago, it would have been difficult to find much in current writing to draw from. One could sit in an air-conditioned city apartment and become a virtual expert on life in a decimated Indian reservation, a hippie commune in the mountains, a steaming ghetto tenement—there were books and books to inform you. But there would have been next to nothing to show you what it was like to live on the wages of a mailman in Corona less than a half-hour's drive away. Only the recent mail strike has begun to bring that home.

The first aim of this book, then, is to provide some of the feel as well as the hard facts about life for most white Americans today: growing up, going to school, hanging around, going to war, going to work, marrying, raising children, settling down, getting by. Just barely getting by.

Part of the reason for the general lack of understanding of workers' problems may be that we are so used to hearing public issues defined in upper-middle-class terms. We all know, for example, that inflation has made many an affluent man tighten his belt, but we have heard very little about what it has meant for the workingman who never loosened his belt in the first place.

Moreover, say the words "alienation" and "drugs" and "generation gap" and you immediately conjure up an image of affluent rebelling youth in the suburbs and on campus. But, as a number of the authors in this book reveal, we have barely begun to realize that alienation is every bit as present among working-class youth in schools, in factories and in dubious battle in Indochina, and that pot and harder drugs have now completely crossed class lines. If affluent youth are being pushed by their horror of America to the left, working-class youth—it would seem from the Wallace statistics at least—are being pushed to the right.

Finally, say the words "women's liberation" and you generally think of a movement for affluent educated women who have learned that marriage can be a burden in disguise for those who forsake their individuality and talent for *Kinder, Kirche, Küche*. Yet a much stronger case could be made, as Mirra Komarovsky shows, for a movement to protest "blue-collar marriage" where the concept of friendship and equality between husband and wife is now as rare as the working-class husband who would be caught doing the weekly wash. And for those women who—to expand the family budget, not for self-fulfillment—spend their days in factories and offices, the exploitation by males is even more severe.

There is a danger, I know, of subsuming under one broad title like "The White Majority" (or, for that matter, "The Silent Majority") people of infinite variety who, like Walt Whitman and everyone else, contradict themselves, who contain multitudes. All generalizations are to some degree incorrect. In Part Three of the book, however, we do try to break down some of the major differences—in income, ethnicity, occupation, sex and age—and learn how the impact of these differences affect people's attitudes toward each other, their tolerance or intolerance for other groups and their political beliefs in general.

In the final section the authors look at the various strategies—Southern and otherwise—now being proposed by the different suitors for the vote of the white majority. They make some political predictions as well as suggesting what needs to be done.

The key question, says S. M. Miller, is whether the objective is "only to abate some of the flames of antiblack anger or to improve the position of a group which is nibbling at the edges of affluence." If the objective is the first, we can expect to find politicians on all sides tempering or terminating their attacks on discrimination and segregation. And to a tragic degree, that is what is happening at present. If, however, the objective is to reach real people with real grievances, we will have to understand far more about them before we can expect to stop their move to the right. That, I believe, is what the young black man in New York was asking us to do. And that is the aim of this book.

L.K.H.

June 1970

THE REVOLT OF THE WHITE LOWER-MIDDLE CLASS

by Pete Hamill

Author and syndicated columnist, Pete Hamill describes himself as a son of the white working class.

They call my people the white lower-middle class these days. It is an ugly, ice-cold phrase, the result, I suppose, of the missionary zeal of those sociologists who still think you can place human beings on charts. It most certainly does not sound like a description of people on the edge of open, sustained and possibly violent revolt. And yet, that is the case. All over New York City tonight in places like Inwood, South Brooklyn, Corona, East Flatbush and Bay Ridge, men are standing around saloons talking darkly about their grievances, and even more darkly about possible remedies. Their grievances are real and deep; their remedies could blow this city apart.

The white lower-middle class? Say that magic phrase at a cocktail party on the Upper East Side of Manhattan and monstrous images arise from the American demonology. Here comes the murderous rabble: fat, well fed, bigoted, ignorant, an army of beer-soaked Irishmen, violence-loving Italians, hate-filled Poles, Lithuanians and Hungarians (they are never referred to as Americans). They are the people who assault peace marchers, who start groups like the Society for the Prevention of Negroes Getting Everything (S.P.O.N.G.E.), the people who hate John Lindsay and vote for George Wallace, presumably because they believe that Wallace will eventually march every black man in America to the gas chambers, sending Lindsay and the rest of the Liberal Establishment along with them. Sometimes these brutes are referred to as "the ethnics" or "the blue-collar types." But the bureaucratic, sociological phrase is white lower-middle class. Nobody calls it the working class any more.

But basically, the people I'm speaking about *are* the working class. That is, they stand somewhere in the economy between the poor—most of whom are the aged, the sick and those unemployable women and children who live on welfare—and the semiprofessionals and professionals who earn their way with talents or skills acquired through education. The working class earns its living with its hands or its backs; its members do not exist on welfare payment; they do not live in abject, swinish poverty, nor in safe, remote suburban comfort. They earn between five thousand and ten thousand dollars a year. And they can no longer make it in New York.

"I'm going out of my mind," an ironworker friend named Eddie Cush told me a few weeks ago. "I average about eighty-five hundred a year, pretty good money. I work my ass off. But I can't make it. I come home at the end of the week, I start paying the bills, I give my wife some money for food. And there's nothing left. Maybe, if I work overtime, I get fifteen or twenty dollars to spend on myself. But most of the time, there's nothin'. They take sixty-five dollars a week out of my pay. I have to come up with ninety dollars a month rent. But every time I turn around, one of the kids needs shoes or a dress or something for school. And then I pick up a paper and read about a million people on welfare in New York or spades rioting in some college or some fat welfare bitch demanding—you know, not askin', *demand-ing*—a credit card at Korvette's . . . I *work* for a living and *I* can't get a credit card at Korvette's . . . You know, you see that, and you want to go out and strangle someone."

Cush was not drunk, and he was not talking loudly, or viciously, or with any bombast; but the tone was similar to the tone you can hear in conversation in bars like Farrell's all over this town—the tone was quiet bitterness.

"Look around," another guy told me, in a place called Mister Kelly's on Eighth Avenue and 13th Street in Brooklyn. "Look in the papers. Look on TV. What the hell does Lindsay care about me? He don't care whether my kid has shoes, whether my boy gets a new suit at Easter, whether I got any money in the bank. None of them politicians gives a good goddam. All they worry about is the niggers. And everything is for the niggers. The niggers get the schools. The niggers get the new playgrounds. The niggers get nursery schools. And they get it all without workin'. I'm an ironworker, a connector; when I go to work in the mornin', I don't know if I'm gonna make it back. My wife is scared to death, every mornin', all day. Up on the iron, if the wind blows hard or the steel gets icy or I make a wrong step, bango, forget it, I'm dead. Who feeds my wife and kid if I'm dead? Lindsay? The poverty program? You know the answer: nobody. But the niggers, they don't worry about it. They take the welfare and sit out on the stoop drinkin' cheap wine and throwin' the bottles on the street. They never gotta walk outta the house. They take the money outta my paycheck and they just turn it over to some lazy son of a bitch who won't work. I gotta carry him on my back. You know what I am? I'm a sucker. I really am. You shouldn't have to put up with this. And I'll tell ya somethin'. There's a lotta people who just ain't gonna put up with it much longer."

It is very difficult to explain to these people that more than 600,000 of those on welfare are women and children; that one reason the black family is in trouble is because outfits like the Iron Workers Union have practically excluded blacks through most of their history; that a hell of a lot more of their tax dollars go to Vietnam or the planning for future wars than to Harlem or Bed-Stuy; that the effort of the past four or five years was an effort forced by bloody events, and that they are paying taxes to relieve some forms of poverty because of more than one hundred years of neglect on top of three hundred years of slavery. The working-class white man has no more patience for explanations.

"If I hear that four-hundred-years-of-slavery bit one more time," a man said to me in Farrell's one night, "I'll go outta my mind!"

One night in Farrell's, I showed the following passage by Eldridge Cleaver to some people. It is from the recently published collection of Cleaver's journalism: "The very least of your responsibility now is to compensate me, however inadequately, for centuries of degradation and disenfranchisement by granting peacefully—before I take them forcefully—the same rights and opportunities for a decent life that you've taken for granted as an American birthright. This isn't a request but a *demand* . . ."

The response was peculiarly mixed. Some people said that the black man had already been given too much, and if he still couldn't make it, to hell with him. Some said they agreed with Cleaver, that the black man "got the shaft" for a long time, and whether we like it or not, we have to do something. But most of them reacted ferociously.

"Compensate him?" one man said. "Compensate him? Look, the English ruled Ireland for seven hundred years, that's hundreds of years longer than Negroes have been slaves. Why don't the British government compensate me? In Boston, they had signs like 'No Irish Need Apply' on the jobs, so why don't the American government compensate *me?"*

In any conversation with working-class whites, you are struck by how the information explosion has hit them. Television has made an enormous impact on them, and because of the nature of that medium—its preference for the politics of theater, its seeming inability to ever explain what is happening behind the photographed image—much of their understanding of what happens is superficial. Most of them have only a passing acquaintance with blacks, and very few have any black friends. So they see blacks in terms of militants with Afros and shades, or crushed people on welfare. Television never bothers reporting about the black man who gets up in the morning, eats a fast breakfast, says goodbye to his wife and children, and rushes out to work. That is not news. So the people who live in working-class white ghettos seldom meet blacks who are not threatening to burn down America or asking for help or receiving welfare or committing crime. And in the past five or six years with urban rioting on everyone's minds, they have provided themselves (or been provided with) a confused, threatening stereotype of blacks that has made it almost impossible to suggest any sort of black-white working-class coalition.

"Why the hell should I work with spades," he says, "when they are threatening to burn down my house?"

The Puerto Ricans, by the way, seem well on the way to assimilation with the larger community. It has been a long time since anyone has written about the "Puerto Rican problem" (though Puerto Rican poverty remains worse than black poverty), and in white working-class areas you don't hear many people muttering about "spics" any more.

"At least the Puerto Ricans are working," a carpenter named Jimmy Dolan told me one night, in a place called the Green Oak in Bay Ridge. "They open a grocery store, they work from six in the mornin' till midnight. The P.R.'s are willing to work for their money. The colored guys just don't wanna work. They want the big Buicks and the fancy suits, but they jus' don't wanna do the work they have ta do to pay for them."

The working-class white man sees injustice and politicking everywhere in this town now, with himself in the role of victim. He does not like John Lindsay, because he feels Lindsay is only concerned about the needs of blacks; he sees Lindsay walking the streets of the ghettos or opening a privately financed housing project in East Harlem or delivering lectures about tolerance and brotherhood, and he wonders what it all means to *him*. Usually, the working-class white man is a veteran; he remembers coming back from the Korean War to discover that the GI Bill only gave him $110 a month out of which he had to pay his own tuition; so he did not go to college because he could not afford it. Then he reads about protesting blacks in the SEEK program at Queens College, learns that they are being paid up to $200 a month to go to school, with tuition free, and he starts going a little wild.

The working-class white man spends much of his time complaining almost desperately about the way he has become a victim. Taxes and the rising cost of living keep him broke, and he sees nothing in return for the taxes he pays. The Department of Sanitation comes to his street at three in the morning, and a day late, and slams garbage cans around like an invading regiment. His streets were the last to be cleaned in the big snowstorm, and they are now sliced up with trenches that could only be called potholes by the myopic. His neighborhood is a dumping ground for abandoned automobiles, which rust and rot for as long as six weeks before someone from the city finally takes them away. He works very hard, frequently on a dangerous job, and then discovers that he still can't pay his way; his wife takes a Thursday-night job in a department store and he gets a weekend job pumping gas or pushing a hack. For him, life in New York is not much of a life.

"The average working stiff is not asking for very much," says Congressman Hugh Carey, the Brooklyn Democrat, whose district includes large numbers of working-class whites. "He wants a decent apartment, he wants a few beers on the weekend, he wants his kids to have decent clothes, he wants to go to a ball game once in a while, and he would like to put a little money away so that his kids can have the education that he never could afford. That's not asking a hell of a lot. But he's not getting that. He thinks society has failed him and in a way, if he is white, he is often more alienated than the black man. At least the black man has his organizations, and can submerge himself in the struggle for justice and equality, or elevate himself, whatever the case might be. The black man has hope, because no matter what some of the militants say, his life is slowly getting better in a number of ways. The white man who makes seven thousand dollars a year, who is forty, knows that he is never going to earn much more than that for the rest of his life, and he sees things getting worse, more hopeless. John Lindsay has made a number of bad moves as mayor of this town, but the alienation of the white lower-middle class might have been the worst."

Carey is probably right. The middle class, that cadre of professionals, semiprofessionals and businessmen who are the backbone of any living city, are the children of the white working class. If they are brought up believing that the city government does not care whether they live or die (or how they live or die), they will not stay here very long as adults. They will go to college, graduate, marry, get jobs and depart. Right now, thousands of them are leaving New York, because New York doesn't *work* for them. The public schools, when they are open, are desperate; the private schools cost too much (and if they can afford private schools they realize that their taxes are paying for the public schools whose poor quality prevent them from using them). The streets are filthy, the air is polluted, the parks are dangerous, prices are too high. They end up in California, or Rahway, or Islip.

Patriotism is very important to the working-class white man. Most of the time he is the son of an immigrant, and most immigrants sincerely believe that the Pledge of Allegiance, the Star-Spangled Banner, the American flag are symbols of what it means to be Americans. They might not have to become rich in America, but most of the time they are much better off than they were in the old country. On "I am an American" Day they march in parades with a kind of religious fervor that can look absurd to the outsider (imagine marching through Copenhagen on "I am a Dane" Day), but that can also be oddly touching. Walk through any working-class white neighborhood and you will see dozens of veterans' clubs, named after neighborhood men who were killed in World War II or Korea. There are not really orgies of jingoism going on inside; most of the time the veterans' clubs serve as places in which to drink on Sunday morning before the bars open at 1 P.M. or as places in which to hold baptisms and wedding receptions. But they are places where an odd sort of know-nothingism is fostered. The war in Vietnam was almost never questioned until last year. It was an American war, with Americans dying in action, and it could not be questioned.

The reasons for this simplistic view of the world are complicated. But one reason is that the working-class white man fights in every American war. Large numbers of poorly educated blacks are rejected by the draft because they can't pass the mental examinations; the high numbers of black casualties are due to the disproportionate number of black career NCO's and the large number of blacks who go into airborne units because of higher pay. The working-class white man

and his brothers, sons and cousins only get deferments if
they are crippled; their educations, usually in parochial
schools, are good enough to pass Army requirements, but
not good enough to get them into the city college system
(which, being free, is the only kind of college they could
afford). It is the children of the rich and the middle class
who get all those college deferments.

While he is in the service, the working-class white hates it;
he bitches about the food, the brass, the living conditions; he
tries to come back to New York at every opportunity, even
if it means two fourteen-hour car rides on a weekend. But
after he is out, and especially if he has seen combat, a romantic glaze covers the experience. He is a veteran, he is a
man, he can drink with the men at the corner saloon. And
as he goes into his thirties and forties, he resents those who
don't serve, or bitch about the service the way he used to
bitch. He becomes quarrelsome. When he gets drunk, he
tells you about Saipan. And he sees any form of antiwar
protest as a denial of his own young manhood and a form of
spitting on the graves of the people he served with who died
in his war.

The past lives on. When I visit my old neighborhood, we
still talk about things we did when we were eighteen, fights
we had, and who was "good with his hands" in the main
events at the Caton Inn, and how great it was eating sand-
wiches from Mary's down near Oceantide in Coney Island.
Or we talk about the Zale-Graziano fights, or what a great
team the Dodgers were when Duke Snyder played center
field and Roy Campanella was the catcher, and what a
shame it was that Rex Barney never learned how to control
the fast ball. Nostalgia was always a curse; I remember one
night when I was seventeen, drinking beer from cardboard
containers on a bench at the side of Prospect Park, and one
of my friends said that it was a shame we were getting old,
that there would never be another summer like the one we

had the year before, when we were sixteen. It was absurd, of course, and yet it was true; the summer we were seventeen, guys we knew were already dying on the frozen ridges of Korea.

A large reason for the growing alienation of the white working class is their belief that they are not respected. It is an important thing for the son of an immigrant to be respected. When he is young, physical prowess is usually the most important thing; the guy who can fight or hit a ball or run with a football is initially more respected than the guy who gets good marks in school. But later, the man wants to be respected as a good provider, a reasonably good husband, a good drinker, a good credit risk (the worse thing you can do in a working-class saloon is borrow twenty dollars and forget about it, or stiff the guy you borrowed it from).

It is no accident that the two New York City politicians who most represent the discontent of the white working class are Brooklyn Assemblyman Vito Battista and Councilman Matty Troy of Queens. Both are usually covered in the press as if they were refugees from a freak show. (I've been guilty myself of this sneering, patronizing attitude toward Battista and Troy at times.) Battista claims to be the spokesman for the small homeowner and many small homeowners believe in him; but a lot of the people who are listening to him now see him as the spokesman for the small homeowner they would like to be. "I like Battista," a guy told me a couple of weeks ago. "He talks our language. That Lindsay sounds like a college professor." Troy speaks for the man who can't get his streets cleaned, who has to take a train and a bus to get to his home, who is being taxed into suburban exile; he is also very big on patriotism, but he shocked his old auditors at the Democratic convention in Chicago in 1968 when he supported the minority peace plank on Vietnam.

There is one further problem involved here. That is the failure of the literary intellectual world to fully recognize the existence of the white working class, except to abhor them. With the exception of James T. Farrell, no major American novelist has dealt with the working-class white man, except in war novels. Our novelists write about bull-fighters, migrant workers, screenwriters, psychiatrists, failing novelists, homosexuals, advertising men, gangsters, actors, politicians, drifters, hippies, spies and millionaires; I have yet to see a work of the imagination deal with the life of a wirelather, a carpenter, a subway conductor, an ironworker or a derrick operator. There hasn't been much inquiry by the sociologists; *Beyond the Melting Pot*, by Nathan Glazer and Pat Moynihan, is the most useful book, but we have yet to see an Oscar Lewis-style book called, say, *The Children of Flaherty*. I suppose there are reasons for this neglect, caused by a century of intellectual sneering at bourgeois values, etc. But the result has been the inability of many intellectuals to imagine themselves in the plight of the American white working man. They don't understand his virtues (loyalty, endurance, courage, among others). The result is the stereotype. Black writers have finally begun to reveal what it means to be black in this country; I suppose it will take a working-class novelist to do the same for his people. It is certainly a rich, complex and unworked mine.

But for the moment, it is imperative for New York politicians to begin to deal with the growing alienation and paranoia of the working-class white man. I really don't think they can wait much longer, because the present situation is working its way to the point of no return. The working-class white man feels trapped and, even worse, in a society that purports to be democratic, ignored. The tax burden is crushing him, and the quality of his life does not seem to justify his exertions. He cannot leave New York City because he can't afford it, and he is beginning to look for someone to blame. That someone is almost certainly going to be the black man.

This does not have to be the situation, of course. If the government were more responsive to the working-class white man, if the distribution of benefits were spread more widely, if the government's presence were felt more strongly in ways that benefit white communities, there would be a chance to turn this situation around. The working-class white man does not care if a black man gets a job in his union, as long as it does not mean the loss of his own job, or the small privileges and sense of self-respect that go with it. I mean it; I know these people, and know that they largely would not care what happens in the city if what happens has at least the virtue of fairness. For now, they see a terrible unfairness in their lives, and an increasing lack of personal control over what happens to them. And the result is growing talk of revolt.

The revolt involves the use of guns. In East Flatbush, and Corona, and all those other places where the white working class lives, people are forming gun clubs and self-defense leagues and talking about what they will do if real race rioting breaks out. It is a tragic situation, because the poor blacks and the working-class whites should be natural allies. Instead, the black man has become the symbol of all the working-class white man's resentments.

"I never had a gun in my life before," a thirty-four-year-old Queens bartender named James Giuliano told me a couple of weeks ago. "But I got me a shotgun, license and all. I hate to have the thing in the house, because of the kids. But the way things are goin', I might have to use it on someone. I really might. It's comin' to that. Believe me, it's comin' to that."

The working-class white man is actually in revolt against taxes, joyless work, the double standards and short memories of professional politicians, hypocrisy and what he considers the debasement of the American dream. But George Wallace received ten million votes in 1968, not all of them from red-necked racists. That should have been a warning, strong and clear. If the stereotyped black man is becoming the working-class white man's enemy, the eventual enemy might be the democratic process itself. Any politician who leaves that white man out of the political equation does so at very large risk. The next round of race riots might not be between people and property, but between people and people. And that could be the end of us.

PART 2

A DAY
IN THE LIFE

LIFE WITH CAPPELLI
ON $IOI A WEEK

---

by Harvey Aronson

Harvey Aronson is a staff writer for Newsday.

Eugene Cappelli, Jr., is driving home from work in the well-kept, second-hand Chevy II (a '63 with about 41,000 miles) that his parents gave him as a present last Christmas to replace a tottering '60 Studebaker. He is a pleasant-faced young man in a white shirt, tie and slacks and he still has on the white-lettered red badge that says "Gene–Psychiatric Asst." It's his badge of employment, and the salary that goes with it signifies his membership in the great army of the struggling class.

Cappelli works the 7:30 A.M. to 4 P.M. shift as an attendant at New York's Pilgrim State Hospital in Brentwood; he received a small raise recently and earns $200.75 every two weeks. That means he takes home $174.60, or about $87 a week. One reason he likes the job is that "it has satisfactions; you see results in people." And another reason is economic. "The idea is that the money's steady, even though it's low," he says. At twenty-nine, Cappelli, a high-school graduate and one-time Air Force jet mechanic, is intensely concerned with job security.

He has a variety of reasons for his concern. He has a special checking account that rarely has more than $200 in it,

and he has no savings account. He has a wife and two children, a $26-a-month life insurance policy, a $24-a-month
oil bill and a home in Ronkonkoma with a thirty-year mortgage. It's a six-room ranch with a full cellar, and it cost
$13,990 when he bought it new five years ago with a down
payment of $650. The monthly carrying charges were origi-
nally quoted at $104 but they were $118 by the time the
family moved in four months later, and now they are $141.
It's a sizable chunk for Cappelli and his wife, Andrea, who
is twenty-six and works part time as a teacher's aide at a
grade school just off her backyard for $2.10 an hour. Last
year, she made about $550, and their combined income was
$5,378. About $217 of that went for income taxes. (This
year they expect their income to be $5,500.)

With Andrea's average take-home pay added to her husband's the couple has a weekly cash income of $101, or
$404 a month for themselves and their children, Debbie,
six, and Sandy, five. Andrea says that after they take out for
the mortgage, life insurance, oil, electricity, phone and car
expenses, they have about $150 a month left for food, cloth-
ing, incidentals and medical care (they had been entitled to
Medicaid for the children, but won't be after June 1). "The
way I figure it," she says, "that is about a dollar twenty-five
per day a person, which is less than the amount some poor
people on welfare receive." In understanding the Cappellis'
situation, it is important to know that if they wanted to earn
a few hundred dollars less a year and to pay rent instead of
having a mortgage, they could probably qualify for welfare.
However, what is important is this: it wouldn't be part of
their life style.

They consider themselves working-class people but not
needy people, and it is a distinction that has to do with
pride. "It's the way I brought him up," says Cappelli's
mother, who works as an attendant with him at the new
Hempstead Psychiatric Division in Pilgrim State, and that's

part of the sociology. His mother also says that "you help your children," and that, too, is part of the sociology—Eugene and Andrea get help in the form of gifts from their parents. The car and their bedroom set from his parents, for example, and the refrigerator and the wallpaper and linoleum in Debbie's room from Andrea's parents. And their living-room furniture, which is twenty years old, once belonged to Andrea's grandmother. But they would break their backs before they asked the government to support them.

"Welfare?" says Gene Cappelli. "No, I can't sit back and try to get money. I can't see that it's mine. I went through that a little when I got out of the service and collected some unemployment insurance. People acted like they were doing you a big favor. I figured the hell with this. I like to feel self-sustaining."

"I'm not against welfare, but I think it's getting out of hand," says Andrea. "Everybody is moving to New York to get on welfare and we're paying for it. I don't mind people getting welfare who need it, and an awful lot really need it. But I don't feel that I should feel sorry for them. They have about as much as me and nobody feels sorry for me and I don't want them to. It wouldn't be fair for us to take it because Gene can work. Why should he sit home? And poor people, people who are in my bracket now, would have to support me."

So, it's time for the little people's luxury of self-respect as Gene Cappelli heads home to his share of the American dream—a chili dinner with his wife and children, time to read the paper, and a chance to watch TV on the nineteen-inch portable he and Andrea bought four years ago along with the kitchen table and the washing machine, after he received a $1,000 settlement in an auto accident case. They do a lot of family things—"Sometimes our life rotates around our children," says Andrea—like picknicking and going to the beach, and they get together with friends for coffee and cake and cards and Monopoly and conversation about kids and money, and they belong to a $7-a-year club that enables you to get one free meal for every one you buy at certain restaurants, and they have used the card twice in the last six months. About once every six months, Gene goes out with the boys. Two years ago, the Cappellis saw *The Arabian Nights* at Jones Beach, and they haven't gone to a movie for about a year. As Andrea says, "You can stay home and watch movies on television."

Instead, they talk and read. Andrea subscribes to *Woman's Day, Family Circle, True Story* and *Redbook,* and Gene likes *Popular Science* and *Popular Mechanics,* and they get *Life,* and listen to records—especially Sonny and Cher, The Righteous Brothers and the Tijuana Brass—and give the TV a workout. Andrea prefers quiz shows and he likes Westerns and anything else with action. At 11 P.M. they watch the news on Channel 7, and the real-life action gets Gene upset. "It's just the way the world's image is at this time," he says. "The war and all the unrest in the world. You know, if a lot of these higher-up people discussed some of this and tried to see it like the lower-class people, it might help. When you see the news, you don't see anything good any more."

"Things bother him more than they bother me," says Andrea. But she, too, knows the world is less than perfect. "When I was around seventeen," she says, smiling—she has brown hair and green eyes, and the smile brings out a dimple in her right cheek—"I said to my mother, 'What's wrong with this world?' My mother said, 'It's been this way all the time. You just never noticed.'"

The day starts at about 7 A.M. for Eugene and Andrea Cappelli, who have been married for eight years, and are young enough to dig rock 'n' roll, and old enough to be mystified by the disorder in the schools. "I think all those kids on those college campuses should be put over somebody's knee and spanked," says Andrea, who took a secretarial course at the Long Island Agricultural and Technical Institute for nine months after graduating from Newfield High School in Centereach. Gene, who put in a four-year Air Force hitch after graduating from Smithtown High, says, "They're holding back the ones who want to learn." It is relevant that the Cappellis compare student troubles to race problems. "I think there are a few militants who are making it bad for the rest of the people," says Andrea in discussing black unrest. "It's the same as with the students." She and Gene preface this by denying bias. "In the service," says Gene, "I had some very close friends who are colored people."

In the morning, Andrea gets Debbie ready for school and gives her breakfast—cereal or eggs—and makes coffee for her husband. About twice a week she drives him to work so she can have the car for the day. When she has the car, she uses it to shop or visit her mother or occasionally see a girl friend in Patchogue. She has a charge account that costs her $15 a month at Sears, but she does most of her shopping, both food and clothing, at Billy Blake's in Sayville. She spends $20 a week for food. "I don't know how she does it," says Gene. But Andrea knows exactly how she does it. "I spend like two hours doing the shopping," she says. "I have to make a list. I check the newspaper and go over the food ads. And I go over the shelves. You have to check the shelves and find out what you don't have enough of. You can't go in the store cold. If you do that, then you could spend forty dollars. And it's all mathematics. You have to sit for hours with your checkbook."

It is a Monday afternoon, and she is in her neat, well-cleaned living room talking about her budget. The family's two Siamese cats, Peppy and Samantha (who is still a kitten), are walking about, and Debbie and Sandy are playing outside. Andrea Cappelli, who married when she was eighteen ("In junior high, I wanted to be a nurse or a laboratory technician, but then in my senior year I met my husband, and I still wanted to do something with my life, but nothing that involved"), has just started the spaghetti sauce for supper. This particular night they are having spaghetti with meat sauce, Italian bread and salad. On Tuesday, they will probably have chili. If there is enough spaghetti left over, they will have that on Wednesday, or she will make a chuck pot roast. She has a two-and-a-half-pound roast and is hoping to get a soup out of it for another night. When she makes spaghetti, she uses a half pound of chopped meat for the sauce. She usually buys a pound of meat and freezes the rest for another night.

When it comes to buying meat, she says, "Anything over chuck steak is out. Chops, for instance, pork chops and lamb chops, are out. We eat a lot of chopped meat and a lot of fish. We have a lot of spaghetti and macaroni. And they won't drink the instant nonfat dry milk, but I use it in cooking, in puddings and things like that. And I invent things. I take some chopped meat and macaroni and a little garlic and throw it together. I love casseroles. And anything that's left over gets tossed in a pot."

She estimates that they spend $10 a month on clothing, although it is hard to figure. For instance, Debbie's shoes cost $10.99. The children, who are blond and healthy-looking, seem nicely clothed. It helps that there are hand-me-downs from Debbie to Sandy, and from an eight-year old niece to Debbie. As for her own clothes, Andrea says, "I have enough to keep me dressed." She buys dresses only when she needs them, usually for a special occasion, and spends from $10 to $15. Gene has bought only one suit since they were married, and it cost about $45. He wears sport jackets and slacks, and spends $15 or $20 on a sport coat when he needs one. The only things they feel guilty about spending money on are cigarettes. Both husband and wife are pack-a-day smokers, and the habit costs them about $15 a month.

Merchandise stamps help. "One day last week," she says, "I spent two hours in the Plaid Stamp store in Bay Shore. I got an ironing-board cover and sheets for the children's beds, and a vaporizer that was a baby present for a friend. I have a hangup about sheets. It's just a piece of cotton and I can't see spending three or four dollars for it."

When she's not shopping, she tries to get some housework done. In any case, the morning goes like quicksilver, and at 11 A.M. she has to be at her job as teacher's aide in a kindergarten class. On Mondays, a neighbor, Mrs. Barbara Roth, whose son is in Mrs. Cappelli's class, watches Sandy. The rest of the week, Andrea's mother, Mrs. Henry Brauns, watches the child either at the Cappelli home or at her own house in Centereach. At 2 P.M., Andrea gets home, finishes her cleaning and starts dinner. If she has the car, she picks up Gene at 4 P.M.

Is she happy? "Yes." Not that there aren't things she wants. She worries about being able to send her children to college, and she and Gene wouldn't mind having another child, but as she says, they couldn't afford one—"if we had more children right now, we'd be sunk."

But she feels her children have as much as she and Gene had when they were growing up (both of them come from working-class homes; her father is a radio technician for LILCO and Gene's father, who is convalescing from an operation, is a painter at Pilgrim State), and her own life is a busy one. "Before I started to work," she says, "I had times when I felt awful. Now my life is too full. I have a lot—a home, a car, two healthy kids, no big problems. I've known people that had a lot of money, and in some ways, I think they are not as well off as I am. I don't have this hangup about money."

A few minutes later, Debbie and Sandy come in with a friend and ask for oranges, and Mrs. Eugene Cappelli, Jr., laughs. "Okay," she says, "but it's still a week till payday."

When he got out of the Air Force, Gene Cappelli, who had been stationed in Las Vegas, came back to Long Island with his family. He did aircraft work at a couple of places but there wasn't any security. "I had two or three jobs like that," he says. "As long as they have a contract you work. But if you are the last one on the list, and they cut back, you lose the job. It's touch and go. We couldn't live like that." He also worked as a luggage handler and aircraft cleaner for American Airlines at Kennedy Airport, "but riding in every day was a strain on the car—it was fifty-two miles each way, and in the wintertime, forget it. I made a little more than I do now, but it went on the car and I wound up with less. And my father talked to me and said that I was foolish, that I should work at the hospital. With the state you have security—the job is always there." Cappelli spent a year and a half working in the narcotics division at Pilgrim before he was selected for the new Hempstead unit, which includes day patients and tries to provide a nonhospital atmosphere.

On a recent afternoon at the unit, Gene Cappelli is in the hall talking to patients. He is cool and very much at ease, and the patients seem to respond to him. "He's very good at his job," says Mrs. Judy McCollum, the nursing director. "Both he and his mother are very good."

Cappelli says he has aspirations for the future. "But it's hard to say how right now. I would like to try to better myself, but it's a little hazy right now."

Eugene and Andrea Cappelli are Lutheran, and their children attend Sunday School. For the most part, they vote

Republican—they voted for Richard Nixon last year, but not with any wild enthusiasm. Gene feels that unions are good and bad ("Working people have a right to ask for more money," he says, "but sometimes the unions are atrocious in their demands"), and he and his wife are as confused about the war as most Americans. "We can't walk out, but we have to do something else," says Andrea. And Gene says, "I don't have anything against these kids who don't want to get shot . . . And I don't think half the boys over there know what it's about. You don't know what's right and what's wrong."

They don't have it easy, but they get by. As Andrea says, they have healthy kids and they own their own home. Their house is on a 50-by-150-foot plot on Louis Kossuth Avenue in a comparatively uncrowded neighborhood of homes that range from small bungalows to large split-levels, and there are still a good many wooded areas around. E. J. CAPELLI, JR., it says in large black letters on the mailbox, and that means something.

At least to Gene Cappelli, it means something. Whether it means anything to the people who run the government is something he's not sure about. "It's hard to say whether the higher-ups care about us," he says. "They say so, but sometimes I don't really believe it. Unless they come down to the little guy's level, they don't really know how it is."

THE CAPPELLIS' MONTHLY INCOME AND EXPENSES

Eugene's monthly income	$403.50
Andrea's monthly income	56.00
Total income	459.50
Monthly expenditures	
State health insurance	$ 7.26
Social Security	19.36
State income tax	2.60
Federal income tax	25.08

Mortgage principal	16.95
Mortgage interest	62.20
Property taxes, insurance	61.85
Property tax deficiency	10.00
Life insurance	26.00
Oil	24.00
Electricity	9.00
Phone	6.00
Car maintenance	40.00
Entertainment	4.00
Cigarettes	15.00
Newspapers	1.20
Clothing	10.00
Credit charge	15.00
Food	80.00
Garbage collection	3.75
Medical expenses, drugs	12.00
Haircuts	4.00
Miscellaneous	4.25
Total expenses	$459.50

BLUE-COLLAR
MARRIAGES AND
FAMILIES

by Mirra Komarovsky

Mirra Komarovsky is professor of sociology at Barnard College, Columbia University. In addition to numerous articles in professional journals, she is author of The Unemployed Man and His Family, Women in the Modern World *and a book-length report,* Blue-Collar Marriage, *of the study she discusses in this article.*

In 1964, William Jovanovich wrote in the *Saturday Review* that "the working class as a proportionately large and socially identifiable segment of our society is all but disappearing" and that "the generic middle class now includes skilled and semiskilled laborers." Earlier than that, the United States Department of Labor asserted (*How American Buying Habits Change,* 1959) that "the wage earner's way of life is well-nigh indistinguishable from that of his salaried co-citizens. Their homes, their cars, their babysitters, the style of the clothes their wives and children wear, the food they eat, the bank where they establish credit, their days off . . . all of these are alike and are becoming more nearly identical."

Is it a valid assumption that because blue-collar workers

have acquired the buying habits of the salaried middle class, the way of life for both has become the same? Can we assume that a spread in patterns of "having" has been accompanied by a spread in ways of thinking, in values and attitudes? I do not think we can. I have recently completed, under a grant from the National Institute of Mental Health, a sociological study of blue-collar families, and I shall here record some of my impressions, especially as they contrast with those gained in my earlier studies among the college-educated.

For the study, sixty working-class couples were interviewed about their marriages—their ideals and expectations, their sexual relations, the marriage dialogue, the nature of friendship between the spouses, the differences between masculine and feminine roles, and ties with their relatives. Most of the couples interviewed were white Protestant and born of native parents. The average husband was a semiskilled worker in his early thirties, had less than a high school education, and earned wages of approximately eighty dollars a week. He and his wife had three children. They lived in an industrial community about fifteen miles from an Eastern metropolis.

The physical scene in which the blue-collar workers live is familiar enough. The homes are pleasant, if modest by middle-class standards; they are decorated with modern furniture and equipped with washing machines and television sets. But the intangible realm of values and attitudes is reminiscent of the past, for the blue-collar world is insulated from contemporary currents of thought. For example, in this age when even the children in middle-class families of college-educated parents prattle about inferiority complexes and mother fixations, the blue-collar parents have retained a pre-Freudian innocence about human behavior. Their concepts of child-rearing are few and simple. If they puzzle over the rebelliousness or obedience of their children, they seek the explanation in discipline, and wonder if they have been "too easy" with one who is rebellious; if that explanation fails, they decide it is because "he has his father's temper."

Incidentally, it is often alleged that the psychological advances of the twentieth century have robbed college-educated parents of self-confidence. College-educated parents do, in fact, report more frequent feelings of inadequacy than uneducated parents. But my respondents are far from complacent. Blue-collar mothers worry about their irritability and say, "It's real hard to know what to do; I shake and beat them and then I feel lousy." As a rule, they have not discovered Dr. Spock, and their guide is still the grandmother.

The goals of child-rearing are expressed in moral terms: "To bring up kids in a respectable manner, to live a decent life, honest and true." They do not speak of "emotional security," "creativity," "capacity to grow," or of "relating to others." These ideas, which middle-class parents get from college courses and child psychologists, from the magazines they read and the social gatherings they attend, have not yet reached the average blue-collar worker. As the interviews progressed, I felt further and further removed from the world of the twentieth century—transported as if by a Wellsian time machine into an older era.

For me, perhaps the most surprising aspect of the blue-collar world had to do not with manners and morals but with the cognitive style of the people. The interviews, which took six hours each, were meant to focus on psychological relationships, but the respondents almost without exception thought in terms of the situational and material conditions of life. My impressions coincide with those of the British observer Richard Hoggart, author of *The Uses of Literacy*, who wrote that the essence of working-class life is the

" 'dense and concrete' life, a life whose main stress is on the sensory, the detailed . . . (and) is characterized by a low level of abstraction."

To the standard question, "Does your husband have any favorites among the children?" my respondents frequently answered, "No; if he gets something for one kid, he always brings something for the other." "Think back over the past week or two. Has your husband done anything that hurt your feelings, made you mad, surprised you?" The word "surprise" was usually taken to mean an unexpected present. The word "help" meant money or services, not help in the psychological sense. "When you feel that way [low for no apparent reason] can your mother help you?" The woman might pause for a moment, being puzzled by the *non sequitur,* and say, "No, she doesn't have any cash to spare."

The interviewer had no need for parrying phrases to deflect the interview from himself to the respondent. College-educated men and women in similar interviews frequently intersperse their talk with such questions as "Don't you agree?" or "Don't you think that was unfair?" They appear to be telling their story and at the same time listening to it. They are concerned with the interviewer's reaction and make self-conscious remarks such as "Don't get me wrong," or "I guess I make him seem selfish." College-educated respondents are concerned not only with the interviewer's moral judgment but also with the accuracy of his understanding. Realizing that behavior may result from a variety of motives, they are quick to anticipate and correct possible misconceptions.

In contrast, only a few of the working-class men and women exhibited this psychological subtlety and self-consciousness. That is not to say, of course, that they opened their hearts to an interviewer without guile or reticence. But whatever they were disposed to tell they told flatly, without punctuating the narrative with asides.

A woman when asked whether her husband was easy or difficult to talk to replied, "I can tell him anything I need to say." She did not perceive that the question might lend itself to qualifications; refinements had to be brought out by painstaking inquiry.

The days may be full of joy and resentment, pity and pride, anger and love, boredom and frustration, but these emotions are not labeled, distinguished, or reflected upon. The charge is often made in this age of self-awareness that family life in the middle class suffers from the constant scrutiny of motivations and that the endless flow of words quenches genuine feeling and spontaneity. Nothing of the kind threatens the blue-collar families.

It is said further of middle-class couples that they are troubled by ambiguity of marriage roles; that neither mate is sure of what he may ask of the other or demand of himself. Should a husband be expected to help with the dishes or to take turns during the night with the baby's bottle? For working-class couples there is no issue over who does what around the house. Not only the men, but even the women, accept the traditional division of masculine and feminine tasks, and the women do not expect assistance from their husbands in everyday circumstances. Moreover, whereas educated women have misgivings about being "just a housewife," not a trace of this attitude appears in the blue-collar class. Attempts to tap feelings about the domestic role evoke a puzzled "Why, it's regular, isn't it? It can't be anything else."

Contrast this simple acceptance of a woman's status with the soul-searching of a college senior of my acquaintance who wrote on the eve of her marriage: "When I get married I want to be a homemaker and raise a family. But I foresee some possible conflicts. I wonder whether it will be difficult to adjust my ego to being just a housewife; I may feel guilty because I do not use my college education in some occupation. I wonder whether I will be intellectually stimulating to my husband. My mother's unfortunate experience adds to my fears; she is bored and lacks direction now that her children are grown."

How unself-conscious the working-class wife appears, with her simple view of her place when compared with my college friend. The one is exposed to the diverse ideas of family, school, and books, and will never possess her blue-collar sister's certainty and single-mindedness. The other is limited to a small circle consisting of parents, relatives and two or three friends who set her standards in life—from food and house furnishings to politics, sex, religion and recreation—and the moral universe seems to have the unity of the simple society of the past. It would appear that it is the working-class girl, rather than her middle-class sister, who leads the sheltered life.

For the happiest third of blue-collar couples in my study, life contains many satisfactions. The birth of a child ("I get real set up when one of them gets born"); the down payment on a house; a good carpentry job; an unexpected gift brought by the husband ("a real classy box of candy"); a good report card brought by a child; sexual satisfaction ("Sex is a big thing with us"); a family reunion of relatives; watching the children at play ("They are really comical"); a new bedroom set—these and other things are sources of pleasure. And for many, there is the satisfaction of feeling they are honorably fulfilling the roles of provider, mate and parent.

But the moral certainties of the blue-collar world, for all their allure, do not insure happiness, and the fact is that by and large these working-class couples are less satisfied with marriage and less happy with life in general than the better-educated middle-class couples.

The assessment of marital happiness is a precarious venture, but the indications are that marital happiness rises with the ascent from working-class to middle-class status. Thus, at a time when nostalgia for moraĺ simplicities appears particularly acute, my journey into the past has a certain relevance. If many of our social ills are the product of the moral confusion that has grown out of exposure to diverse ideas and changing circumstances, it does not follow that clear moral directives and consensus are synonomous with social health.

Marriage roles may be clearly defined, yet unsatisfactory. The isolation that shields the blue-collar workers from some of the ills of modern life serves also to bar them from its benefits. It prevents the dissemination of values and ideas that would promote marital happiness under conditions of modern life. Whereas middle-class couples today regard companionship as one of the functions of marriage, those in the working class tend to differentiate sharply between the mental worlds of the sexes, and do not include friendship between the spouses in their model of marriage.

Marriage without friendship may have been viable when married couples remained close to relatives and trusted friends, but these working-class families do, after all, live in an industrial and changing society and are subject to many of its pressures; geographical mobility is increasing.

A spokesman for the Department of Labor was quoted in the *New York Times* as saying: "Many more of our workers than in the past must have, or develop, the mobility to shift jobs . . . Many may have to change their residence." Separated from kin and friends, married couples must increasingly turn to each other for emotional support and friendship.

A family I shall call the Robinsons illustrate some of the problems of these couples. Mr. and Mrs. Robinson, aged twenty-five and twenty-three respectively, are grammar school graduates, married three years, and the parents of two infants. Mr. Robinson earns about $4,000 a year.

Mr. Robinson leaves the child care and housework completely to his wife and spends most of his leisure away from the home with male friends. He and Mrs. Robinson accept this as normal. "If you do right by your job and by the woman (sexually), they owe you some rest to yourself." "The husband earns the money, don't he? He has the right to get away as often as he wants." Of friendship between the sexes, Mrs. Robinson says, "Regular guys don't mess around with women except when they want what a woman's got to give them. Men and women are different; men don't feel the same as us. The fellows got their interests and the girls got theirs, they each go their separate ways." Mr. Robinson asks, "What is it about women that they want to talk about things when there is really nothing to talk about? Why do they have to hash it over? They talk about screwy things. Keep quacking, like beating a dead horse."

Mrs. Robinson, though she accepts her husband's absences, feels lonely and trapped at home with her two infants. Her mother works, and Mrs. Robinson has no relatives or close friends in the neighborhood. She is irritable and depressed, and an atmosphere of gloom pervades the home. This perplexes Mr. Robinson—all the more so because their sexual relations are highly satisfactory to both. As he behaves in ways sanctioned by their circle, it never occurs to him that there may be some connection between his wife's irritability and his own behavior.

Mrs. Robinson's dissatisfaction with her life is great, but she is at a loss to explain it. Her husband's neglect of her appears quite normal, as does his occasional violence, and she never expected companionship in marriage. But accepting these circumstances does not alleviate her loneliness. Mr. and Mrs. Robinson's conception of marriage without friendship and their lack of mutual understanding combine to intensify their unhappiness. But being largely isolated from the intellectual mainstream of society, they are slow to modify their conceptions of marriage in ways that might help them to happiness.

What may we infer from the plight of the Robinsons and others in their circumstances? It seems fair to conclude from my study that the spread of the middle-class habits of consumption to the semiskilled and the less educated wage earners has not been accompanied by a similar spread of mental outlook and social behavior. From all appearances, the working-class style of life—its values, attitudes, institutions—remains in many respects quite distinct from the dominant middle-class patterns of contemporary American society.

Life at its best is economically comfortable, but for the great majority it is narrowly circumscribed by the family, the relatives, a few friends, the union, the boss, the church. Nothing is visible in the vast darkness beyond this limited circle but a few movie stars, athletes and some national officeholders. Social life is limited to two or three couples, and many have no joint social life whatever, apart from visiting relatives. Television, radio and the newspapers bring in something of the outside world, but past research has revealed how selected is the response to the mass media and how weak the impact when compared with the influence of close associates.

Blue-collar families lack even such links with society as may be provided by membership in women's clubs or the Rotary. The labor union occasionally provides this sort of link for the men, but only infrequently. In short, these working men and their wives—English-speaking, well dressed and well mannered—do not enjoy full membership in the American society.

We know from other studies that only about one-third of the children of manual workers can be expected to rise to a higher stratum of society. What of the remaining two thirds? Almost without exception, the fathers hope their sons will not become semiskilled workers; they want them to "go a lot further." Yet whatever their hopes, the milieu in which they live will be perpetuated for the majority of their children unless measures are taken to help them to a better life.

The restricted environment and the low cultural level of the home hinder the development of working-class children from the first years of life on, retard the development of intellectual interests and motivation, and diminish the children's chances for higher education. The resources of the schools must be improved so that these children can be given from an early age the stimulation they lack at home. Vocational counseling—a commonplace in the better schools—is sorely needed in the schools blue-collar children attend. And civic organizations must somehow make the effort to reach their parents.

Until such steps are taken, there will remain a gap between the wage earners and the salaried middle classes, socially as well as materially; the working class will live on the fringe of society, and the antipoverty movement directed at the stratum below theirs will go only part way toward fulfilling the American promise.

WORKING-CLASS YOUTH

Alienation without
an Image

---

by William Simon
and John H. Gagnon

William Simon is currently program supervisor (sociology and anthropology) at the Institute for Juvenile Research in Chicago; John Gagnon is associate professor of sociology at the State University of New York at Stony Brook, Long Island. The findings reported in this article are being pursued through a study financed by a Public Health Service Grant.

To a degree possibly never experienced before, ours is a society whose image of youth is one of discontent and alienation. This holds true in both the professional literature and in the mass media. However accurate or inaccurate this image may be, it is marked by a crucial shortcoming: it appears to be drawn exclusively from the upper and lower reaches of society. There is a void between the largely upper-middle-class and middle-middle-class youth who are expected to go on to college and the economically deprived who are said to live in "cultures of poverty."

Clearly there are more than two Americas. But possibly

only those who are greatly articulate or dramatic in expressing their discontent can today command attention. In the
absence of public displays from that large group of young
people of the lower-middle or working classes, intellectuals
have tended to conclude, without bothering to look, that all
is well. Perhaps one positive outcome of the surprising
strength shown by the Wallace third-party candidacy will be
a desire to focus both attention and social programing
upon this segment of the population.

One way society acts to contain tendencies toward alienation that it sees among its young people is to respond by
offering minimal public images of the assumed attitudes.
This, if nothing else, lessens the isolation to some degree by
saying to the young, "We know you are there and that you
are unhappy." In the recent past one of the reasons noted
for the alienation of black youth was society's failure to
offer some validating or bolstering image of this group
within the society. Today that is essentially the situation for
working-class youth.

In some sense the working class has never been substantially represented in the cultural iconography of the society.
In the past, however, there were enough near-heroes, and,
more important, the image of America itself was sufficiently
based on working-class values as to be supportive. Now, as
the postindustrial society advances and changes, the possibilities for working-class youth to recognize themselves in
the emerging images of man have significantly lessened.
They may well be looking to society for some sense of confirmation as to who they are and who they might become,
and they may be looking increasingly in vain.

Part of the problem has been the failure of the society's
cultural middlemen, its intellectuals, even to begin to recognize this population. Among those intellectuals most identified with alienation as a growing consumer industry, one
finds an initial commitment to their own alienation; they

tend to be, almost without exception, anti-Establishment. The voices of discontent in the ghettos and on the campuses, the rapidly fading hippie experience, and the equally rapidly expanding use of drugs by the young are defined by such intellectuals as confirmation of their own view of the prevailing social order. Indeed, it is not uncommon for such movements or phenomena to be described by these men as a kind of Children's Crusade that will lead to a transformation of middle-class society and its attending malaise—a transformation that middle-class intellectuals could not manage for themselves.

From another perspective, however, these anti-Establishment intellectuals may be hard to distinguish from the Establishment itself. They and their rhetoric have become essential to the communications media that provide the society with images of itself. As the early discoverers, if not partial inventors, of popular modes of discontent, they find frequent employment as guides and commentators. For working-class populations, particularly the young, these anti-Establishment groups have become the Establishment, at least to the degree that they set the tone for the surface imagery of our times. For example, much is said of the crisis of the colleges and ghetto schools, both apparently requiring growing investments of society's resources. Does anyone for a moment think that the quality of education in the working-class schools in this country—both public and parochial—is any better? That the slaughter of human potential and sensibility is any less severe? Or that a crisis of identity equal in magnitude to that of the children of the affluent middle class or those of the ghetto is not going on among the youth of the working class?

One of the models for our thinking about alienation is that of a Stephen Dedalus desperately trying to free himself from the suffocating effects of a conservative, bigoted Ireland, an Ireland obsessed with its own mythic past. The young of the United States working class represent an unfamiliar and unattractive form of alienation: they are like Ireland—still conservative, bigoted, and obsessed with the past, their sense of alienation growing as they cling to versions of traditional values in a society that has become less traditional or at least less willing to glamorize traditional values.

And though the routes to alienation may be different and less romantic for these young people than they were for others, it does not follow that the consequences are any less disordering, pathogenic or painful. Moreover, it does not follow that the consequences for society are less costly. For all the talk of a youth revolution and the constant reminders of the proportion of the total population under twenty-five, we should also bear in mind that not all of this swelling tide comes from suburban homes or ghetto tenements. The images of Holden Caulfield and poor Benjamin the Graduate have become commonplace. So has the discovery of Claude Brown. Perhaps what is missing is a portrait of Studs Lonigan, a Studs frustrated, however, not by a depression but by the more ambiguous context of an affluent society.

"Intense commitment to change may be one of the elements in neurosis-building. Change is accelerating at a rapid pace, as students of the modern American family have so well documented. The 'healthy' population demonstrates little participation in this rapid pace, nor have their parents. They move ahead slowly at a pace which does not overly strain them." This is the observation of Roy R. Grinker in his impressive study entitled *Mentally Healthy Young Males* (*Homoclites*), one of the very rare studies in the literature of lower-middle-class or working-class youth. (Similar observations were recently made by David Riesman.) Grinker continues: "Within the general population of the United States this group is relatively silent. Its members are goal-directed, anxious only in striving to do their jobs well in which they will have moved up from their fathers' positions, but with little ambition for upward social or economic mobility. By the nature of their aspirations *to do well, to do good* and *to be well liked,* they plan to carry on their lives quietly in simple comfort, marry and raise their families, and retire on small pensions plus security." In essence, then, they represent the solid, if not stolid, center of society.

From some points of view, shaking them out of this somewhat bland commitment might be defined as progress. However, just as this "shaking-out" process appears to be affecting larger and larger sections of this population, it is experienced by many as both discomfiting and demoralizing. As transformations occur in the society, people are asked to cope with precisely that dynamic against which their very training and life styles have protected them. Change itself becomes the enemy. Much of the current racism may derive not so much from the factors we once associated with prejudice but with the increasing complications that the image of the Negro community now represents the most powerful symbol of "disruptive" changes in their lives. Moreover, this symbol is perceived by working-class youth as being endorsed or at least tolerated by the major institutions of the society. Its potential for generating a kind of "white rage" was typified in the comment of a young man who participated in the occasionally violent counterdemonstrations to Martin Luther King's open-occupancy marches in Chicago a few summers ago. For him, a Catholic, the presence in the march of clerics was anything but a constraint; rather they were part of his motivation to violence. He was intensely angry: *"They* even got to *them;* now no one stands for us."

For him, and for many others like him, racial integration (and the disruption of community life that he feels, not without justification, must follow) is part of an organized effort within which agents of government, the mass media and even the church are co-conspirators. Thus he too becomes anti-Establishment, but for him it is a Liberal Establishment, and before it he feels increasingly powerless. Adding to his frustration is the fact that he cannot take the alternative of "dropping out"—there is no place to drop out to. He did not seek out change; it sought him.

The Vietnam war is perceived by these alienated youth in somewhat hawkish ways. Recently, when the movie *The Graduate* attracted so much talk and commentary, as well as being the top moneymaker of the year, little attention was paid to the second big moneymaker, John's Wayne's *The Green Berets*. Just as college kids lined up to see *The Graduate*—two or three times in some cases—working-class kids were off to the drive-ins to see *The Green Berets* two or three times. Many of them have mixed feelings about the war. They see it as being inconvenient in some ways, but this tends to be overshadowed, since the war presents one of the few available images that allows them to see themselves as important or at least relevant to some sense of national purpose. They still believe in John Wayne and that he could lead us to victory in Vietnam were it not for the sabotage of the Liberal Establishment.

For many of these youths the emergence of a blandly mod style for middle-class American life—particularly as it is reflected in the mass media—is frequently more threatening than the more extreme expressions observable in the hippie subculture. The hippie phenomenon it can easily distance—it is something very freaky—but the style of the urban middle class hits too close to home. Here there is a striking difference in attitude on the part of males and females. Working-class girls are a great deal more responsive to national trends in feminine styles—they tend to adopt partial mod styles, although, even here, there is an unusual persistence of older styles. For the boys there has been a wondrous consistency in dress over the years. It is not just that the more well-to-do have more or better things—it is that they increasingly appear to be into something that is different. This, too, increases a sense of cultural isolation, or possibly cultural desertion. Along with the hippie, *Playboy* has joined the enemy.

The current phase of the technological revolution is obviously beginning to pose problems for the working-class young man. Some are sufficiently obvious not to require more than casual reference. Technology produces a trend toward professionalization that cuts the middle out of occupational hierarchies within given industries. This in turn produces growing difficulty in translating technical skills—often learned informally—into formal certification. Other skills that are currently available or where entry is facilitated because of informal connections—as in many of the building trades—become obsolete, or the formal requirements of organizational or governmental intervention operate to lessen the ability of relatives to be helpful.

After working-class youth leave secondary school—which for most of them is not seen as deprivation but as something natural and even desirable—their movement in the world of work and the process of making occupational commitments is uncertain.

And here it should be noted that no small part of this premature detachment from educational opportunities is facilitated by both the values of their parents and the values of the educational system itself. Parents frequently reinforce negative attitudes toward education. Schoolteachers and counselors go beyond their normal incompetence and act toward most working-class youth (particularly the boys) as if early termination of education is the expected thing. Despite the glib TV commercials about the importance of education, these young people who appear to *drop out* are actually as much victims of the process of being *pushed out* as are any children of the ghetto.

The range of work opportunities runs from formal apprenticeship programs to a whole spectrum of jobs for youth that require little training and are essentially dead-end. For great numbers there is just accidental drift and opportunity. Many justify their work by what it makes possible during nonwork time. That, in turn, is for boys very much an extension of their utilitarian attitudes toward high school. For girls the job itself is more important as a source of social contacts and off-the-job social attachments; the jobs for girls also frequently involve more social-class heterogeneity, and as a result, girls tend to feel less separated from major current fads and fashions.

The military remains an important post-high-school alternative for working-class youth, and it probably provides more technical training and certification than any other area of employment. It is also one of the few major institutions that reaffirm traditional values.

Entry into the military becomes, ironically, one way a working-class youth can be assured the protection of youth status. Young men in the military, like college students, are allowed margins of acting out that are reasonably permissive: they can be disorderly or engage in sexual misbehavior with greater indulgence on the part of authorities than will be true for any of their civilian counterparts. However, unlike the college student, the military experience reinforces a style of all-male socializing that is general in working-class culture.

The working-class boy tends to be object-oriented in his work preferences. Technical competence, however informally learned, remains an important aspect of his sense of self. This, curiously, provides another instance of a kind of reverse alienation. Descriptions of alienation in work have almost universally focused not on critiques of job procedures but on a failure in the quality of the social relations and nontechnical social activity within the work environment. As industry and the military have responded in varying degrees to criticism focusing upon alienating aspects of the work situation, there have been increasing attempts to make work more engaging of the total personality and more responsive to the work situation as a social environment. This, however, while satisfying essentially middle-class notions of what work should be like, is felt as threatening by many working-class youth. One detects a confusion and sense of discomfort among them as the very procedures designed to lessen what others have defined as alienating work conditions often impose an obligation to be socially integrated and socially competent—an imposition that has the reverse effect of making work more fearful.

There is, as we have said, a tendency among working-class youth to prefer working with things rather than with people. From some points of view this may be seen as a critical failure of full character development and indeed it may be just that. However, there is no immediate solution in modifying the work situation; rather we must look to more fundamental stages and processes of character development itself. Meanwhile, it is worth underscoring the possibility that the very strategies for ameliorating those aspects of work defined by some as alienating may well be creating alienation for others.

It is noteworthy that almost none of the talk about the generation gap current in our society finds an appropriate working-class imagery. Possibly this is because there is less difference in the values held by different generations in the working class than among those of middle-class populations, where there is a greater commitment to modernity. One basis of difference, however, that is shared across class lines is that youth who grew up in the years following World War II do not have the memories of deprivation and resignation that gave meaning and validity to the values their parents supported. At the same time, working-class youth do not have the same trust in affluence that middle-class youth do. This is one reason that middle-class "mod styles," with their frivolous air, are frequently threatening. They may serve to alter the credibility of an older generation, although they may not alter a larger sense of shared experiences and shared values.

Working-class youth have little access to a distinct youth culture or to youth-serving institutions that reinforce a commitment to a youth culture. As a result, much of the fashionable imagery and rhetoric of the "now generation" only leaves them feeling even more like strangers in their own society. This is not total—there is a great deal of ambiguity. Having themselves grown up in relative affluence, they also have a greater commitment to pleasure than their parents, but the available and best-advertised forms of pleasure appear so remote to their own sense of themselves and their worlds that they cannot identify with them.

One point where the problem of access to images and sources of pleasure has become particularly acute is the drug question. During the early stages of our current research we noted a seeming immunity of working-class neighborhoods to the drug problem which for some time has been epidemic in the urban ghettos and had begun moving toward the same state in numerous middle-class communities. However, with remarkable swiftness working-class communities were permeated by drug use and, in an uneven way, by drug knowledge. One source of supply was the local city or community colleges, where many "hip" middle-class dropouts and underachievers continued to play the game of waiting out the draft. A second source, of perhaps equal and possibly greater significance, were the older brothers who were currently serving or had recently served in the military. If our present sense of the importance of this second source is at all accurate, the military establishment has clearly failed to report—or even failed to understand—the extent of drug use among its personnel.

The potential effect of drugs current among the working-class youth (essentially the same drugs that have become part of the college scene) is hard to determine. It may well be a mixed outcome. Risks for working-class youth, unlike their counterparts in the middle class, multiply because both parents and community agents are more likely to view drug use in moral terms rather than in terms of the psychological metaphors that often shelter the children of the middle class. On the other hand, drug use can provide a link to a culture which is essentially middle class, and some working-class youth may form an attachment to more sophisticated youth cultures as a result of taking drugs. However, their risks of ultimately becoming alienated are great, for while drug culture often becomes a basis for detachment from working-class culture, it does not necessarily assure subsequent attachment to social life once one ages out of youth culture. Other than the minority of such youth who become "hip," drug use is rapidly absorbed into the neighborhood peer culture. For the most part, it replaces or becomes an addition to liquor. And in this largely facilitative function one can observe a refutation of the claims of the ideologists of drug use about the ability of chemistry to transform both social and personal visions.

The greatest strain in the area of family life may not be found in the families into which they were born, but in the families they themselves create—and they tend to marry fairly young. Here a gender difference may be of crucial significance. If women are more often and more systematically the consumers of popular culture in our society, they are particularly so in the working class. There is also, we would like to argue, far greater homogeneity in much of the content of the messages addressed to women than is found in the cultural messages addressed to men. Just as women respond to the norms of the national society in terms of make-up and fashion more immediately than men do, so do they also respond to the general life styles.

This has been suggested in Mirra Komarovsky's *Blue-Collar Marriage* (with a relatively young sample) in the wives' growing desires not only for increased sexual experiences with their husbands but for a heterosexuality reinforced or accompanied by increased *heterosociality*. In some very limited interviewing of young wives of military enlisted personnel, each of us discovered much the same: considerable dissatisfaction with their husbands' social incompetence or lack of interest in social life and with what they perceived as their husbands' somewhat indifferent attitude toward involvement in family life. They were extremely explicit in their discontent with their husbands' too exclusive concern with their own technical competence and preoccupation with a world of things the wives cannot share. Like their middle-class counterparts, they have fully absorbed the rhetoric of sharing and, implicitly, the value of interpersonal competence. For the men, middle-class styles are often felt as an additional pressure to become something they have not been trained to be—indeed, to become something that might involve a very fundamental transformation of their sense of self. In the man's view of marriage he often values service, support and esteem, refuge and relaxation. The strain that becomes increasingly evident to him in the community and on the job begins to follow him home.

As has already been suggested, the typical young working-class male is a great deal like his father. With his father he essentially shares an outlook characterized by resignation, but resignation without a basis in experience. He is, in relative terms, active rather than introspective. He is not a moralist. He is prepared to take life as it comes, expecting frighteningly little as long as it comes in predictable ways. It is when it does not come this way, when it becomes unpredictable, and he is required to respond, that he does so as a moralist, and a very rigid moralist indeed. (Moral language may well be the only language he has been trained in that can be used to describe events, persons and relationships beyond the most pedestrian. This is unlike, for example, his middle-class counterpart, who increasingly is trained to respond in psychological or even psychiatric language.)

His political participation is rather episodic and largely nonorganizational, passionate rather than programatic. In content, his stance tends to be defensive and protective rather than offensive and expanding. And in his present mood he feels increasingly cornered and slightly paranoid. Simultaneously, he sees other groups effectively using government for ends that are self-serving, and with a particular sense of outrage he sees government going out to involve other groups in ways that exclude him. If he delights in the politics of George Wallace it is because these politics appear to him as a politics of restoration, restoration of an incomplete and somewhat mythic sense of the past. He sees himself as a "natural man"—even more than do the participants of hippie culture. For him all bureaucracies are evil; all are sources of frustration and threaten the natural order of things.

A significant difference between the young worker and his father is that he realizes his status of being young affords special opportunities and freedoms, but he is not very sure of how they should be used. This is partly because of his uncertain relation to youth culture and partly because the line between adolescence and adulthood is far less certain for him than for middle-class youth. One young worker described his youth as a period when "you had a good time," something you couldn't do when you grew up.

Asked what he is or would like to be, he would most likely say, "A good guy." This translates to some degree into someone who is both tough and sentimental, someone who

can be pushed just so far, but no one—including himself—
appears to know just how far that is. He has a distinct commitment to a somewhat unrealistic notion of manhood, a
major part of which involves a valuing of silence and a mask-
ing of emotion that tends to dignify his own fundamental
inarticulateness.

Behind it all, however, and with very little language with
which to describe it, he is a classic instance of alienated
man. He feels powerless and often feels himself to be the
object of manipulation, someone who is exploited or poorly
served by the central institutions of his society. He feels that
other groups in the society—both above and below him—
are getting more than their share and getting it by not playing by the rules, particularly the rule that says you have to
pay for what you get. If he is not isolated, he feels an increasing sense of cultural desertion—the society may be involved in too many things he cannot experience or get to.
He has social values that he shares with his friends and family, but not necessarily with the larger society.

For a female much of this same picture applies. To the
degree that it differs, owing to her greater exposure or
stronger receptivity to the mass media, it does not necessarily make life any easier and in fact may make it more complicated. If she is less estranged from the national society
than the men in her life, she is to that extent estranged from
the men among whom she will find a husband.

It is possible, of course, that we have overstated a case.
Clearly, given the very informal nature of our research at
this stage—largely a limited number of ethnographic interviews—much of what we have said should be treated as tentative. But it must be remembered that not all children of
the affluent upper-middle class become hippies, not all college students are disaffected activists, and not all the young
in the ghetto have affiliated with the black-power move-

ments. We pay attention to such elements not only because they are dramatic and compelling but also because they represent responses to strains that others feel and respond to differently. The same may be said of our alienated working-class youth.

Alienation is a relational concept describing a kind of painful relation between individuals and their surrounding social structure. Too often intellectuals have turned it into a substantive concept, and too often the substance has involved liberal, middle-class values, tastes and styles. But the rear guard of a society may, in decidedly different ways, be every bit as alienated as that society's vanguard and perhaps more so. To very few intellectuals or professionals are the values of the rear guard attractive; the rear guard is seen as the enemy of the values we approve and strive for and as obstacles to social progress (as we define it). Its members are not only villains, they are also victims—tragic victims requiring more attention and social concern than they have received thus far.

GREASERS, DUPERS AND HIPPIES

Three Responses to the Adult World

by Stephen A. Buff

Mr. Buff is a graduate student in sociology at North-western University and is currently doing research* on white working-class youth with Dr. William Simon at the Institute for Juvenile Research in Chicago.

This essay is about the working-class youth of a place we shall call Grey Park, a community area, on the southwest side of Freight City, a sprawling, industrial, Midwestern metropolis. The neighborhood area is about two miles square, nearer to the city limits than to the central business district. Factories, warehouses, and city facilities are spread throughout the area, making Grey Park a mixed residential and light-industry neighborhood, intersected by two major highways and two railway systems.

* This investigation is being supported by a General Research Support Grant, FR–05666–02, from the General Research Support Branch, Division of Research Facilities and Resources, National Institute of Health, and a Public Service Grant (HD–02257). The author gratefully acknowledges the generous help and advice of his colleagues, Mary Jane Nelson and Alan P. Berger.

Streets are laid out, for the most part, along a monotonously flat terrain, broken only by the raised superhighways. Every half-dozen blocks or so, one comes to a long commercial thoroughfare, treeless, arched by electric cables for the buses, lined with stores, restaurants, and neighborhood taverns, advertised by neon signs. Large late-model cars (few of them more than three or four years old) dominate the scene—parked bumper to bumper at night on the side streets or filling the back-alley garages—while the main streets are filled with bright dealers' showrooms, gas stations, and crowded used-car lots. One cannot tell when the storefronts were built, and the only structures which give an impression of a particular era are the garish drive-ins and carry-out restaurants of the sixties—all surrounded by ample parking areas—that serve *Kentucky Fried Chicken, Burger-King, Tastee-Freeze.*

The dwellings vary from rows of bungalows to rectangular three-story apartment buildings of darkened brick to large two-family houses sided with wooden clapboard or shingles, whose paint jobs haven't stood up well against the smog, harsh winters, and blistering summers. On some residential streets there are few trees and narrow front lawns, while on others there is more space between houses and lovely old trees which make the houses shady and pleasant in summer and hide their imperfections in winter.

Nothing in Grey Park rises much over two stories and those few structures that do are massive and uninviting—a beige concrete Sears department store and a thick-walled public high school with steep garrets reminiscent of some Victorian institution. There are many churches in the area —large Catholic churches of sculptured, light-gray stone, and modest Methodist and Baptist churches of red brick, fitting into the neighborhood unobtrusively. Residential areas are dotted with small parks taking up one or two blocks with grass or concrete, filled with small shrubbery, a red brick field house, swings, benches and playing fields of grass or a basketball court of concrete.

The people who live in Grey Park are white, working-class and lower-middle-class, and predominantly Catholic. The ethnicity is heterogeneous, with most people claiming Irish, Polish, Eastern European or Italian ancestry. Sections of Grey Park were once predominantly Jewish, but now only elderly Jews remain and their children have moved to the suburbs. Appalachian whites, Puerto Ricans, and some blacks are moving closer to the area as they move out from the central city, but few have moved into Grey Park.

Throughout the vast white working-class neighborhoods of northwest Freight City, people of high school and college age (fourteen to twenty-four) congregate in parks, on street corners, and at small restaurants and drive-ins—at whatever central locations adults and police allow or tolerate their presence.

For my own work, I have "hung" with various groups of kids, participating in their recreational activities in the evening and night (e.g., going to parties with them, taking their side in any confrontation with adults, going to the police station with them when they were called in, leaving street corners with them when the police chased them away). A recurrent and fascinating theme that struck me from the outset of my observations was the existence of different categories that young people would use to describe themselves, one another, and outside groups. Three major types emerged: greasers, hippies and dupers. When inquiring how they differed, these three would be identified, first of all, in terms of dress.

Greasers are boys accurately identified as those wearing "black leathers"—not the motorcycle jackets of the fifties, but hip-length jackets with patch pockets of a fairly soft leather or simulated leather. They often wear work clothes

—gray denim shirts and gray or green work trousers (baggies)—black laced shoes, sometimes pointed in the European style, or high black combat boots. In the summer they usually wear sleeveless undershirts (dago-tees) but may go bare-chested, and even in the winter they frequently keep their jackets and shirts unbuttoned. Their pants are generally black and tight and they wear Ban-lon sweaters of a dark shade. Depending on the style of the particular group, they may wear floppy British style working-class caps with a brim, or berets. Hair is worn fairly long, about collar-length, combed back from the forehead in a pompadour, unparted, and always aided by some hair cream or oil.

Duper boys are characterized by bright shirts, penny loafers or sneakers, and wheat jeans. Their dress is patterned in some way after the "collegiate" style of the early sixties. Trousers usually have cuffs and are narrow (but not pegged like those of some greasers), or they may be cut like jeans in any number of colors or fabrics. They wear wool sweaters and woodsman-style wool jackets and, later in the year, ski jackets or wool winter coats. They usually have shorter hair than greasers, parted, with their forelocks combed diagonally over part of their foreheads—"pulled all over to one side," as a greaser has described it.

Hippies (or long-hairs) costume themselves with jeans, usually with flared cuffs (bellbottoms), sneakers (or they go barefoot), floppy-brimmed hats, blue cotton work shirts, army-surplus jackets, beads and other decorations, such as painted tee-shirts or the peace symbol, on the back of their jackets. But the most notable features, according to nonhippies, are beads and long hair, which is worn over the ears, sometimes shoulder-length, often parted in the center and tied with a headband.

The most pronounced differences and the items of dress are summarized in the table which follows.

DISTINCTIVE TYPES OF CLOTHING WORN BY MALES
IN GREASER, DUPER, AND HIPPIE GROUPS

Type of Clothing	Greaser	Duper	Hippie
Jackets			
black leather jacket (hip-length)	common	very rare	rare
quilted nylon jacket	common	occasional	rare
team jackets and sweaters with school emblem	never	common	never
army jackets	common	common	common
Shirts			
dark-colored "knits" (Ban-lons)	common	rare	rare
work shirts	common	never	common
brightly colored or plaid sport shirts	never	common	never
Trousers			
"baggies" (work pants)	common	never	occasional
black pegged pants	common	rare	occasional
wheat jeans	never	common	rare
bellbottoms	very rare	rare	common
Shoes			
heavy work shoes or combat boots	common	never	very rare
penny loafers	never	common	never
pointed black shoes (European style)	common	rare	rare
tennis sneakers	never	common	occasional

Type of Clothing	Greaser	Duper	Hippie
Other			
outlandish costume	never	never	common
beads	never	never	common
Grooming			
shoulder-length hair	never	never	occasional
clean-cut	very rare	common	never
pompadour and slicked-back hair	common	very rare	very rare

The males show greater differentiation in their apparel than the females. Greaser girls used to be easily identified— and can still be to some extent—by their ratted hair, black leather jackets and heavy make-up. But they now seem to be tending more and more toward a common middle-class style. Bouffant hairdos are declining, and straight hair with less teasing is in vogue. When youths describe differences in dress among greasers, dupers, and hippies, they mention male dress primarily, because, given the similar "natural" hair styles, bellbottoms, and suede jackets that are increasingly common to all groups of girls, it is often difficult to identify girls in one of these three modalities if they aren't accompanied by boys.

Greasers

Differences among greasers, hippies, and dupers begin but certainly do not end with dress. As one hippie said, "The dress goes along with it [the behavior]. If you dress like a greaser, of course you're going to act like a shit-stud dude [a tough guy]." Hippie or long-hair kids refer to the greaser kids as tough, ready for a street battle, thinking it cool to fight and push guys around. The hippie girls described what greaser girls are like in these two comments:

"It's ninety degrees out and their hair's all ratted up and they wear black sweaters and it's ninety degrees out and they stand there sweating and try to get picked up."

"A whole bunch of make-up and ratted hair and black leather and black sweaters and they like to beat up other girls."

Seen from the hippie's point of view, then, a dominant trait of greaser boys and girls is their "toughness." More generally, they seem to conform to the middle-class stereotype of working-class, street-corner gang kids (although the groups observed thus far are gangs only in the sense in which sociologist Walter B. Miller uses the term—loose aggregates who "hang together" with a very limited sense of territoriality and without any necessary formalization of leadership roles).

The greaser groups that I have been most involved with are fairly stable in terms of the ages of the members. Members of each age-graded group know members in the older and younger grades, know where they hang out, and expect to hang out in the older spot when their grade moves up.

Many of the interests and activities of greasers are not out of the ordinary: they play the traditional sports, especially baseball and football, and are avidly interested in repairing old autos and "souping up" the newer ones, and many of them are caught up in the drag-racing scene. But their relationship to the adult world, especially The Law, is problematic. School appears to be a punishing and/or boring experience for the boys, though not necessarily for the girls. There is a high dropout rate (perhaps over 50 percent after age sixteen); however, many boys do get their diplomas eventually at night school or in the armed forces.

The attitude of greasers to police is complex and ambiguous. Police, more than any other group, set close limits around their freedom. Aside from fighting, petty thievery, car thefts, or other more spectacular delinquent acts, the greasers, and other groups for that matter, are very often in a position to be harassed for some minor delinquent act or annoyance: being out late after the ten-thirty weekday curfew, possessing grass or any other drug, drinking beer out of doors, being too noisy on a street corner so that neighbors complain, or becoming too numerous in a business establishment, so that the manager complains. Cops, in turn, are to be outwitted, to be beaten at their own game, to be provoked and confronted and put on.

On the other hand, these kids might secretly dig cops—they have the fast cars, the authority, and the legitimate opportunity for violence—but this is pure speculation at this point. There is further ambivalence because, after all, this is the population from which many cops are recruited. The cop-hating kid, when confronted with an occupational choice, may well choose police work. The more knowledge of the street the kid has, the better neighborhood cop he will eventually make and the tougher he will probably make it in turn for street kids because he knows how "bad" they are and how to catch them at their own game. The system of passage from oppressed to oppressor, then, seems to resemble a fraternity hazing system in which those who have been "hassled" the most are the most oppressive in hazing the next incoming cohort. The major difference is that freshmen join a fraternity while greasers or street kids seem to back into police work.

An early identification with the world of work is evident among greasers. There is a great deal of shopping around by trial and error for a job that isn't too boring, routine or dead-end. A job in "the trades" is highly preferred but police work also pays well. The service is often seen as an avenue for job advancement, offering a second chance to receive a high school diploma and the best possible chance to receive vocational, highly technical or college-level training. If one adopts an instrumental approach the years of military service can fit in with one's career plan; it serves as the IBM, the paternalistic corporation, for much of this population (see Paul Goodman, *Growing Up Absurd*). Those not planning to use the military in this way experience the expectation of the draft as two or more years of discontinuity with any of their life plans. The draft may function to postpone any serious decisions or a realistic future orientation. Since the draft will certainly disrupt one's future plans, why make any?

Greaser kids take pride in their mechanical and vocational skills. Pride and investment in work is often dependent on getting into the trades or going to vocational school. If their horizons are not broadened, if they are not allowed to exercise a body of skills, as in a trade, they may stay in their jobs out of inertia, or just for the money. Kids are often tied to their jobs because of (1) the pressure to contribute to family income and (2) the financial drain that comes from owning and caring for cars.

The recreational life of the group involves the camaraderie of hanging together, cars, sports, "boozing, balling and blowing pot," parties, and music. Boys and girls meet at the park and may pair off later, but much of their time together is spent with the entire group. I'm not sure if a double standard exists in terms of a value being placed on virginity. Girls who make themselves available are "sluts," but any girl will make love, according to some boys, if she is going with a guy for more than four to six months. According to the social workers, however, the girls are "prick teasers" and not as available as they may appear to be.

Taking drugs (virtually any "soft" drug) and drinking are the main pastimes. All greasers that I have met drink, and many also take drugs. Drinking starts in early adolescence as does glue-sniffing. Most kids have tried marijuana before they have tried LSD, psilocybin, amphetamines, mescaline, or any other "soft" drug. The main impediment to the use of hard drugs is the fear of addiction and the fear of "needles." Anything that can be swallowed, however, is acceptable and is experimented with in many combinations. "Uppers" and "downers," wine, and beer may be taken within a short time span. They may "trip" one evening and get drunk the next, or they may take alcohol and drugs almost simultaneously. The greasers who don't take drugs have tried them but they don't "do anything for them." (They may partake of a culture in which drug use is valued, but they may not value the use of that drug themselves.) Drug use is seen as cool, fun, enjoyable, and is a valued experience among "heads" (those greasers who take drugs), but its use has not brought other notable changes in behavior along with it as it has among the hippies. Although the use and abuse of drugs has become a major pastime, it seems to be incremental and adaptive to the other concerns of the greasers rather than a main element. The vocabulary of motives for the use of drugs is far slimmer among greasers than among hippies. No outstanding change in life style or world view seems to accompany or to be induced by the use of drugs.

Hippies

"Grease" is the most widespread cultural mode of dress and behavior. Most hippies are "greaser converts," although some were formerly dupers. Grease may be an irresistible form of posturing for young adolescents (twelve to fourteen) who wish to express their toughness. But the newest subcultural style of working-class youth is the hippie style.

Only greasers, hostile to the adult world, and dupers,

tractable to the adult world, existed in the area beforehand. The long-hair, among youth in this area, is relatively new. The diffusion of the hippie life style into the working class is interesting in itself and may point more to general processes altering the consciousness of this population.

Hippie culture was originally a middle- and upper-middle-class movement, with its images coming from the mass media, from acid or hard-rock groups, the large psychedelic dance halls and, to a much lesser extent, from the underground press. But to point out these sources is not saying anything, necessarily, about the process of becoming a working-class hippie. I have not, as yet, been able to locate all the contingencies in this process. One important element in understanding the change from a grease to a hip style of life is to learn what differences hippies see in themselves since the conversion.

Firstly, hippies realize that "it isn't cool to beat up on other people" or to push them around as greaser boys and girls are reputed to enjoy doing. Hippies have stopped fighting. If they are insulted by greasers, they ignore it rather than fight. They look down on greasers as kids who have not matured past a certain hostile stage of development, who aren't with it and who cannot see the foolishness of their own ways.

Secondly, drugs are believed by the hippies to have brought about this conversion to peacefulness. Either marijuana or LSD is purported to bring about a nonbelligerent attitude toward life—"Acid and fighting just don't mix." Drugs, in addition to being peace-instilling, exciting, and a groove, help a person with his life: acid opens up one's world; speed makes one able to live faster, to attain one's goals more quickly because everything is speeded up; grass makes one mellow and peaceful and helps one to think things through. In the weekly bull sessions (or "drug sessions") of the local youth with social workers, the hippies' ideological justifications for drug use are better developed, better integrated, and more subtle than the "straight" arguments for non-use put forward by the youth workers.

Thirdly, the hippies see themselves "hassled" by a square adult world which has nothing to offer them except condemnation, discrimination by storekeepers and neighbors, police repression, deadly boring jobs, "bullshit rules" of dress and conduct in schools which teach them nothing. Much of this seems to be objectively true: the pizzeria owner on the corner won't let them in because he is afraid they're "holding" drugs. Neighbors complain, and cops chase them off corners, perhaps with much more vehemence than they would with the other groups of kids.

Unlike the greasers, who admit the existence of a generation gap but avoid an up-front conflict with adults, the hippies enjoy actively "putting on" adults. They sometimes like to "freak them out" by bizarre dress or actions—panhandling, exploring the drainage sewers, drinking on the rooftop of a factory. Their hijinks are put-ons intended to "blow the minds" of the adult world, a flaunting of the world taken for granted, while a similar infraction by a greaser would be a testing of the authority or coercive power of the adult world and the indication of one's own "badness," or manliness. A greaser, insofar as he acts against the adult world, tries to *outwit* the authorities; a hippie tries to blow their minds while blowing his own mind in the process.

The hip flaunting of the conservative adult-dominated world may have far more harsh consequences in a working-class milieu than in some sectors of the more permissive upper-middle-class milieu—whose members not only tolerate but attempt to coopt and derive vicarious satisfaction from the iconoclastic cultural forms of youth. One indication of this is the very high drop-out rate among local hippies over the age of sixteen. Only one boy in the area has graduated from high school and only one other that I know of is still in school. The hippies' rejection of ordinary career goals, and their refusal to comply with the strict standards of dress (short hair and conventional clothing) and conduct imposed by the school administration, probably contribute to this rate, but it also appears to be an effort of the administration at the high school to get rid of people they consider to be undesirable and potentially or actually disruptive. Career planning, if it exists at all, is vague, and the boys are usually not engaged in, or they put off, the steps that *they* see as necessary to their plans—"I'll start going back to night school. I'd like to get my diploma." But the *time* of that start remains undefined. With little or no orientation toward the future and vague or unrealistic career plans, the kids concentrate on and seem fully immersed in (the enjoyment of) the present.

Jobs are regarded as a source of sustenance ("bread") rather than a vehicle for self-advancement. The youth switch from one dead-end job to another, not working unless they have to. One boy has refused to engage in any more repetitive "robot-like" work and has taken up dealing in drugs as a source of income. Hippies may hold jobs for an even shorter length of time than the greasers, but most of the members of both groups show irregular and unstable job trajectories. I have yet to sort out how much of the hippies' tenuous situation is due to a self-fulfilling prophecy, how much is a consequence of their choice to drop out, and how much is due to actual discrimination and repression by school authorities, police, courts, and employers which make their situation more difficult than that of other youths.

The hippies are interested in music, and those at the center of the group (those who are most "hip") are more experimental in their listening tastes. The hippies of long standing have catholic tastes in music—any acid or hard-rock variations or most forms of jazz are popular, but soul music is frowned upon, while it is popular with greasers and with the recent greaser converts to a hip style—those who have been dropping acid for a few months to a year. The greaser converts are therefore considered to be a few months or even a few years behind in their musical tastes. While greaser kids and greaser converts listen to music avidly and know the lyrics, the old-time hippies are not only just as familiar with the music but they also own instruments and have their own jam sessions.

Hippies tend to be somewhat apolitical, discounting much of what they read and hear as "bullshit." But they are strongly against the war, and when one recent greaser convert backslid to join the Air Force, the rest of the group derided him behind his back. Another boy had clear-cut plans for becoming a jet-maintenance expert, but when he was rejected for physical reasons he was pleased with his non-draftable status. I said, "I hear you had problems with the military." He said, "They rejected me; that's a problem?" None of them ever plan to go into police work or into a military career, and many of them devise elaborate plans (even going so far as to assume a new identity) to evade or avoid the draft. They are unimpressed by national achievements such as the exploration of the moon, which they described jokingly as "no more significant than our own explorations of the neighborhood sewers." Some of the hippies participated in the protests surrounding the 1968 Democratic National Convention and were gassed. But this event was not seen entirely as a highly political act but as an exciting and dangerous kind of "high." This is not to say that they learned no political lessons from the confrontation.

As hippies, kids have picked up other parcels of cultural baggage. They dig the underground newspaper and they like science fiction and fantasy. They are more knowledgeable about drugs than the greasers, and insist that they know how to "pace" their drug intake so they will not abuse themselves.

Dupers

The word "duper" or "dooper" comes from the acronym of "Dear Old Upton Parker." Upton Park is an old, slightly declining, respectable middle-class suburb, so a duper is one who affects middle-class dress, behavior, or life style. Dupers do not hang on street corners like other groups. According to one hippie in the area, they hang in back alleys near the garages of residential homes or flats so they will not have to confront hostile greasers or be tempted by hippies.

Greasers view dupers as "sissified," and they probably have a lot more to say about them, while hippies consider the duper kids to be conceited snobs, who put on a real "clean-cut front" and act as if they are better than everybody else. Here are some hippie opinions about dupers:

"They're snots, real snots."

"The guys, their whole life ambition is to be insurance salesmen and the girls want to be housewives and Marlo Thomases . . ."

"They like to look rich, even if they're from the slums they walk around . . ."

"They look on the hippies and greasers as if they're mud. If you're not a duper, you're shit to them."

"They hate us. We are everything they want to be and can't be. They just listen to their parents and follow them, even though they may not know what's going on either. We're doing what we want to do and that's something they just can't do."

Dupers seem to be close, then, to all adult socialization institutions, especially their families, their schools and, to a lesser extent, the church. One greaser male told me, "The greasers hang out in the stores and commercial places . . . The dupers hang in the school or schoolyards." But their involvement in school is not merely limited to "hanging." Not only do they tend to stay in school but they seem to be well integrated into the student culture of the school and are the mainstay of extracurricular activities, especially sports. This is what gives dupers the reputation for being "jocks." Sports and school life seem to be a central theme for dupers, just as cars and booze are central for greasers, and music and drugs are central for hippies.

Dupers are rarely labeled or defined as "bad kids" by the police and the courts; they do not pose a "problem" for adults. Social workers of a local youth agency provide guidance and sponsorship for some of their activities, such as chaperoning dances, but they do not regard dupers as alienated youth, while greasers and hippies often fall in this category.

Youth Cultures

Peer groups and the cultures that are generated and adopted by them are quite pervasive, so much so that Herbert Gans, in *The Urban Villagers,* has typified his entire working-class population as a "peer-group society" because most of their relationships are with peers of the same age, sex, and life-cycle status. The types of working-class youth cultures attached to these peer groups are quite widespread and show remarkable similarity to the ones we have described (see James Q. Wilson's "The Young People of North Long Beach," in *Harper's,* December 1969, and Jeremy Bugler's article on "skinheads"—Great Britain's version of greasers—in *New Society,* November 13, 1969). Let us inquire, all too briefly, into some of the sociological reasons for the prevalence and pervasiveness of these youth cultures.

Peer-group cultures can be seen as a collective response to the problems that youths find in their life situations, particularly to the demands that adult authorities make upon them. The peer-group cultures that we have described contain many elements, but the most outstanding ones are, first, *the nature of the response to adult authority,* and second, *the nature of the generalized stance toward the adult world and the amount of preparation for that world.* Members of duper cultures seem to respect adult authorities, accept the adult world and prepare for membership in that world (preferably in the more middle-class segments of that world). Greasers participate in a culture that stresses rejection of adult authorities (especially law-enforcement officials and, to a lesser extent, teachers) but emphasizes a positive relationship to the adult world and preparation for adult (mostly blue-collar) occupations. Those socialized to hippie culture, however, reject the legitimacy of the adult world and also seem to avoid serious planning or preparation for future adult status.

These various cultures associated with peer groups serve as the normative screens and the arbiters of reality through which many of the demands and pleas of the adult world are perceived, accepted, acted upon, or rejected. Whether one should stay in school or drop out, get a job, or become a "bum," enlist in the military or steer clear of it, get married or remain single, etc., are often discussed, interpreted and decided upon within the framework of common perspectives arrived at by the peer group. Participation in the peer group not only influences attitudes but also leads to concrete behavior that may alter one's path or paths in and out of schools, jobs, the military, reformatories, or jails. The thrusts and emphases of greaser, duper, and hippie cultures may act as significant links in the youthful careers of individuals as they move or are impeded in their paths toward adulthood, and thereby may significantly enter into the process of personal and social change.

WHY THEY FIGHT

U.S. Combat Soldiers in Vietnam

by Charles C. Moskos, Jr.

Charles C. Moskos, Jr., is associate professor of sociology at Northwestern University. Awarded a Faculty Research Fellowship, 1969–70, by the Ford Foundation, he is currently observing United Nations peacekeeping operations in Cyprus. His book The American Enlisted Man *is being published by the Russell Sage Foundation.*

The most popular notion of how men are brought to kill and be killed in combat has to do with the presumed national character of the soldiers. Different national armies perform better or worse according to the putative martial spirit of their respective citizenries. Italians make "poor" soldiers, Germans "good" ones. Another view has it that combat performance is basically a consequence of the operation of the formal military organization—the strict discipline, military training, unit esprit de corps and so forth. This viewpoint is, naturally enough, found in traditional military thought; but the importance of military socialization is similarly emphasized, albeit from different premises, by antimilitarists concerned with the perversions that military life allegedly inflicts on men's minds. Another interpretation— often the hallmark of political rhetoric—holds that combat performance depends on the soldier's conscious allegiance to the stated purposes of war. Whether motivated by patriotism or a belief that he is fighting for a just cause, the effective soldier is ultimately an ideologically inspired soldier.

Yet another explanation of combat motivation developed out of the social sciences' studies of World War II. This interpretation deemphasizes cultural, formal socialization and ideological factors and focuses attention instead on the crucial role of face-to-face or "primary" groups. The motivation of the individual combat soldier rests on his solidarity and social intimacy with fellow soldiers at small-group levels. This viewpoint was characteristic of the studies that Samuel Stouffer and his associates reported in *The American Soldier,* as well as of the analysis of the *Wehrmacht* by Edward Shils and Morris Janowitz.

My own research among American soldiers in Vietnam has led me to question the dominant influence of the primary group in combat motivation. Put most formally, I would argue that combat motivation arises out of the linkages between individual self-concern and the shared beliefs of soldiers as these are shaped by the immediate combat situation.

The information for this article is based on my observations of American soldiers in combat made during two separate stays in South Vietnam. During the first field trip in 1965, I spent two weeks with a weapons squad in a rifle platoon of a paratrooper unit. The second field trip in 1967 included a six-day stay with an infantry rifle squad and shorter periods with several other combat squads.

In both field trips, I collected data through informal observations and personal interviewing of combat soldiers.

During the second field trip I also conducted thirty-four standardized interviews with the men of the particular squads with whom I was staying.

A prefatory comment is needed on the social origins of the men I interviewed. The thirty-four soldiers had the following civilian backgrounds prior to entering the service: ten were high-school dropouts, only two of whom were ever regularly employed; twenty-one were high-school graduates, six directly entering the service after finishing school; and three were college dropouts. None were college graduates. Eighteen of the thirty-four men had full-time employment before entering the service, twelve in blue-collar jobs and six in white-collar employment. About two-thirds of the soldiers were from working-class backgrounds, with the remainder being from the lower-middle class.

As for other social-background characteristics: eight were black; one was a Navajo; another was from Guam; the other twenty were white, including three Mexican-Americans and one Puerto Rican. Only seven of the squad members were married (three after entering the service). All the men, except two sergeants, were in their late teens and early twenties, the average age being twenty years. Again excepting the sergeants, all were on their initial enlistments. Twenty of the men were draftees and fourteen were regular army volunteers. Importantly, except for occasional sardonic comments directed toward the regulars by the draftees, the behavior and attitudes of the soldiers toward the war were very similar, regardless of how they entered the service.

To convey the immediacy of the combat situation is hard enough for the novelist, not to say the sociologist. But to understand the fighting soldier's attitudes and behavior, it is vital to comprehend the extreme physical conditions under which he must try to live. It is only in the immediate context of battle that one can grasp the nature of the group process developed in combat squads. For within the network of his relations with fellow squad members, the combat soldier is also fighting a very private war, a war he desperately hopes to leave alive and unscathed.

The concept of relative deprivation—interpreting an individual's evaluation of his situation by knowing the group he compares himself with—has been one of the most fruitful in social inquiry. We should not, however, forget that there are some conditions of life in which deprivation is absolute. In combat, a man's social horizon is narrowly determined by his immediate life chances in the most literal sense. The fighting soldier, as an absolutely deprived person, responds pragmatically to maximize any and all short-run opportunities to improve his chances of survival. For the soldier the decisions of state that brought him into combat are irrelevant, meaningless.

Under fire the soldier not only faces an imminent danger of his own death and of being wounded but he also witnesses the killing and suffering of his buddies. And always there are the routine physical stresses of combat life—the weight of the pack, tasteless food, diarrhea, lack of water, leeches, mosquitos, rain, torrid heat, mud and loss of sleep. In an actual firefight with the enemy, the scene is generally one of terrible chaos and confusion. Deadening fear intermingles with acts of bravery and, strangely enough, even moments of exhilaration and comedy. If prisoners are taken, they may be subjected to atrocities in the rage of battle or its immediate aftermath. The soldier's distaste for endangering civilians is overcome by his fear that any Vietnamese, of any age or sex, could very well want him dead. Where the opportunity arises, he will often loot. War souvenirs are frequently collected, either to be kept or later sold to rear-echelon servicemen.

For the individual soldier, the paramount factor affecting

combat motivation is the operation of the rotation system. Under current assignment policies Army personnel serve a twelve-month tour of duty in Vietnam. Barring his being killed or severely wounded, then, every soldier knows exactly when he will leave Vietnam. His whole being centers on reaching his personal DEROS (Date Expected Return Overseas). It is impossible to overstate the soldier's constant concern with how much more time—down to the day —he must remain in Vietnam.

Overall, the rotation system reinforces a perspective which is essentially private and self-concerned. Somewhat remarkably, for example, I found little difference in the attitudes of combat soldiers in Vietnam over a two-year interval. The consistency was largely due, I believe, to the fact that each soldier goes through a similar rotation experience. The end of the war is marked by the date a man leaves Vietnam, and not by its eventual outcome—whether victory, defeat or stalemate. Even discussion of broader military strategy and the progress of the war—except when directly impinging on one's unit—appears irrelevant to the combat soldier: *"My* war is over when I go home."

When the soldier feels concern over the fate of others, it is for those he personally knows in his own outfit. His concern does not extend to those who have preceded him or will eventually replace him. Rather, the attitude is typically: "I've done my time; let the others do theirs." Or, as put in the soldier's vernacular, he is waiting to make the final entry on his FIGMO chart—"Fuck it, got my order [to return to the United States]." Whatever incipient identification there might be with abstract comrades-in-arms is flooded out by the private view of the war fostered by the rotation system.

Conventionally, the primary group is described as a network of interpersonal relationships in which the group's maintenance is valued for its own sake rather than as a mechanism that serves one's own interests. And, as has been noted, social science descriptions of combat motivation in World War II placed particular emphasis on the importance of groupings governed by intimate face-to-face relations. Roger Little's observations of a rifle company during the Korean War differed somewhat by pointing to the two-man or "buddy system" as the basic unit of cohesion rather than the squad or platoon.

My observations in Vietnam, however, indicate that the concept of primary groups has limitations in explaining combat motivation even beyond that suggested by Little. The fact is that, if the individual soldier is realistically to improve his survival chances, he must *necessarily* develop and take part in primary relationships. Under the grim conditions of ground warfare, an individual's survival is directly dependent upon the support—moral, physical and technical—he can expect from his fellow soldiers. He gets such support to the degree that he reciprocates with the others in his unit. In other words, primary relationships are, at their core, mutually pragmatic efforts to minimize personal risk.

Interpreting the solidarity of combat squads as an outcome of individual self-interest can be corroborated by two illustrations. The first deals with the behavior of the man on "point" in a patrolling operation. The point man is usually placed well in front of the main body in the most exposed position. Soldiers naturally dread this dangerous assignment, but a good point man is a safeguard for the entire patrol. What happens, as often as not, is that men on point behave in a noticeably careless manner in order to avoid being regularly assigned to the job. At the same time, of course, the point man tries not to be so incautious as to put himself completely at the mercy of an encountered enemy force. In plain language, soldiers do not typically perform at their best when on point; personal safety overrides group interest.

The dominance of individual self-interest in combat units is also indicated by the letters soldiers write. Squad members who have returned to the United States seldom write to those remaining behind. In most cases, nothing more is heard from a soldier after he leaves the unit. Perhaps even more revealing, those still in the combat area seldom write their former buddies. Despite protestations of lifelong friendship during the shared combat period, the rupture of communication is entirely mutual, once a soldier is out of danger. The soldier writes almost exclusively to those he expects to see when he leaves the service: his family and relatives, girl friends, and civilian male friends.

Do these contrasting interpretations of the network of social relations in combat units—the primary groups of World War II, the two-man relationships of the Korean War, and the essentially individualistic soldier in Vietnam described here—result from conceptual differences on the part of the commentators, or do they reflect substantive differences in the social cohesion of the American soldiers being described? If substantive differences do obtain, particularly between World War II and the wars in Korea and Vietnam, much of this variation could be accounted for by the disruptive effects on unit solidarity caused by the introduction of the rotation system in the latter two wars.

I propose that primary groups maintain the soldier in this combat role only when he has an underlying commitment to the worth of the larger social system for which he is fighting. This commitment need not be formally articulated, nor even perhaps consciously recognized. But the soldier must at some level accept, if not the specific purposes of the war, then at least the broader rectitude of the society of which he is a member.

Although American combat soldiers do not espouse overtly ideological sentiments and are extremely reluctant to voice patriotic rhetoric, this should not obscure the existence of more latent beliefs in the legitimacy, and even superiority, of the American way of life.

Quite consistently, the American combat soldier displays a profound skepticism of political and ideological appeals. Somewhat paradoxically, then, anti-ideology itself is a recurrent and integral part of the soldier's belief system. They dismiss patriotic slogans or exhortations to defend democracy with: "What a crock," "Be serious, man," or "Who's kidding who?" In particular, they have little belief that they are protecting an outpost of democracy in South Vietnam. United States Command Information pronouncements stressing defense of South Vietnam as an outpost of the "Free World" are almost as dubiously received as those of Radio Hanoi which accuse Americans of imperialist aggression. As one soldier put it, "Maybe we're supposed to be here and maybe not. But you don't have time to think about things like that. You worry about getting zapped and dry socks tomorrow. The other stuff is a joke."

In this same vein, when the soldier responds to the question of why he is in Vietnam, his answers are couched in a quite individualistic frame of reference. He sees little connection between his presence in Vietnam and the national policies that brought him there. Twenty-seven of the thirty-four combat soldiers I interviewed defined their presence in the war in terms of personal misfortune. Typical responses were: "My outfit was sent over here and me with it," "My tough luck in getting drafted," "I happened to be at the wrong place at the wrong time," "I was fool enough to join this man's army," and "My own stupidity for listening to the recruiting sergeant." Only five soldiers mentioned broader policy implications—to stop Communist aggression. Two soldiers stated they requested assignment to Vietnam because they wanted to be "where the action is."

Because of the combat soldier's overwhelming propensity to see the war in private and personal terms, I had to ask them specifically what they thought the United States was doing in Vietnam. When the question was phrased in this manner, the soldiers most often said they were in Vietnam "to stop Communism." This was about the only ideological slogan these American combat soldiers could be brought to utter; nineteen of the thirty-four interviewed soldiers saw stopping Communism as the purpose of the war. But when they expressed this view it was almost always in terms of defending the United States, not the "Free World" in general and certainly not South Vietnam. They said, "The only way we'll keep them out of the States is to kill them here."

Fifteen of the soldiers gave responses other than stopping Communism. Three gave frankly cynical explanations of the war by stating that domestic prosperity in the United States depended on a war economy. Two soldiers held that the American intervention was a serious mistake initially, but that it was now too late to back out because of America's reputation. One man gave a Malthusian interpretation, arguing that war was needed to limit population growth. Nine of the soldiers could give no reason for the war even after extensive discussion. Within this group, one heard responses such as: "I only wish I knew" and "I've been wondering about that ever since I got here."

I asked each of the nineteen soldiers who mentioned stopping Communism as the purpose of the war what was so bad about Communism that it must be stopped at the risk of his own life. The first reaction to such a question was usually perplexity or rueful shrugging. After thinking about it, and with some prodding, twelve of the men expressed their distaste for Communism by stressing its authoritarian aspects in social relations. They saw Communism as a system of excessive social regimentation which allows the individual no autonomy in the pursuit of his own happiness.

Typical descriptions of Communism were: "That's when you can't do what you want to do," "Somebody's always telling you what to do," or "You're told where you work, what you eat, and when you shit." As one man wryly put it, "Communism is something like the army."

While the most frequently mentioned features of Communism concerned individual liberty, other descriptions were also given. Three soldiers mentioned the atheistic and antichurch aspects of Communism; two specifically talked of the absence of political parties and democratic political institutions; and one man said Communism was good in theory but could never work in practice because human beings were "too selfish." Only one soldier mentioned the issue of public-versus-private-property ownership.

I could stress once again that the soldiers managed to offer reasons for the war or descriptions of Communism only after extended discussions and questioning. When left to themselves, they rarely discussed the goals of America's military intervention in Vietnam, the nature of Communist systems, or other political issues.

To say that the American soldier is not overtly ideological is not to deny the existence of salient values that do contribute to his motivation in combat. Despite the soldier's lack of ideological concern and his pronounced embarrassment in the face of patriotic rhetoric, he nevertheless displays an elemental American nationalism in the belief that the United States is the best country in the world. Even though he hates being in the war, the combat soldier typically believes—with a kind of joyless patriotism—that he is fighting for his American homeland.

The soldier definitely does *not* see himself fighting for South Vietnam. Quite the contrary, he thinks South Vietnam is a worthless country, and its people contemptible. The low regard in which the Vietnamese—"slopes" or "gooks"— are held is constantly present in the derogatory comments on the avarice of those who pander to GI's, the treachery of all Vietnamese, and the numbers of Vietnamese young men in the cities who are not in the armed forces. Anti-Vietnamese sentiment is most glaringly apparent in the hostility toward the ARVN (Army of the Republic of Vietnam, pronounced "Arvin"), who are their supposed military allies. Disparaging remarks about "Arvin's" fighting qualities are common.

A variety of factors underlies the soldier's fundamental pro-Americanism, not the least of them being his immediate reliance on fellow Americans for mutual support in a country where virtually all indigenous people are seen as actual or potential threats to his physical safety. He also has deep concern for his family and loved ones back home. These considerations, however, are true of any army fighting in a foreign land. It is on another level, then, that I tried to uncover those aspects of American society that were most relevant and important to the combat soldier.

To obtain such a general picture of the soldier's conception of his homeland, I asked the following question, "Tell me in your own words, what makes America different from other countries?" The overriding feature in the soldier's perception of America is the creature comforts that American life can offer. Twenty-two of the soldiers described the United States by saying it had high-paying jobs, automobiles, consumer goods and leisure activities. No other description of America came close to being mentioned as often as the high—and apparently uniquely American—material standard of living. Only four of the soldiers emphasized America's democratic political institutions; three mentioned religious and spiritual values; two spoke of the general characteristics of the American people; and one said America was where the individual advanced on his own worth; another talked of America's natural and physical beauties; and one black soldier described America as racist. Put in another way, it is the materialistic—and I do not use the word pejoratively—aspects of life in America that are most salient to combat soldiers.

The soldier's belief in the superiority of the American way of life is further reinforced by the contrast with the Vietnamese standard of living. The combat soldier cannot help making invidious comparisons between the life he led in the United States—even if he is working-class—and what he sees in Vietnam. Although it is more pronounced in the Orient, it must be remembered that Americans abroad—whether military or civilian—usually find themselves in locales that compare unfavorably with the material richness of the United States. Indeed, should American soldiers ever be stationed in a country with a markedly higher standard of living than that of the United States, I believe they would be severely shaken in their belief in the merits of American society.

Moreover, the fighting soldier, by the very fact of being in combat, leads an existence that is not only more dangerous than civilian life but more primitive and physically harsh. The soldier's somewhat romanticized view of life back home is buttressed by his direct observation of the Vietnamese scene, and also by his own immediate lower standard of living.

The materialistic ethic is reflected in another characteristic of American servicemen. Even among front-line combat soldiers, one sees an extraordinary amount of valuable paraphernalia. Transistor radios are practically *de rigueur*. Cameras and other photographic accessories are widely evident and used. Even the traditional letter-writing home is becoming displaced by tape recordings. It seems more than coincidental that American soldiers commonly refer to the United States as "The Land of the Big PX."

Another factor that plays a part in combat motivation is

the notion of masculinity and physical toughness that pervades the soldier's outlook toward warfare. Being a combat soldier is a man's job. Front-line soldiers often cast aspersions on the virility of rear-echelon personnel ("titless WAC's"). A soldier who has not experienced combat is called a "cherry" (i.e., virgin). Likewise, paratroopers express disdain for "legs," as nonairborne soldiers are called. This he-man attitude is also found in the countless joking references to the movie roles of John Wayne and Lee Marvin. These definitions of masculinity are, of course, general in America, and the military organization seeks to capitalize on them with such perennial recruiting slogans as "The Marine Corps Builds Men" and "Join the Army and Be a Man."

Needless to say, however, the exaggerated masculine ethic is much less evident among soldiers after their units have been bloodied. As the realities of combat are faced, more prosaic definitions of manly honor emerge. (Also, there is more frequent expression of the male role in manifestly sexual rather than combative terms, for example, the repeatedly heard "I'm a lover, not a fighter.") That is, notions of masculinity serve to create initial motivation to enter combat, but recede once the life-and-death facts of warfare are confronted. Moreover, once the unit is tempered by combat, definitions of manly honor are not seen to encompass individual heroics. Quite the opposite, the very word "hero" is used to describe negatively any soldier who recklessly jeopardizes the unit's welfare.

On both of my trips to Vietnam I repeatedly heard combat soldiers—almost to a man—vehemently denounce peace demonstrators back in the United States. At first glance, such an attitude might be surprising. After all, peaceniks and soldiers both fervently want the troops brought home. In fact, however, the troops I interviewed expressed overt political sentiments only when the antiwar demonstrations came up in the talk. Significantly, the soldier perceived the peace demonstrations as being directed against himself personally and not against the war. "Did I vote to come here? Why blame the GI?" There was also a widespread feeling that if peace demonstrators were in Vietnam they would change their minds. As one man stated: "How can they know what's happening if they're sitting on their asses in the States? Bring them here and we'd shape them up quick enough." Or, as one of the more philosophically inclined put it, "I'd feel the same way if I were back home. But once you're here and your buddies are getting zapped, you have to see things different."

Much of the soldier's dislike of peace demonstrators is an outcome of class hostility. To many combat soldiers—themselves largely working-class—peace demonstrators are socially privileged college students. I heard many remarks such as the following: "I'm fighting for those candy-asses just because I don't have an old man to support me." "I'm stuck here and those rich draft dodgers are having a ball raising hell." "You'd think they'd have more sense with all that smart education."

The peace demonstrators, moreover, were seen as undercutting and demeaning the losses and hardships already suffered by American soldiers. Something of this sort undoubtedly contributed to the noticeable hawklike sentiments of combat soldiers. "If we get out now, then every GI died for nothing. Is this why I've been putting my ass on the line?" Here we seem to have an illustration of a more general social phenomenon: the tendency in human beings to justify to themselves sacrifices they have already made. Sacrifice itself can create legitimacy for an organization over a short period of time. It is only after some point, when sacrifices suddenly seem too much, that the whole enterprise comes under critical reevaluation. But sharp questioning of past and future sacrifices does not generally occur among combat soldiers in Vietnam. I believe this is because the twelve-month rotation system removes the soldier from the combat theater while his personal stake remains high and before he might begin to question the whole operation. The rotation system, in other words, not only maintains individual morale but also fosters a collective commitment to justify American sacrifices.

The soldier's hostility toward peace demonstrators is reinforced by his negative reactions to the substance of certain antiwar arguments. For while the combat soldier is constantly concerned with his own and his fellow American's safety, as well as being a fundamental believer in the American way of life and being profoundly apolitical to boot, the radical element of the peace movement mourns the suffering of the Vietnamese, is vehement in its anti-Americanism, and is self-consciously ideological. At almost every point, the militant peace movement articulates sentiments in direct opposition to the basic values of the American soldier. Statements bemoaning civilian Vietnamese casualties are interpreted as wishes for greater American losses. Assertions of the United States' immorality for its interventionism run contrary to the soldier's elemental belief in the rectitude of the American nation. Arguments demonstrating that the Viet Cong are legitimate revolutionaries have no credence both because of the soldier's ignorance of Vietnamese history and, more important, because the Viet Cong are out to kill him. As one man summed it up: "I don't know who are the good guys or the bad guys, us or the V.C. But anybody who shoots at me ain't my friend. Those college punks are going to answer to a lot of us when we get back."

It must be stressed, however, that the soldier's dislike of peace demonstrators is reactive and does not imply any preexisting support for the war. Paradoxically, then, the more militant peace demonstrations have probably created a level of support for the war among combat soldiers that would otherwise be absent. This is not to say that the soldier is immune to antiwar arguments. But the kind of arguments that would be persuasive among soldiers (e.g., Vietnam is not worth American blood; South Vietnam is manipulating the United States; the corruptness of the Saigon regime and ineptitude of the ARVN make for needless U.S. casualties) are not the ones usually voiced by radical peace groups. The *combat soldier is against peace demonstrators rather than for the war.* For it should also be known that he has scant affection for support-the-boys campaigns in the United States. Again, the attitude that "they don't know what it's all about" applies. As one soldier succinctly put it—and his words spoke for most: "The only support I want is out."

HOW THEY GET
AWAY FROM IT ALL

---

by Gurney Williams
and Jerry Parker

Gurney Williams and Jerry Parker are both staff writers for Newsday.

The song says anyone can have a good time, regardless of wealth. "Not much money," the words say, "but ain't we got fun?" Well, yes and no.

What's your idea of fun? Two on the aisle at a big Broadway musical? Catching a movie (at $2.50 a ticket) at its first Long Island showing? Dinner at an expensive North Shore restaurant or a fancy South Shore seafood place? Two weeks of April in Paris?

Or is it bowling followed by a couple of beers, a backyard barbecue with the folks, Sundays with the kids at Jones Beach, curling up in front of the television or behind a red-hot paperback best seller, and living *en famille* in a tent pitched somewhere in the great outdoors for a week or so?

For many there is no choice. For the average Joe trying to run a house, keep a wife and raise a couple of kids on a salary that falls on the right side of the poverty line but the wrong side of affluence, the sweet life so easily accessible on

Long Island or Manhattan might as well be on the moon.

"Fun?" said the mental-hospital attendant when asked what he did for it. "By the time I get all the bills paid I have nothing left over for fun."

"Fun?" said the factory worker when asked what he did for it. "I work two jobs every day and sometimes pump gas for extra cash on the weekends. I got no time for fun and I got no energy for it. When I come home I flop."

For the lower-middle-income working man, enjoyment is often both rare and simple. Few families seem to budget for entertainment as such. They are not poor, but they do not often have spare cash. When they do, they use it for fun. "For really big things we save up special," one man said. "Otherwise, if we have a few dollars, we go to the movies or go bowling. If we don't, we don't."

Perhaps the most common form of enjoyment for the working family is the cheapest—visiting friends. The immediate cost is almost nil, though the visitor does feel obliged to be the host at some later date, which means stocking up on beer, soda and crackers. It's just a few dollars once or twice a month. Older people with grown children say they prefer to visit the children, especially if there are grandchildren. Younger couples take turns holding small get-togethers at each other's homes.

Perhaps nothing so dramatically illustrates the working-man's lack of entertainment outside the home than the testimony of so many of them that they almost never go to the movies. "I haven't been to a movie in at least five years," one man said. For two generations, motion pictures had been the average man's bedrock entertainment. Now they are often out of his reach.

A survey commissioned last year by the Motion Picture Association of America showed that although 60 percent of all moviegoing is done at suburban theaters and drive-ins, it is the young and better-educated suburbanite who is doing the bulk of it. The survey showed that persons between sixteen and twenty-four account for 48 percent of all adult admissions. Persons between sixteen and forty accounted for 74 percent of admissions.

Education, which generally parallels income, also is directly related to moviegoing. Thirty-nine percent of college-educated persons go to the movies regularly, meaning once a month or more. But among those who have only finished high school, only 27 percent regularly attend movies, and the percentage is lower still for those who have not graduated from high school.

Partly this is because moviegoing has become expensive. In Long Island, N.Y., for example, an early showing of a relatively new movie costs $2.50 a ticket, though some second-run theaters are experimenting with $1 admissions. Another reason is that many workingmen like to take their children to movies, partly because baby-sitters are expensive and partly because they don't see enough of their children, and fewer children's movies are being made these days.

What has replaced the movies for many lower-middle-income families is, of course, television, which may explain why so many men are willing to add to their already heavy debt burden by buying a color TV set on a time-payment plan. According to the Nielsen Television Index for the heavy-viewing winter months, the average household in the $5,000–$9,000 income range had its TV set on for 15.5 of the 24.5 prime-time viewing hours each week. Actually, this was just six minutes a week more than the viewing of more affluent families, those with more than $10,000 a year. Rich or poor, it seems that anyone who owns a television set has it on from two to two-and-a-half hours a night. But there is a striking difference in the programs they prefer. The tastes of lower-middle-income viewers run to the

more folksy, down-home shows (the *Glen Campbell Show,
Bonanza, Mayberry RFD, Beverly Hillbillies*). The more
affluent viewers watch the relatively more sophisticated
shows such as *Mission Impossible,* the *Dean Martin Show*
and *Julia.*

Laugh-In is No. 1 with both groups, but the late
Smothers Brothers Show, No. 9 with the affluent viewers,
was not even on the top twenty among lower-middle-income
viewers. The Nielsen survey showed that about 45 percent
of the total national audience earns between $5,000 and
$9,000 a year, and though there is a trend among advertis-
ers toward appealing to more affluent, youthful viewers,
network officials concede it is still the lower-middle-income
adult whose tastes are paramount.

Contrary to the stereotype of the dull, nearly illiterate
worker, many lower-middle-class people read quite a lot.
They don't buy very many new hard-cover books, which
start at about $5 a copy these days, but many hold library
cards, and use them, or buy paperbacks. About 350 million
paperbacks were sold in the United States last year. John
Hummler, the national chain-store-jobber sales manager
for Bantam Books, Inc., one of the five big paperback pub-
lishers, doesn't know how many were bought by people in
the lower-middle class. But obviously plenty were.

"We do a lot of our business in the discount stores and
in the dime stores," said Hummler, whose company said
working families account almost entirely for the success of
some authors. Take, for example, Emilie Loring. She is not
exactly a giant of twentieth-century literature, but 20 million copies of her books have been sold under thirty-five
different titles. Nearly all Loring books are sold in discount
stores and dime stores.

Music apparently does little to soothe the average workingman, except the music he may hear on a TV variety
show. Record dealers say they believe few albums are sold

to lower-middle-income adults, though their children like rock music that the parents, especially those of middle age, often find distracting. One form of music that does seem popular with workers, especially women, is country and Western.

When a working family does go out, it is often a big night planned long in advance and hopefully remembered for some time, until they can afford to do it again. Right now, Pasquale (Pat) Iadevia, thirty-four, and his wife are planning a night out with five other couples. They are saving up the $30 or $40 they figure it will cost to get a baby-sitter for their three daughters, buy tickets to see comedian Pat Cooper at the Westbury Music Fair, and have dinner at a restaurant.

Iadevia earns $8,600 a year as a landscaper at Salisbury Park and sometimes picks up some extra cash working at a gas station on weekends. The Iadevias rarely go out, have never taken a real vacation trip, and spend all their surplus time and money on improving their two-bedroom Westbury bungalow.

On Long Island, there are nearly as many bowling alleys as there are movie theaters, at least sixty-five in Nassau and forty in Suffolk. But bowlers all seem to be what one bowling-alley cocktail waitress described as "just plain working people." When a person likes bowling, he really likes bowling.

Mrs. Stella Daskauskas, a Westbury housewife, mother of two teenage sons and wife of a New York City motorman, stood waiting her turn to bowl one recent night at the Garden City Bowl. Asked what her leisure activities were, she replied, "Bowling, what else?" Mrs. Daskauskas bowls Tuesday and Wednesday nights, as part of a bowling league. Her husband's league bowls Friday nights. The Daskauskases often go out with other couples on Saturday nights.

"We go bowling," she said. "We have to practice up. Then we go to somebody's house for beer and cold cuts or coffee and dessert."

It is perhaps at vacation time when the lack of money hurts most. Josephine Iadevia, who has seen all those "Come on down" television commercials, would like to go to Florida. Carol Boyle, a Carle Place housewife, and her airlines mechanic husband manage to go on vacation by camping out with their four sons. "I like camping," she said. "I recommend it to everyone." But she concedes that if she didn't like it, her family would have to stay home: "With four boys, staying at motels would be out of the question."

Most workers do not go away on vacation. They stay home and work around the house, which is all they have of value in the world. Sometimes they save up for a weekend trip to relatives, a night at the movies, a week's camping. In the meantime, they work very hard.

PART 3

PRIDE AND
PREJUDICE

A BLACK VIEW
OF THE WHITE WORKER

by James Boggs

*Auto worker and revolutionary theoretician, James
Boggs has been exploring the concept of black power
in relation to the impact of cybernation ever since
1963, when his book* The American Revolution:
Pages from a Negro Worker's Notebook *appeared.
He has written widely here and abroad on the ideology of the black revolution.*

In my book *The American Revolution* I traced the decline
of organized labor in the United States from a *movement*
(which once launched the social productive forces of this
highly advanced society onto the road of control of production) to a *bureaucracy* that does not move today except in
support of the Establishment. Its relationship to the Establishment in every sphere—industrial, political and military
—is that of a force that accepts the American capitalist system as the best in the world and only wants it reformed and
refined a little to give workers a bigger share of the pie.

When we speak of the labor movement in the United
States, it is necessary to remember that we are talking primarily of a Northern movement. Organized labor never
really could or would tackle the question of the division of
labor in the South between whites and blacks. Only in the

mines and mills, where the ethnic structure was already firmly entrenched, did labor organize in the South.

Until World War II the industrial work force of the United States consisted chiefly of immigrants from Europe who had come to this country to escape regimented and impoverished lives and who had a vision of the United States as a land where one could rise from rags to riches in a few years. With this view of the land to which they were coming, it was only natural that these workers accepted the attitude toward black people held by the whites already here. It is true that these workers waged many militant struggles against the American capitalists, but these struggles were always limited by the workers' acceptance of racist policies by which the blacks were kept beneath them and by the fact that they themselves were willing to keep the blacks down as a basis for their own elevation.

In the early days of the civil rights movement, labor, especially its national leadership and the CIO wing, fought for legislation against both the poll tax and lynching. Since such legislation had little concrete meaning for rank-and-file Northern workers, they supported these activities passively and without protest. In the early days of the King movement in the South, local unions even sent donations to the civil rights cause, usually under the influence of the few socially conscious radicals who still remained in or around the unions, having weathered the McCarthy witch hunts that virtually purged the labor movement of those with any serious social consciousness.

I am not suggesting that the labor organizations would have been very much different if the socially conscious radicals had not been purged, for not even these radicals ever seriously dreamed of blacks becoming a social force in this country that would be demanding social changes far beyond labor's wildest dreams.

In *The American Revolution* I said that *if* it had been possible, around 1948, to incorporate the black work force into production, and into the labor movement, then it might have been possible to visualize the integration of the races in the United States. That was speculation. What has happened is that blacks themselves have begun to struggle outside the labor apparatus and in so doing have put severe tests and strain on the labor unions.

For when blacks demanded equal job opportunities, the unions replied that, although they were on record as favoring such opportunities, only management and the government had the power to provide jobs. They preferred to shift the responsibility for stimulating jobs, even make-believe ones like the WPA jobs of the thirties, to government, because, as long as it was government's responsibility, the unions would not have to confront their predominantly white memberships on this question. The unions obviously were not prepared to suggest that white workers give up their jobs to blacks. The alternative was to suggest that all suffer together and thus find a basis for struggling together. A few black workers in the labor organizations suggested this, but received no support from the labor leadership. Instead, the leadership evaded the issue and thus allowed the wrath and fears of the white workers to simmer and increase as blacks pressed their demands for equal job opportunities.

Older black workers inside the union tended to become complacent and even now are not a serious factor either inside the labor organizations or in the black movement. They can best be described as conservative, while the older white workers must be characterized as reactionary.

Actually, it is putting it mildly to call white workers reactionary. The AFL is dominated by the skilled trades—construction workers, carpenters, brickmasons, electricians, sheet-metal workers, ironworkers, painters—who for the most part are arrogantly hostile to black workers. The AFL leadership is comfortable with the counterrevolution at home and abroad. Merely supporting the foreign policy of the United States is not enough for it; it screams for more extreme counterrevolutionary measures. It is not only anticommunist but profascist. AFL workers, spurred on by their leaders and spurring on their leaders, have become the staunchest supporters of the Vietnam war and the most militant enemies of protesting students and pacifists.

The leaders of UAW and CIO unions are little better. Far from guiding their membership in a struggle *against* the war in Vietnam most have encouraged support of the war. The main difference is that the UAW-CIO unions attempt to maintain a liberal image through association with allegedly liberal politicians.

Except where questions of higher pay are involved, the rank-and-file white worker in the United States is more conservative than most politicians and industrialists in relation to the black movement. Many industrialists and politicians see the need to make concessions to blacks for the sake of social peace, at home and abroad. But the average white worker only sees the black movement as a direct threat to himself and his own position and privileges.

Fascism in the United States is unique because it is developing from the grass roots rather than from the top down. Today such organizations as the Minutemen, the White Citizens Council, the America Firsters and scores of others that have been organized to defend the United States against black demands for justice are made up of workers, skilled and unskilled. These workers are the ones who work with blacks inside the shop during the day and then return to their homes in the suburbs at night to organize against the same blacks. Sometimes they will confide in some black worker with whom they have worked for many years that their hostility is not against him but against those "jitterbugs" and "guerrillas" in the black ghetto. They are completely insensitive to the fact that the black jitterbugs and guerrillas to whom they refer are the sons of the black workers in whom they are confiding. They don't seem to care that their unconcealed antagonism is educating even some of the older, passive blacks into more militant positions.

White workers tend to see blacks as threatening their jobs when in fact their jobs are being threatened by automation and cybernation. Instead of accepting the technical progress of automation and using it as a basis to demand the right to a decent livelihood for everyone, working or not, they have chosen the road of fighting blacks not only on the job market but even in other arenas involving the black community, such as schools and police, where white workers are not directly threatened. Often afraid to confront blacks at the point of production, they organize outside the plant with the aim of inflaming not only white workers but other groups in the white population not engaged in the process of production. Thus, side by side with the development of the black revolutionary forces are growing the counterrevolutionary forces of white workers.

Today, when the police force of every major city is actually an occupation army for black people, white workers have become the chief supporters of the "Support Your Local Police" movement. Wherever you find a community consciously excluding blacks on the basis of race, it turns out to be a community of workers. (Bourgeois communities exclude blacks on the basis of economics.) In every major urban center there is a suburb notorious for its exclusion of blacks. In Detroit it is Dearborn, which is composed mainly of Polish workers who fled from Hamtramck, which is inside the Detroit city limits and was once the largest Polish settlement outside of Warsaw. Dearborn's residents are refugees from a Hamtramck encircled by blacks. Dearborn's mayor is elected year after year on the slogan "Keep Dearborn

Clean"—meaning, of course, clean from black people. Chicago has Cicero, where Italian workers keep the neighborhoods "clean." Cleveland has a Slavic section and an Italian section, both of which mobilize periodically for pitched battles with blacks. These two ethnic groups stand out, but they only express more dramatically what is deeply embedded in every ethnic grouping of the white working class.

"White working class" does not have the same meaning in the United States as in the classical European interpretation, because white workers, by the very nature of the country's historical development, are in a class above all blacks. "The worker" (i.e., the white worker) supports the system precisely because it has provided him with this superior position even when he is worse off economically than some blacks.

Of all the classes in the United States the worker feels most threatened by the blacks. Today the worst thing that could happen in this country would be the arming of these workers. In fact, fascist tendencies are growing so rapidly among them and they are already arming themselves at such a rapid rate that even the power structure is deeply disturbed, fearful that white workers will turn on it if it makes any concessions to the black movement. At this stage, however, these workers are content to vent their hate and frustration on the blacks. Wherever possible, these workers join the special forces that have been set up by the police or by city administrations to assist in time of emergency in putting the blacks back in their place.

Blacks in the United States have long since bypassed the labor organizations. No one knows this better than the labor leaders themselves, who cannot relate to the young blacks either inside or outside the labor force and find the few old blacks whom they have incorporated into their political machines of little use in trying to relate to young blacks. Younger blacks are extremely sensitive to the antagonism of white workers and cannot distinguish them from oppressors. Already in Detroit, home of the UAW and of the late Walter Reuther, labor's most progressive spokesman, young black workers are rallying to DRUM (Dodge Revolutionary Union Movement). DRUM is made up of young black production workers who have now organized local groups inside the Ford and General Motors plants after a series of successful wildcat strikes at the Chrysler Hamtramck plant. These black workers represent the new street force whose allegiance is to the black community, not to labor. Unlike the older black workers who were grateful for any job, these younger men believe that their confinement to the old backbreaking jobs on the production line is strictly a manifestation of the racism in American society. From their point of view, these jobs, no matter how much they pay, are no better than the field-hand jobs their slave forefathers were forced to perform in the South. What the union and an older generation of workers accept as the company's prerogative, these young blacks challenge. To them, the statement that the "company has the sole right to run the plant as it sees fit" expresses not a truth but a popular prejudice.

The demands and the expectations of these young black workers far exceed the wildest dreams of the labor movement and of earlier generations of workers even in their most militant days. The white workers who monopolize the skilled jobs—plumbers, electricians, tool-and-die men, machine repairmen—think only in terms of more money per hour. The DRUM member, at the bottom of the production ladder, demands the hiring of black plant doctors, fifty black foremen and even a black chairman for the board of directors. He is not satisfied with any old job; he wants control of the plant itself.

Inside the plant, white workers are being shaken up, not

just by these demands but by the fact that older black workers who once seemed so docile are becoming increasingly sympathetic and even supportive of the young blacks, thus threatening the peaceful coexistence between white and black inside the plant that was once so comforting to the white workers.

Since white racism is expressing itself at the present time most clearly inside the white work force, and since black power is regarded by the white worker as the main threat to his hard-won comforts, a clash is inevitable. This clash is being staved off today only because the military forces of this country, whether in the form of the police, the National Guard, state troopers or the United States Army, have made it clear that they will be employed to crush the blacks. Thus reassured, the unofficial white forces have not felt it necessary to rush into the ghetto.

The inevitable clash cannot be averted by the labor leaders. In fact, labor leaders are irrelevant to it. They have waited too long to intervene. For too many years they have allowed white workers to go their merry and not-so-merry way, joining and supporting the system until their policies have become indistinguishable from the racist policies of the system and are in fact the system's main prop.

In the United States the alienation of man from man started long before the alienation of man from production. It is from this alienation that blacks and whites of the lowest strata of the society will bleed the most.

WHITE AGAINST WHITE

The Enduring Ethnic Conflict

---

by Andrew M. Greeley

The Rev. Andrew M. Greeley is program director of the National Opinion Research Center at the University of Chicago. His article is excerpted from Why Can't They Be Like Us? Facts and Fallacies About Ethnic Differences and Group Conflicts in America, *published by the Institute of Human Relations Press of the American Jewish Committee.*

A number of social scientists, most notably Lewis Coser, have argued that social conflict is a good thing, that it is a safety valve permitting society or groups within it to let off excess steam, which, if contained, could lead to violent explosions. Coser argues that when the patterns of relationships in society are no longer adequate to the social realities, group conflict is a way of forcing a restructuring without destroying the patterns completely. Thus, if a given ethnic group has less political power than its size, conflict between this group and other groups with more power than their size seems to warrant is a way of restructuring the social order before frustration and dissatisfaction tear it apart.

In the context of Coser's very wise theorizing, black mili-

tancy can be seen as highly constructive for society, because
it has forced concessions to the blacks of positions, prestige,
power, control and responsibility appropriate to their numbers, their stake in society and their emerging self-consciousness. If there was no social conflict to force this restructuring, there might be an eruption that would tear apart the
total society. Although some black extremists use a rhetoric
of destruction, it still seems safe to say that, thus far, black
militancy seems to have restructuring rather than destruction
as its goal.

The late John Courtney Murray wrote and spoke frequently of the "conspiracies" within American society. He
argued that the various religious groups were indeed competing for power and influence, but at least within some
vaguely agreed-upon "rules of the game"—rules that everyone was careful not to make too explicit, lest the very expli-
citness become a source for conflict. Social conflict is likely
to lead to destruction when there is not even a vague agreement. The nonviolent phase of the civil rights movement op-
erated under rather explicitly agreed-upon rules of the
game, and even though the nonviolent phase is now assumed to be over, a substantial segment of the black leadership still seems willing to settle, in reality if not in rhetoric,
as did other ethnic groups before them, for "more" within
the existing structure. The struggle between the black school
districts and the white, largely Jewish teachers' union in
New York seems to bode ill for the future of the city precisely because it springs from a disagreement on the rules of
the game.

Most of the conflicts between ethnic and religio-ethnic
groups currently going on in American society are well
within the rules of the game. Violence may occasionally
break out, especially between the races and on the fringes
where one ethnic ghetto brushes against another, either
physically or psychologically. But given the size, complexity

and newness of American society, the astonishing fact is not that there is inter-ethnic conflict but that it is not more destructive.

There is, first of all, the conflict of political competition. In New York, there is the struggle between Jews and Catholics for control of the Democratic Party—a struggle that has led some Jews to form what is basically their own political party, the Liberal Party. And among the Catholics there is conflict between the Italians and the Irish for control of the Democratic Party. The Republican Party is still basically white Protestant, though it has managed to attract some liberal Jews who find the liberal and aristocratic WASP more to their liking than either the unsophisticated Catholics of the Democratic Party or the socialistically oriented Jews in the Liberal Party. The blacks and the Puerto Ricans are generally within the confines of the Democratic coalition, and have been accorded some positions of power and prestige, but nowhere in keeping with their numbers.

The second focus for ethnic conflict is housing. As each group improves its economic situation, it seeks new housing —new, at least, for it—and begins to move from its original location into neighborhoods that have previously been the preserve of other ethnic groups. Generally speaking, the first neighborhoods to be so "invaded" are already declining, either out of physical obsolescence or because the most ambitious of its citizens are already seeking better housing for themselves. But invasion by a "foreign" ethnic group is a profound threat; not only does it imply (despite overwhelming evidence to the contrary) a decline in sales value of one's own house, it also is a challenge to friendship patterns, churches, familiar landscape and shopping areas, and all those things a man has come to value in that particular area he thinks of as his own.

The conflict between white and black has been so well publicized in recent years that we tend to forget that other ethnic groups have "battled" for neighborhoods, and that such conflicts continue even today. When I was growing up on the west side of Chicago, an Italian family was only a little more welcome in an Irish neighborhood on the south side than a Negro family would have been; and while the replacement of Poles by Puerto Ricans in Chicago is more peaceful than the replacement of whites by blacks, there is still tension and potential conflict in the replacement of one ethnic group by another.

Education provides another focus for inter-ethnic conflict. Again, the most obvious conflict today is between blacks and whites over attempts to create racial balance in the public school system and the efforts of black militants to gain more and more control of the schools in their own communities (which means, in part, control over white teachers who work in these schools). But various white ethnic groups have fought among themselves for control of the public school system, with Catholics warring against Protestants and various Catholic groups fighting each other.

Ethnic battles also rage in the trade unions, where leadership, once Irish or German or Jewish, has recently shifted somewhat toward the Italians and the Slavic immigrant groups. In the meantime, the blacks have become conscious that they are under-represented at the middle and higher levels of union leadership and are beginning to demand what they deem to be adequate representation in the upper councils of labor.

In the business world, particularly the world of the small shop or the small entrepreneur, such as the construction contractor, vigorous if not vicious and cut-throat competition exists along ethnic lines, though there is little documentation on the subject. Similarly, in the underworld of the rackets, the Italian (which is to say, generally, Sicilian) leadership of years gone by now finds itself beginning to be threatened by restless black allies.

While it is difficult in our present state of knowledge to sort out the different influences of race, ethnicity and religion, it is not always important for practical purposes that we do so. But we must remember that it is not merely religious theory that makes Catholics and Jews suspicious of each other, nor merely racial history that creates the problem in Ocean Hill-Brownsville. The struggle between Catholic and Jew over the public schools, for example, is not so much rooted in religious differences as in the political and social styles of two immigrant groups jockeying for prestige and power in an urban world where they are closely juxtaposed. Only if we understand that the battle is between two groups searching for more power lest it be used against them, can we understand the depth of the passions and fears involved.

In both the Catholic-Jewish and the Negro-Jewish conflicts, religion and race and class are, of course, involved in many different ways, but I am suggesting that even if all these factors could be drained out of the conflict, the basic resentment toward a group of "strangers" who are trying to take something from us, or keep something from us that is rightfully ours, will make the conflict almost as serious as it is at the present time.

We now turn from speculation and theory about ethnicity to some concrete findings about differences among ethnic groups in America. Data obtained from a number of national and neighborhood studies conducted in the 1960's by the National Opinion Research Center, though sometimes difficult to tie together in a coherent pattern, do allow us to make the following generalizations.

The earlier immigrant groups are both the most socially successful and the most tolerant, but there are enough differences between, say, the Irish and the Germans, or between the Italians and the Poles, to suggest that other factors are at work besides the time at which one's parents washed up on American shores.

Of all the ethnic and religious groups the Jews are politically the most liberal and socially the most active, as well as economically the most successful. They are close to their parents, relatively less close to their siblings, and given to worrying.

Italians are conservative in their child-rearing practices and extremely close to their relatives—to their parents, basically because they live close to them, and to their siblings, because the sibling relationship is apparently very important to them. They are only moderately successful socially and economically, relatively uninvolved in organizational activity (perhaps because of their heavy family commitment) and liberal on some political questions, though more likely to leave the Democratic Party than are other Catholic ethnic groups. Though they think of themselves as very sociable, they are likely to have a lot of worries. They score rather low in measures of canonical religiousness, and fairly high on prejudice, though not as high as the Poles or the French. A college education apparently reduces, but does not completely eliminate, these differences in degree of prejudice.

The Irish are economically and socially the most successful among Catholic immigrant groups, and the most liberal, politically and socially. They have very strong ties with their siblings, are the most devoutly Catholic and least prejudiced, and their view of themselves ranks them as the happiest and most self-confident.

The Poles score lowest, economically and socially, of all Catholic immigrant groups; those in the Midwest who are not college graduates are the most likely to be prejudiced against blacks and Jews. They are very loyal to the Catholic Church (but in a more "ethnic" way than the Irish or the Germans). They are the most likely to be Democrats, and if they are college graduates, to be liberal Democrats. They are low in morale and sociability, and high on measures of anomie.

The many historical, sociological and psychological processes that are involved in producing these ethnic differences are still frustratingly obscure, but to me they constitute one of the most fascinating questions for social research still open in the American culture. And yet, anyone who argues that ethnic research is important is generally told, first, that the question is quite irrelevant because of the workings of the assimilation process, and, second, that it is a highly sensitive issue which might offend people if pushed too vigorously. How something can be irrelevant and sensitive, no longer an issue and still offensive, is one of those great paradoxes that we gentleman-adventurer sociologists must learn to live with.

But without knowledge, how is society to cope with the problems that ethnicity generates? For it seems to me that we must, above all, recognize that ethnic problems are likely to persist, and that it does little good to lament them or moralize about them. We must also be carefully aware of our own ethnic biases and not permit ourselves the luxury of superior attitudes toward behavior which, if the truth be told, we dislike mostly because it's not the sort of thing "our kind of people" might do. And, finally, we must be wary of turning correlations into causes. For example, if correlations between "Polishness" and certain ethnocentric attitudes are described, it would be quite easy to make a leap and say that being Polish "causes" the ethnocentric attitudes, even though there are no grounds for such an assumption. There may be something in the Polish cultural background to explain anti-Semitism, but there is nothing I can think of that would explain racism. Thus I would be much more inclined to see the conflict between the Poles and the

blacks in terms of the particular stage in the ethnic assimilation process that the Poles happen to have reached at the
time when the black group has become militant. In other
words, I am inclined to think we can explain the conflict
between the Poles and the blacks almost entirely in economic, social and psychological terms without having to fall
back on cultural traditions at all.

It is easy enough for liberals, intellectuals and other upper-
middle-class types to dismiss Slavic homeowners' fears as
primitive and uneducated, but they are still very real fears
and, up to a point, valid. Unless we can find ways to lessen
these fears—and I for one do not yet know how this can be
done—there is little ground for reasonably expecting that
racial hatred will decline.

The problem is not much easier with respect to the somewhat less intense controversies separating white ethnic
groups from one another. We simply do not know enough;
not enough data are available, not enough experiments have
been done, and all too few theories have been advanced to
enable us either to understand what is going on or to pre-
scribe remedies for the pathology we may observe.

It does seem to me, however, that it is essential for political leaders, social planners and influential figures in the ethnic communities to abandon the rather foolish controversy
of whether ethnicity is a good thing or a bad thing—particularly since it clearly has both good and bad effects—and
settle down to a better understanding of what it means and
how we may live with it, not merely tolerably, but fruitfully.

THE FEAR OF
EQUALITY

by Robert E. Lane

Professor of political science at Yale University, Robert Lane has for years been studying the social and psychological roots of political beliefs. Two of his major works are Political Life: Why People Get Involved in Politics *and* Political Ideology: Why the American Common Man Believes What He Does, *from which this article is taken. It should be noted that the interviews reported were made about a decade ago, before the onset of the racial and political ferment of the sixties.*

Since 1848 it has been assumed that the drive for a more equalitarian society would come from the stratum of society with the most to gain: the working classes. This was thought to be the revolutionary force in the world—the demand of workers for a classless society sparked by their hostility to the owning classes. It was to be the elite among the workers, not the *Lumpenproletariat*, not the "scum," who were to advance this movement. Just as "liberty" was the central slogan of the bourgeois revolution, so "equality" was the central concept in the working-class movement. Hence it was natural to assume that whatever gains have been made in equalizing the income and status of men in our society came about largely from working-class pressure.

But on closer investigation the demands for greater liberty or "freedom" prove to have been of an ambiguous nature. The middle classes sought freedom of speech and action in large part for the economic gains that this would give them, and moralized their action with the theology of freedom. But the freedom that they gained was frightening, for it deprived them of the solidarity in social relationships and the ideological certainty that often gave order and meaning to their lives. On occasion, then, as Erich Fromm has noted, they sought to "escape from freedom." The older unfree order had a value the earlier social commentators did not appreciate.

There is a parallel here with the movement toward a more equalitarian society. The upper working class and the lower-middle class support specific measures, embraced in the formula "welfare state," that have equalitarian consequences. But, actually, I shall argue, many members of the working classes do not want equality. They are afraid of it. In some ways they already seek to escape from it. Equality for the working classes, like freedom for the middle classes, is a worrisome, partially rejected by-product of the demand for more specific measures. Inequality has values to them that have been overlooked. It is these attitudes on status and equality that I shall explore here.

How to Account for One's Own Status

Attitudes toward equality rest in the first instance upon one's attitude toward one's own status. Like a large number of social beliefs, attitudes toward equality take their direction from beliefs about self, the status of the self, one's self-esteem or lack thereof. It is necessary, therefore, first to explore how people see themselves in American hierarchical society.

The American culture and the democratic dogma have given to the American public the notion that "all men are created equal." Even more insistently, the American culture tells its members: "Achieve," "Compete," "Be better, smarter, quicker, richer than your fellow men"; in short, "Be unequal." The men I interviewed (for *Political Ideology,* a study of "the common man"—i.e., upper-working-class and lower-middle-class men) had received these inequalitarian messages, some eagerly, some with foreboding. Having heard them, they must account for their status, higher than some, lower than others. They must ask themselves, for example, "Why didn't I rise out of the working class, or out of the 'housing-project class,' or out of the underpaid office-help class?" And, on the other hand, "Why am I better off than my parents or than the fellows down the road in the low-rental project or than the fellows on relief?" Men confronted with these questions adopt a variety of interesting answers.

Is It Up to Me?

The problem of accounting for status is personally important for these men only if they think that their decisions, effort, and energy make a difference in their position in life. Most of my subjects accepted the view that America opens up opportunity to all people, if not in equal proportions, then at least enough so that a person must assume responsibility for his own status. Thus O'Hara, a maintenance mechanic in a factory, in a typical response, comments that the rich man's son and the poor man's son "have equal opportunity to be President . . . if they've got the education and the know-how." But, he goes on to say, "Some of them have a little more help than others." This is the constant theme: "All men can better themselves"; the circumstances of American life do not imprison men in their class or station —if there is such a prison, the iron bars are within each man.

There were a few, of course, who stressed the differences of opportunity at birth, a mockery of the phrase "All men are created equal." Here, as only rarely in the interviews, a head of steam builds up that might feed radical social movements. But this is true for only a few of the sample. Three or four angry young or middle-aged men deny the Jeffersonian phrase. Rapuano, the packing-house clerk, says:

"How could you say we were born equal when, for instances when I was born, I was born in a family that were pretty poor. You get another baby born in a family that has millions."

And Kuchinsky, a roofer, says:

"Are we created equal? I don't believe we are, because everybody's got much more than another and it's not right, I think. Of course, ah, we have no choice. I mean we can't do nothing about it. So we're not as equal as the next party, that's for sure."

And Ferrera, a shoe salesman, says:

"All men created equal? Ah, very hypocritical, 'cause all men are not created equal—and—I don't know—you really pick some beauties, don't you? . . . The birth of an individual in a [social] class sort of disputes this."

To these men, then, subordination and life position are attributable not so much to the efforts of the individual, something for which we must assume responsibility, as to the circumstances of birth, over which he has no control. Yet for each of those men the channels of advancement were seen as only partly blocked. Rapuano, for example, says elsewhere that income is generally proportionate to ability. Like the theme of "moral equality," the theme of differential life chances from birth is easily available. What is surprising is not that it is used at all but rather that it is used so infrequently.

Reducing the Importance of the Struggle

When something is painful to examine, people look away, or, if they look at it, they see only the parts they want to see. They deny that it is an important something. So is it often with a person's class status when the reference is upward, when people must account, not for the strength of their position, but for its weakness. How do they do this?

In the first place they may *insulate* themselves, limit their outlook and range of comparisons. Ferrera, who says, "It's pretty hard for me to think there is anyone in the upper class and I'm not in the upper class," slides into a prepared position of insulated defense:

> "I think a lot of people place a lot of stress on the importance of social classes, [but] I feel that I have a job to do, I have my own little unit to take care of. If I can do it to the best ability that is instilled in me at birth or progress through the years, I feel that I rightly deserve the highest classification you can get. I don't particularly like the headings 'upper, middle, working, and lower.' "

It is a resentful narrowing of focus in this case: two years at an inferior college may have led to ambitions that life then failed to fulfill. Contrast this with Woodside, a railroad guard and auxiliary policeman with a Midwestern rural background, who accepts the "categories" of social class rather willingly. He says, after dealing with the moral and intangible aspects of equality, and after being asked, "Are there any people whom you regard as not being equal to you?"

"Well, that is a tough question. Well, in fairness, I'd say all people are equal to one another in his own category. When I say category, I mean you couldn't exactly expect a person that had very little knowledge to be, we'll say, should have a position where a person with a lot more education had it."

Equality must be treated within classes, not between them, to be meaningful—and in this way the problem of placing oneself becomes tolerable, or sometimes rather gratifying.

A second device for reducing the impact of class position is to deny its importance. This does not mean denying the importance of getting ahead, but limiting this to the problem of job classification or occupational choice—nothing so damaging to the self-esteem as an ordering of persons on a class scale. Rapuano, resisting the class concept, says:

"I don't think it [social class] is important. I mean, whenever I went and asked for a job, the boss never asked me what class I was in. They just wanted to know if I knew my business. Oh, yes, and I don't think in politics it makes any difference."

Others maintain that for other countries social class is important, but not for Americans. There are rich and poor, perhaps, but not status, class, or deference levels to be accounted for.

A third device for reducing the significance of the struggle for status and "success" is resignation, a reluctant acceptance of one's fate. When some men assume this posture of resignation one senses a pose; their secret hopes and ambitions will not down. For others it rings true. When Dempsey, a factory operative, speaks of his situation at the age of fifty-five, one believes him:

"It's hard, very hard. We seem to be struggling along now, as it is, right here, to try and get above our level,.to get out of the rut, as you might say, that we're probably in right now . . . [But] After you get to a certain age, there, you stop—and you say, 'Well, I can't go any further.' I think I've gotten to that point now."

But when Sokolsky reports that he is contented with his station in life, it does not seem authentic:

"Being in the average group [he wouldn't assign himself a class status] doesn't bother me. I know I make a living— as long as I make a living, and I'm happy and I have what I want—try to give my family what they want. It doesn't bother me—no. I'm satisfied."

But then he adds, "I hope to God my children will do better than their father did."

Contrast these views with those of Johnson, a mechanic, who says: "I feel someday, I'll be better off. I feel that way because I believe I have it within me to do it"; and with Flynn, a white-collar worker, who answers:

"No, I'm nowhere near satisfied. It seems to me every-time I start to move up a little bit, all the levels move up one step ahead of me. I can't ever get out of this area. I have a certain desire and willingness to do something extra."

The Working Class Gets Its Share

When comparing their status with those lower on the scale, however each man may define it, it is easy to point with pride to achievement, material well-being, standing in the community. But satisfaction with one's self and one's friends depends on seeing some advantage in one's situation vis-à-vis those who live and work on a higher status level. At first this seems to be a difficult task, but in many simple ways it can be easily done. Our sample, for instance, found ways of ascribing greater happiness, power, and even income to the working class than would be found in the upper class.

The equality of happiness is a fruitful vein. Lower income and status are more tolerable when one can believe that the rich are not receiving a happiness income commensurate with their money income. "Are the rich happier than people who are just average?" O'Hara does not think so:

> "I think lots of times they're never happy, because one thing is, the majority of them that are rich have got more worries. You see a lot more of them sick than you do, I think, the average. I think a lot of your mental strain is a lot greater in the higher class—in the rich class—than in the other."

And Johnson says:

> "Well, even though this rich man can go places and do things that others can't afford, there's only certain things in life that I think make people happy. For instance, having children, and having a place to live—no matter where it is, it's your home . . . the majority of these big men—I don't think they devote as much time and get a thrill out of the little things in life that the average guy gets, which I think is a lot of thrills."

Indeed, hardly a man thought the rich were happier. And yet, O'Hara says, on another occasion: "What is the most important thing that money can buy? Happiness, when you come down to it." Perhaps he means that money buys happiness for the average man but not for the rich. In this way he can cope with a mild envy by appropriating happiness for himself and "his kind."

Power, like happiness, is awarded to the working (or lower-middle) class. The sheer fact of numbers gives a sense of strength and importance. Costa, a factory operative, says, for example, "People like you [the interviewer] are the minority and people like me are the majority, so we get taken care of in the long run." Whether a person sees himself as middle-class or working-class, he is likely to believe that most people belong to his class. This being true, his class, people like him, becomes the most important force in electoral decisions. O'Hara puts it this way:

> "The biggest part of the people in this country are working class. And I think they've got the most to do with— they've got a big part to do with running this country— because the lower class, a lot of them don't vote, when you come down to it, they don't have the education to vote, and your upper class isn't that much—isn't as great as the other, so really when you come down to it, it's your working class that's deciding one way or the other."

Not only do they "have a big part to do with running the country," they are crucial for the economy. This is not only as producers—indeed, no one mentioned the theme romantic writers on the laboring man, the immigrant, have often employed: "they cleared the land and built the cities." Rather it is because of their power to shatter the economy and their power to survive in a depression that they feel they are important. Kuchinsky explains this as follows:

> "I think the lower class of people are the important people. I think so because of the business end of it. Without us, I don't think the businessmen could survive. I mean if we don't work—of course, they have the money, but, ah, a lot of times during the crash, which was an awful thing, too, I think a lot of 'em lived so high that

they couldn't stand it any more when they went broke, and they committed a lot of suicides there. But we were used to living that way, it didn't bother us."

Today, as perhaps never before, the working-class man can see his lack of status, not shared by white-collar workers, as a lack compensated by income advantages. Thus De Angelo, a machine operator and shop steward, reports:

"You got people, working in offices, they might consider themselves upper class, y'know, a little better than the workingman. But nine times out of ten the workingman is making more money than he is."

And in the same vein, Rapuano says:

"I certainly would hate like hell to be a white-collar worker in the middle class and making the money that the white-collar worker does. I would rather be a worker in the lower class, and making their money, see?"

Of course, this assignment of income advantages to the working class hinges upon a narrowing of the range of competition—but this is the range that makes a difference for these men.

Moral Equality

Another device for dealing with subordination in a society where invidious comparison with others is constantly invited represents, in effect, a borrowing from an older classical or religious tradition, an emphasis upon the intangible and immeasurable (and therefore comfortingly vague) spiritual and moral qualities. The only clearly adequate expression of this religious view was given by McNamara, a gentle and compassionate bookkeeper, who said: "All men are created equal? That's our belief as Catholics," implying some sort of religious equality, perhaps such an idea as is captured in the phrase "equality of the soul." Woodside, a Protestant railroad guard, takes, in a way, a secular eighteenth-century version of this view when he says that men are equal, "not financially, not in influence, but equal to one another as to being a person." Being a person, then, is enough to qualify for equal claims of some undefined kind.

But it seems probable that when men assert their own equality in this vague sense, typically phrased in something like O'Hara's terms: "I think I'm just as good as anybody else. I don't think there's any of them that I would say are better," something other than moral or spiritual equality is at issue. These moral qualities are what the educated commentator reads into the statement, but O'Hara means, if I may put words in his mouth: "Don't put on airs around me; I'm trying to preserve my self-respect in a world that challenges it; I therefore assert my equality with all. I won't be pushed around; I know my rights"; and, to the interviewer, "Just because you're a professor and I'm an oiler, it doesn't mean you can patronize me." And when Sokolsky, a machine operator and part-time janitor, says, in the interview: "The rich guy—because he's got money he's not better than I am. I mean, that's the way I feel," he is not talking about moral or spiritual qualities. He is saying, in effect, to his prosperous older brother and his snobbish wife, "Don't look down on me," and to the world at large, "I may be small, but I will protect my self-esteem." These men are posting notices similar to the motto on the early American colonies' flags, "Don't tread on me."

Speaking of moral virtues, we must observe how easy it would have been to take the view that the morality of the middle levels of society was superior because the rich received their wealth illegitimately. None of my clients did this. Nor did they stress the immoral lives of the wealthy classes, as did Merton's sample some two decades ago—a commentary, perhaps, upon changing attitudes toward the upper classes that took place over this period.* The psychic defenses against subordination available in stressing moral equality or superiority were used—but only rarely.

People Deserve Their Status

If one accepts the view that this is a land of opportunity in which merit will find a way, one is encouraged to accept the status differences of society. But it is more than logic that impels our men to accept these differences. There are satisfactions of identification with the going social order; it is easier to accept differences one calls "just" than those that appear "unjust"; there are the very substantial self-congratulatory satisfactions of comparison with those lower on the scale. Thus this theme of "just deserts" applies to one's own group, those higher, and those lower.

So Kuchinsky says: "If you're a professor, I think you're entitled to get what you deserve. I'm a roofer and I shouldn't be getting what you're getting." Furthermore, confidence in the general equity of the social order suggests that the rewards of one's own life are proportionate to ability, effort, and the wisdom of previous decisions. On ability, Costa, a machine operator, says:

> "I believe anybody that has the potential to become a scientific man, or a professor, or a lawyer, or a doctor, should have the opportunity to pursue it, but there's a lot of us that are just made to run a machine in a factory. No matter what opportunities some of us might have had, we would never have reached the point where we could become people of that kind. I mean, everybody isn't Joe DiMaggio."

* Robert K. Merton, *Mass Persuasion: The Social Psychology of a War Bond Drive* (New York: Harper, 1946).

And on the wisdom of earlier decisions, Johnson, the electric-utility mechanic, says:

"I don't consider myself the lower class. In between someplace. But I could have been a lot better off but through my own foolishness, I'm not. [Here he refers back to an earlier account of his life.] What causes poverty? Foolishness. When I came out of the service, my wife had saved a few dollars and I had a few bucks. I wanted to have a good time. I'm throwing money away like water. Believe me, had I used my head right, I could have had a house. I don't feel sorry for myself—what happened happened, you know. Of course you pay for it."

But the most usual mistake or deficiency accounting for the relatively humble position is failure to continue one's education, owing to lack of family pressure ("They should have made me"), or youthful indiscretion, or the demands of the family for money, or the depression of the thirties.

The Upper Classes Deserve to Be Upper

Just as they regard their own status as deserved, so also do they regard the status of the eminently successful as appropriate to their talents. Rapuano, the packing-house clerk, reports:

"Your income—if you're smart, and your ability calls for a certain income, that's what you should earn. If your ability is so low, why, hell, then you should earn the low income. ["Do you think income is proportionate to ability now?"] I would say so. Yes."

But there is a suggestion in many of the interviews that even if the income is divorced from talent and effort, in some sense it is appropriate. Consider Sokolsky again, a machine operator and part-time janitor, discussing the tax situation:

"Personally, I think taxes are too hard. I mean a man makes, let's say, one hundred fifty thousand dollars. Well, my God, he has to give up half of that to the government —which I don't think is right. For instance, if a man is fortunate enough to win the Irish Sweepstakes, he gets one hundred fifty—I think he has about forty-five thousand dollars left. I don't think that's right."

Even if life is a lottery, the winner should keep his winnings. And De Angelo, a machine operator, comes spontaneously to the same conclusion:

"I think everybody needs a little [tax] relief. I mean, I know one thing, if I made a million dollars and the government took nine-tenths of it—boy, I'd cry the blues. I can't see that. If a man is smart enough to make that much, damn it, he's got a right to holler. I'm with the guy all the way."

Because he is "smart enough" to make the money, it is rightfully his. Surely, beyond the grave, there is a specter haunting Marx.

The concept of "education" is the key to much of the thinking on social class and personal status. In a sense, it is a "natural" because it fits so neatly into the American myth of opportunity and equality, and provides a rationale for success and failure that does minimum damage to the souls of those who did not go to college. Thus, in justifying their own positions, sometimes with reference to the interview situation, my clients imply: "If I had gone to college (like you), I would be higher up in this world." Costa, a machine operator, speaks this theme:

"Now, what would be the advantage of you going twenty years to school so you wind up making ten thousand dollars a year and me going eight years to school, making ten thousand? You would be teaching the young men of tomorrow, the leaders of tomorrow, and I would be running a machine. You would have a lot more responsibility to the country as a whole than I would have. Why shouldn't you be rewarded in proportion?"

McNamara, the mild-mannered bookkeeper who went to night school to get his training in accounting and bookkeeping, emphasizes education in response to the question, "Do you think it's easy or hard to get from one class to another?"

"Well, I think it's hard because . . . not because of the class itself, or what the influence they have on you, but you just seem to reach a certain point, and if you don't have it, you just don't—you don't make the grade. I've found that to be true. I always seems to be one step away from a good spot. And it's no one's fault—it's my fault. I just don't have the education—just don't—just don't have what it takes to take that step."

And Sokolsky, machine operator and part-time janitor, says, in his justification of income differences:

"A man that gets out of the eighth grade—I don't think he would have the ability to do the job as a man that got out of college."

But later, he says, of politicians and businessmen:

"If a man with more education has been in politics, he should get the job, but if there's a man that, let's say, just got out of high school, and he's been around in politics all his life, I think he should have a chance too. It's how good he is. There's some big business people who just haven't got it. [But] there could be some men with a gift of gab—maybe just out of eighth grade—they could sell anything."

What is it about education that justifies differences in income? In the above interviews it is clear that education is thought to increase skills that should be suitably rewarded. Furthermore, it appears that the time necessary for educational preparation deserves some reward—a recurrent theme. With education goes responsibility, and responsibility should be rewarded. But there is also some suggestion in the interview material that the pain and hard (unpleasant) work associated with going to school deserve compensation. People who did not like school themselves may be paying homage to those who could stick it out. It is a question whether O'Hara, a maintenance mechanic, implies this when he says:

> "I think a person that is educated deserves more than somebody that isn't. Somebody who really works for his money really deserves it more than somebody that's lazy and just wants to hang around."

In this and other ways, education serves as a peg on which to hang status; and, like "blood," whether a person got the education or not is not his "fault," or at least it is only the fault of an irresponsible youth, not a grown man.*

The Lower Classes Deserve No Better than They Get

By and large those in the lower orders are those who are paid daily (not weekly) or are on relief; they live in slums or in public housing projects (but not middle-income projects); they do not live respectable lives; they have only grammar school education; they may have no regular jobs. Closer to home, those slightly lower in status are people like "the lady next door who has a little less than I have," the

---

* Contrast de Tocqueville: "I never met in America a citizen so poor as not to cast a glance of hope and envy on the enjoyments of the rich or whose imagination did not possess itself by anticipation of those good things that fate still obstinately withheld from him" (*Democracy in America*, II, 129).

man who can't afford to take care of his kids properly in the project, people who spend their money on liquor, the person with less skill in the same line of work.

The rationale for their lower status turns chiefly on several things: their lack of education, and therefore failure to know what they want or failure to understand lifemanship, and their general indifference. It is particularly this not-caring that seems so salient in the upper-working-class mind. This is consonant with the general view that success is a triumph of the will and a reflection of ability. Poverty is for lazy people, just as middle status is for struggling people. Thus, Ruggiero, a building maintenance man, accounts for poverty by saying, "There's laziness, you'll always have lazy people." De Angelo, a factory operative, sees it this way:

> "A guy gets married and, you know, he's not educated too well, he doesn't have a good job and he gets a large family and he's in bad shape, y'know what I mean. It's tough; he's got to live in a lousy rent—he can't afford anything better."

But De Angelo takes away some of this sympathy the next moment when he goes on to say:

> "But then you get a lot of people who don't want to work; you got welfare. People will go on living on that welfare —they're happier than hell. Why should they work if the city will support them?"

In general, there is little sympathy given to those lower in the scale, little reference to the overpowering forces of circumstance, only rare mention of sickness, death of a breadwinner, senility, factories moving out of town, and so forth. The only major cause of poverty to which no moral blame attaches is depression or "unemployment"—but this is not considered a strikingly important cause in the minds of the

Eastport men. They are Christian in the sense that they believe "The poor ye have with you always," but there is no trace of a belief that the poor are in any way "blessed."

What If There Were Greater Equality of Opportunity and Income?

We have examined here the working- and lower-middle-class defenses of the present order. They are well organized and solidly built. By and large these people believe that the field is open and that merit will tell. They may then deprecate the importance of class, limit their perspectives, accept their situation reluctantly or with satisfaction. They may see the benefits of society flowing to their own class, however they define it. They tend to believe that each person's status is in some way deserved.

How would these lower-middle- and working-class men feel about a change in the social order such that they and their friends might suddenly be equal to others now higher or lower in the social order? Most of them wouldn't like it. They would fear and resent this kind of equality.

Abandonment of a Rationale

Changing ideas is a strain not to be lightly incurred, particularly when these ideas are intimately related to one's self-esteem. The less education one has, the harder it is to change such ideas. Painfully these men have elaborated an explanation for their situation in life; it helps explain things to their wives, who take their status from them; it permits their growing children to account for relative social status in school; it offers to each man the satisfactions of social identity and a measure of social worth. Their rationales are endowed with moral qualities; the distribution of values in the society is seen as just and natural. While it gives satisfactions of an obvious kind to those who contemplate those beneath them, it also, oddly enough, gives order and a kind of reassurance to those who glance upward toward "society" or the "four-hundred." This reassurance is not unlike the reassurance provided by the belief in a just God while injustices rain upon one's head. The feudal serf, the Polish peasant, the Mexican peon believed that theirs was a moral and a "natural" order—so also the American workingman.

The Problem of Social Adjustment

Equality would pose problems of social adjustments, of manners, of how to behave. Here is Sokolsky, short and heavy, uneducated, and nervous, with a more prosperous brother in the same town. "I'm not going to go over there," he says, "because every time I go there I feel uncomfortable." On the question of rising from one social class to another, his views reflect his personal situation:

"I think it's hard. Let's say—let's take me, for instance. Supposing I came into a lot of money, and I moved into a nice neighborhood—class—maybe I wouldn't know how to act then. I think it's very hard, because people know that you just—word gets around that you . . . never had it before you got it now. Well, maybe they wouldn't like you . . . maybe you don't know how to act."

The kind of equality with others that would mean a rapid rise in his own status is a matter of concern, mixed, of course, with pleasant anticipation at the thought of "telling off" his brother.

Consider the possibility of social equality, including genuine fraternization, without economic equality. Sullivan, a truck driver, deals with this in graphic terms:

"What is the basis of social class? Well, things that people have in common . . . Money is one, for instance, like I wouldn't feel very comfortable going around with a millionaire, we'll say . . . He could do a lot and say a lot—mention places he'd been and so on—I mean, I wouldn't be able to keep up with him . . . and he wouldn't have to watch his money, and I'd have to be pinching mine to see if I had enough for another beer or something."

And, along the lines of Sokolsky's comments, Sullivan believes that moving upward in the social scale is easier if one moves to a new place where one has not been known in the old connection. Flynn holds that having the right interests and conversational topics for the new and higher social group will make it possible, but otherwise it could be painful. Kuchinsky, the roofer, says: "I suppose it would feel funny to get in a higher class, but I don't believe I would change. I wouldn't just disregard my friends if I came into any money." Clinging to old friends would give some security in that dazzling new world.

De Angelo, a factory operative, also considers the question of whether people of higher status will accept the arriviste, but for himself he dismisses it:

"I wouldn't worry much about whether they would accept or they wouldn't accept. I would move into another class. I mean—I mean—I don't worry much about that stuff. If people don't want to bother with me, I don't bother with them, that's all."

These fears, while plausible and all too human, emerged unexpectedly from the interview material designed to capture ideas and emotions on other aspects of class status. They highlight a resistance to equalitarian movements that might bring the working class and the rejecting superior class—whether imaginary or not—in close association. If these were revolutionaries, one might phrase their anxieties: "Will my victims accept me?" But they are not revolutionaries.

These are problems of rising in status to meet the upper classes face to face. But there is another risk in opening the gates so that those of moderate circumstances can rise to higher status. Equality of opportunity, it appears, is inherently dangerous in this respect; there is the risk that friends, neighbors, or subordinates will surpass one in status. O'Hara has this on his mind. Some of the people who rise in status are nice, but:

> "You get other ones, the minute they get a little, they get big-headed and they think they're better than the other ones—where they're still—to me they're worse than the middle class. I mean, they should get down, because they're just showing their illiteracy—that's all they're doing."

Sokolsky worries about this possibility too, having been exposed to the slights of his brother's family. But the worry over being passed by is not important, not salient. It is only rarely mentioned.

Deprivation of a Meritorious Elite

It is comforting to have the "natural leaders" of a society well entrenched in their proper place. If there were equality there would no longer be such an elite to supervise and take care of people—especially "me." Thus Woodside, the railroad guard, reports:

> "I think anybody that has money—I think their interest is much wider than the regular workingman . . . And therefore I think that the man with the money is a little

bit more educated, for the simple reason he has the money, and he has a much wider view of life—because he's in the knowledge of it all the time."

Here and elsewhere in the interview, one senses that Woodside is glad to have such educated, broad-gauged men in eminent positions. He certainly opposes the notion of equality of income. Something similar creeps into Johnson's discussion of social classes. He feels that the upper classes, who "seem to be very nice people," are "willing to lend a helping hand—to listen to you. I would say they'd help you out more than the middle class [man] would help you out even if he was in a position to help you out." Equality, then, would deprive society, and oneself, of a group of friendly, wise, and helpful people who occupy the social eminences.

The Loss of the Goals of Life

But most important of all, equality, at least equality of income, would deprive people of the goals of life. In this they are like the working class of the Lynds' *Middletown:* "Its drives are largely those of the business class: both are caught up in the tradition of a rising standard of living and lured by the enticements of salesmanship." Every one of the fifteen clients with whom I spent my evenings for seven months believed that equality of income would deprive men of their incentive to work, achieve, and develop their skills. These answers ranged, in their sophistication and approach, across a broad field. The most highly educated man in the sample, Farrel, answers the question "How would you feel if everyone received the same income in our society?" By saying, "I think it would be kind of silly . . . Society, by using income as a reward technique, can often insure that the individuals will put forth their best efforts." He does not believe, for himself, that status or income is central to motivation, but for others, they are. Woodside, whose main concern is not the vistas of wealth and opportunity of the American dream, but rather whether he can get a good pension if he should have to retire early, comes forward as follows:

"I'd say that [equal income]—that is something that's pretty—I think it would be a dull thing, because life would be accepted—or it would—rather we'd go stale. There would be no initiative to be a little different, or go ahead."

Like Woodside, Flynn, a white-collar worker, responds with a feeling of personal loss—the idea of such an equality of income would make him feel "very made." Costa, whose ambitions in life are the most modest, holds that equality of income "would eliminate the basic thing about the wonderful opportunity you have in this country." Then for a moment the notion of his income equaling that of the professional man passes pleasantly through his mind: "Don't misunderstand me—I like the idea"; then again, "I think it eliminates the main reason why people become engineers and professors and doctors."

Rapuano, whose worries have given him ulcers, projects himself into a situation where everyone receives the same income, in this case a high one:

"If everyone had the same income of a man that's earning fifty thousand dollars a year, and he went to, let's say ten years of college to do that, why, hell, I'd just as soon sit on my ass as go to college and wait till I could earn fifty thousand dollars a year—now, that's another question."

But however the question is answered, he is clear that guaranteed equal incomes would encourage people to "sit around on their anatomies" and wait for their pay checks.

But he would like to see some leveling, particularly if doctors, whom he hates, were to have their fees and incomes substantially reduced.

That These Sacrifices Shall Not Have Been in Vain

The men I talked to were not at the bottom of the scale, not at all. They were stable breadwinners, churchgoers, voters, family men. They achieved this position in life through hard work and sometimes bitter sacrifices. In their control of impulse and desire they have absorbed the Protestant ethic. At least six of them have two jobs and almost no leisure. In answering questions on "the last time you remember having a specially good time," some of them must go back ten to fifteen years. Nor are their good times remarkable for their spontaneous fun and enjoyment of life. Many of them do not like their jobs, but stick to them because of family responsibilities, and they do not know what else they would rather do. In short, they have sacrificed their hedonistic inclinations, given up good times, and expended their energy and resources in order to achieve and maintain their present tenuous hold on respectability and middle status.

Now, in such a situation to suggest that men be equalized and the lower orders raised and one's own hard-earned status given to them as a right and not a reward for effort seems to them desperately wrong. In the words of my research assistant, David Sears, "Suppose the Marshall Plan had provided a block and tackle to Sisyphus after all these years. How do you think he would have felt?" Sokolsky, Woodside, and Dempsey have rolled the stone to the top of the hill so long, they despise the suggestion that it might have been in vain. Or even worse, that their neighbors at the foot of the hill might have the use of a block and tackle.

The World Would Collapse

As a corollary to the view that life would lose its vigor and its savor with equality of income, there is the image of an equalitarian society as a world running down, a chaotic and disorganized place to live. The professions would be decimated: "People pursue the higher educational levels for a reason—there's a lot of rewards, either financial or social," says Costa. Sullivan says, "Why should people take the headaches of responsible jobs if the pay didn't meet these responsibilities?" For the general society, Flynn, a white-collar man, believes that "if there were no monetary incentive involved, I think there'd be a complete loss. It would stop all development—there's no doubt about it." McNamara, the bookkeeper, sees people then reduced to an equal level of worth: with equal income "the efforts would be equal and pretty soon we would be worth the same thing." In two contrasting views, both suggesting economic disorganization, Woodside believes, "I think you'd find too many men digging ditches, and no doctors," while Rapuano believes men would fail to dig ditches or sewers, "and where the hell would we be when we wanted to go to the toilet?"

Only a few took up the possible inference that this was an attractive but impractical ideal, and almost none followed up the suggestion that some equalization of income, if not complete equality, would be desirable. The fact of the matter is that these men, by and large, prefer an inequalitarian society, and even prefer a society graced by some men of great wealth. As they look out upon the social scene, they feel that an equalitarian society would present them with too many problems of moral adjustment, which they fear and dislike. But perhaps, most important, their life goals are structured around achievement and success in monetary terms. If these were taken away, life would be a desert.

These men view the possibility of an equalitarian world as a paraphrased version of Swinburne's lines on Jesus Christ: "Thou has conquered, O pale Equalitarian; the world has grown grey from Thy breath."

Some Theoretical Implications

Like any findings on the nature of men's social attitudes and beliefs, even in such a culture-bound inquiry as this one, the new information implies certain theoretical propositions that may be incorporated into the main body of political theory. Let us consider seven such propositions growing more or less directly out of our findings on the fear of equality:

1. The greater the emphasis in a society upon the availability of "equal opportunity for all," the greater the need for members of that society to develop an acceptable rationalization for their own social status.

2. The greater the strain on a person's self-esteem implied by a relatively low status in an open society, the greater the necessity to explain this status as "natural" and "proper" in the social order. Lower-status people generally find it less punishing to think of themselves as correctly placed by a just society than to think of themselves as exploited or victimized by an unjust society.

3. The greater the emphasis in a society upon equality of opportunity, the greater the tendency for those of marginal status to denigrate those lower than themselves. This view seems to such people to have the factual or even moral justification that if the lower classes "cared" enough, they could be better off. It has a psychological "justification" in that it draws attention to one's own relatively better status, and one's own relatively greater initiative and virtue.

4. People tend to care less about *equality* of opportunity than about the availability of *some* opportunity. Men do not

need the same life chances as everybody else; indeed, they usually care very little about that. They need only chances (preferably with unknown odds) for a slightly better life than they have now. Thus popular satisfaction with one's own status is related less to equality of opportunity than to the breadth of distribution of some opportunity for all, however unequal this distribution may be. A man who can improve his position one rung does not resent the man who starts on a different ladder halfway up.

These propositions are conservative in their implications. The psychological roots of this conservatism must be explored elsewhere, as must the many exceptions that may be observed when the fabric of a social order is so torn that the leaders, the rich and powerful, are seen as illegitimate, and hence "appropriately" interpreted as exploiters of the poor. I maintain, however, that these propositions hold generally for the American culture over most of its history, and also that the propositions hold for most of the world most of the time. This is so, even though they fly in the face of much social theory—theory often generalized from more specialized studies of radicalism and revolution. Incidentally, one must observe that it is as important to explain why revolutions and radical social movements do *not* happen as it is to explain why they do.

The more I observed the psychological and physical drain placed upon the men I interviewed by the pressures to consume—and therefore to scratch in the corners of the economy for extra income—the more it appeared that competitive consumption was not a stimulus to class conflict, as might have been expected, but was a substitute for or a sublimation of it. Thus we would say:

5. The more emphasis a society places upon consumption—through advertising, development of new products, and easy installment buying—the more social dissatisfaction will be channeled into intraclass-consumption rivalry in-

stead of interclass resentment and conflict. The Great
American Medicine Show creates consumer unrest, working
wives, and dual job-holding, not antagonism toward the
"owning classes." And, as a corollary of this view:

6. The more emphasis a society places upon consumption, the more will labor unions focus upon the "bread and
butter" aspects of unionism, as contrasted to its ideological
elements.

We come, finally, to a hypothesis that arises from this inquiry into the fear of equality but that goes much beyond
the focus of the present study. I mention it here in a specula-
tive frame of mind, undogmatically, and even regretfully:

7. The ideals of the French Revolution—liberty and
equality—have been advanced because of the accidental
correspondence between these ideals and the needs of the
bourgeoisie for freedom of economic action and the demands of the working class, very simply, for "more." Ideas
have an autonomy of their own, however, in the sense that
once moralized they persist even if the social forces that
brought them to the fore decline in strength. They become
"myths"—but myths erode without support from some
major social stratum. Neither the commercial classes nor
the working classes, the historical beneficiaries of these two
moralized ideas (ideals or myths), have much affection for
the ideals in their universal forms. On the other hand, the
professional classes, particularly the lawyers, ministers, and
teachers of a society, very often do have such an affection. It
is they, in the democratic West, who serve as the "hard
core" of democratic defenders, insofar as there is one. It is
they, more frequently than others, who support the generalized application of the ideals of freedom and equality to all
men. This is not virtue, but rather a different organization
of interests and a different training. Whatever the reason,
however, it is not to "The People," not to the business class,
not to the working class, that we must look for the consist-

ent and relatively unqualified defense of freedom and equality. The professional class, at least in the American culture, serves as the staunchest defender of democracy's two greatest ideals.

WORK LIFE AND POLITICAL ATTITUDES

A Study of Manual Workers

by Lewis Lipsitz

Both a political scientist and a poet, Mr. Lipsitz is a member of the executive council of the Caucus for a New Political Science and the author of Cold Water, *a book of poems. The interviews for the study reported here were completed in 1961.*

For centuries men have speculated about the human consequences of work. Slowly a considerable body of literature has begun to accumulate concerning the relationships between people's jobs and other aspects of their lives. Investigators have pointed out, among other things, the connections between certain types of jobs and certain personality disorders, attitudes toward union and management, productivity, job satisfaction and leisure activities. Extending such findings, the study discussed in this article concludes that a particular job situation can have important effects on a man's political outlook.

Political studies have long classified individuals according to occupation. Yet there have been extremely few efforts to penetrate within specific occupational categories to discover the reasons for differences in attitudes. On the whole, political scientists have been content to work with relatively large groupings, such as "semiskilled" manual workers, "unskilled" manual workers, etc.

Concerning the problem of job satisfaction, Seymour Lipset, writing in 1960, observed that it was yet to be shown that "job satisfaction and creativity contribute independently to political behavior over and beyond differences in status and economic conditions . . ." Our study indicates, however, that at least one particular work situation—that of the automobile assembly line—affects the political and social attitudes of the automobile workers involved. The ways in which the concrete work situation affects the workers' political attitudes are determined by the technology and social setting of the job itself. Specifically, assembly-line workers are found to be more fatalistic, more punitive and more politically radical than other workers of comparable salary and education who work in the same plant.

I

Before proceeding to the findings themselves, it may be helpful to first consider briefly the nature of assembly-line work in comparison with other occupational types.

The factory is a symbol of modern life, and the assembly line in particular has often been thought to embody in extreme form the worst tendencies of industrial work. Other analysts have argued to the contrary, that modern industrial societies offer more individuals more chances for genuine work satisfaction than any previous societies. It would serve little purpose here to get involved in this controversy, for even if the issues raised remain unresolved, certain facts about modern work life relevant to our inquiry are quite clear.

First, manual workers generally indicate lower work satisfaction than nonmanual workers. Second, within the manual group, satisfaction varies with skill: the higher the skills, other things being equal, the greater the satisfaction. The table below provides some frame of reference for dealing with the question of job satisfaction in manual and nonmanual jobs.

PROPORTION IN VARIOUS OCCUPATIONS WHO WOULD CHOOSE
SAME KIND OF WORK IF BEGINNING CAREER AGAIN*

Professional Occupations	*Per-cent*	*Working-Class Occupations*	*Per-cent*
Mathematicians	91	Skilled printers	52
Physicists	89	Paper workers	52
Biologists	89	Skilled automobile workers	41
Chemists	86	Skilled steelworkers	41
Lawyers	83	Textile workers	31
Journalists	82	Unskilled steelworkers	21
		Unskilled automobile workers	16

Beyond the question of how workers respond when asked if they are satisfied with their jobs, a more important question concerns the *effects* of work: what impact the job has on a man's life outside of the factory. Many writers and analysts have speculated about this. Much of the analysis of industrial work emphasizes its destructive or negative aspects and focuses attention on the elimination of skill and the increase of simple, repetitive assembly-line style of work. Yet there have been only a few studies of assembly-line jobs.

The expectation that men would dislike assembly-line work is borne out by current research. Consistently, investigators have found that conveyor-paced jobs in mass-production industries show lower levels of satisfaction than other manual and nonmanual jobs. Robert Blauner has concluded that assembly-line work is more disliked than any

* Robert Blauner, "Work Satisfaction and Industrial Trends in Modern Society," in *Labor and Trade Unionism,* edited by Walter Galenson and S. M. Lipset (New York: John Wiley & Sons, 1960).

other major type of work. Within the automobile industry, which is the setting of this study, the position of the semi-skilled line worker is particularly difficult. Possibilities of advancement within the ranks are extremely slim. Wage differentials between the highest- and lowest-paid production jobs are small.

Automobile assembly-line workers have little control over the pacing of their work. The average worker on the line performs no more than five operations, remains at his station at all times, and repeats the same operation about forty times an hour. For most workers the work cycle is between one and two minutes regulated by the conveyor speed.

Characteristically the assembly-line worker is alone on his job. The technology of the line increases the worker's sense of impersonality and presents barriers to group cohesiveness. Moreover, there appears to be no adjustment to the assembly line as time passes. The longer a man has held an assembly-line job, the more likely he is to have an unfavorable attitude toward all aspects of work experience.

What do we know about the effects of assembly-line work? Compared with other groups of manual workers, assembly-line workers show few open grievances, little use of pressure tactics, and much internal disunity and evidence of suppressed discontent. They permit leadership to gravitate to aggressive individuals with a strong need to dominate. They accept certain aspects of their work life as inevitable, and they lack self-confidence.

When Charles Walker and Robert Guest (in *The Man on the Assembly Line,* Harvard University Press, 1952) compared workers holding "pure" assembly-line jobs with another group of workers whose jobs were more skilled, varied and autonomous, they found that absenteeism was much higher on repetitive, conveyor-paced jobs; repetitiveness was negatively correlated with interest in work; limitations on talking were a source of frustration to line workers; mass-production methods tended to increase the worker's sense of anonymity. My study indicates that the differences that Walker and Guest find between different groups of semi-skilled factory workers carry over into the area of political attitudes.

II

Three samples of workers were used in the study as a basis for comparison: (1) assembly-line workers, or men with jobs approximating those of the assembly line, (2) repair, relief and utility workers and (3) skilled maintenance workers.

Repair, relief and utility workers were chosen for purposes of comparison because their jobs provided them with greater variety and autonomy than the line workers' jobs. Repair jobs, for example, could not be time-studied and were not completely repetitive. Individual judgment and some choice of tools were required. Relief and utility workers both performed as stand-ins for men on the assembly line, but were competent to handle many kinds of line jobs within a given department of the shop. Their work was more varied and likely to lead to a stronger sense of pride and a deeper interest in the task.

The repair, relief and utility workers, like assembly-line operatives, would normally be classified as semiskilled in a social class or occupational breakdown. Skilled workers were also included in the study as they would furnish an important comparison with both semiskilled groups.

Names were selected at random from the files of the local union. Men willing to participate were interviewed in their homes. All of the men interviewed were married, native-born and white. The three groups were closely comparable in many respects. Educationally, all three groups averaged between nine and ten years of education completed. A majority of each group was Catholic. The mean age of each sample was between forty and fifty. Assembly-line workers interviewed had been on their present jobs an average of six years; repair workers twelve years, and skilled workers, thirteen years. Pay rates in the two semiskilled groups varied between $2.40 and $2.74 an hour, while in the skilled group the rates ranged from $2.96 to $3.39.

The assembly plant in which these men worked was located in Linden, New Jersey. At the time of these interviews, between 2900 and 3000 men were employed at the plant. The general effort was to study intensively the political orientations of a relatively small group of men, to gain some insights of general applicability that could then be tested on a larger sample, more systematically.

III

The three work groups showed attitude differences in five areas: the job, the union, the amount of fatalism about social life, the extent of preoccupation with economic problems and the extent of sympathy and tolerance.

The Job

Assembly-line workers view their job with a mixture of anger and resignation. Almost all of them complain bitterly of overwork, physical strain and monotony. They feel subjected to undue pressures because of the excessive speed of the line, but they feel powerless to control this speed. Relationships with supervisors are marked by inequality and anxiety. These men feel expendable. They know there is nothing unique about their performances at work.

As for the repair, relief and utility workers, all of these

men have ambivalent attitudes toward their jobs. Many complain of pressure and overwork, of physical and emotional strain. Yet they also note compensating factors: variety, skill and the very important fact that the men on the assembly line have much more unpleasant jobs than theirs.

The fifteen skilled workers present a picture of their jobs in extremely vivid contrast to those offered by the other two groups. Not a single man dislikes his job, and the degree of satisfaction is high in most cases. By and large, these men note as important the fact that they set their own pace of work, that they are not closely supervised. They speak of pleasure in the creative use of their skills. They feel themselves in a position to perform useful and appreciated services for others. They have relatively good relations with supervisors. They show no sense of resignation to the inevitable; they know they can leave the corporation since they possess skills needed elsewhere. They have a certain self-confidence built on the knowledge that they have something valuable to sell.

The Union

The twelve line workers show slightly favorable attitudes toward unions. Only four are altogether favorable. Five are ambivalent, citing both good and bad features of unionism. Finally, three men are largely hostile toward unions.

Those with anything good to say about unions note "protection" as the most important union function; indeed it is the one positive union function the line workers cite. They see the union as the only force that blunts the exploiting bent of the company. Several of the men mention seniority as an especially important kind of protection. Those who criticize the union concentrate their attention on the idea that unions are not controlled by workers, but rather by a clique which serves its own interests. They assert that unions are corrupt and uninterested in the rank and file. As a group, these men are not closely attached to their unions. They give no indication of participation or solidarity.

The views of the repair, relief and utility workers resemble those of the line workers in several respects, but differ in several others. These workers show more favorable feeling toward unions generally and also toward their own union. Eight of the fourteen men have positive union attitudes, while six are ambivalent. Not one is completely anti-union. Like the line workers, they stress the importance of protection as a union function, but four of the men also note union benefits such as vacations, company-paid insurance, etc. Within the repair group only one man accuses unions of being oligarchical. Criticisms move in other directions and seem to be less intensely felt than among the line workers.

Much as might be expected, the skilled maintenance men also show relatively favorable attitudes toward unions. Seven are wholly pro-union, while the eight others are ambivalent. This group, too, emphasizes the protection the union offers, but stresses union benefits even more than the other groups. None of these skilled workers show the sense of abandonment found in the line sample; and none of them criticize unions as oligarchies.

Attitudes toward the late Walter Reuther were quite revealing. Both the line and repair workers were sharply critical of their union head. A majority in both groups condemned Reuther as a man out for himself, personally ambitious, and uninterested in the fate of the ordinary workers. Even men who praised the UAW as a whole, and unions generally, were wholly negative where Reuther was concerned. The skilled workers, by contrast, were overwhelmingly favorable toward Reuther; they praised his skill and intelligence as well as his honesty and dedication. In all, attitudes toward Reuther were more extreme (both positive and negative) than attitudes toward unions in general or the UAW in particular. The line workers, who were most unhappy at work, were least happy with Reuther and with unions. The skilled workers, who were most satisfied on the job, were largely pleased with Reuther and with unions. The repair group occupied a middle position in both areas.

Fatalistic Attitudes

It is sometimes argued that fatalistic attitudes do not characterize industrial man. Fatalism, it is held, is characteristic of the peasantry, lending support to rigid class distinctions and to the idea that the political order is not to be tampered with.

No doubt, citizens of industrial societies are as fatalistic as their ancestors. Yet it is also clear that the social and technical structures of industrial societies themselves produce certain fatalistic orientations, and that these are related to the specific kinds of work men are engaged in. Those workers who are conscious of having the least control over their own lives at work show the most pronounced tendency to view the social and political worlds as unalterable.

To say the very least, it is difficult to determine the degree of fatalism comprised in an individual's outlook. In an effort to find an approximate means of measurement, individuals were scored on a fatalism scale composed of four open-ended interview questions. The questions that made up the scale were: (1) Will men and nations always fight wars with one another? (2) Will there always be poverty in the world? (3) Do you think the ordinary man is helpless to change some aspect of government he doesn't like, or is there something he can do about it? (4) Some people say they can plan ahead for long-range goals and then carry out their plans;

others say, "Whatever's going to be is going to be and
there's no sense planning"—how do you feel about it?

There are clear differences among the three work groups
and these differences are in the expected direction. The assembly-line workers are the most strongly fatalistic. Though
there isn't space here to explore the types and nuances of
fatalistic attitudes, a few important points need to be made.
First, as a group, the men are most strongly fatalistic about
the problem of war. The idea of the inevitability of aggression fits well with the picture these men have of human nature. Second, fatalistic attitudes are weakest in the area of
the political potency of the ordinary citizen. These men retain the notion that a letter to one's Congressmen will
change things. They hold to this idea despite the fact that on
other questions they indicate their belief that public officials
don't really care about the common person.

The nonfatalistic workers in the sample stand out most
strongly from their fatalistic fellows in two respects. First,
they are indignant rather than merely sullen and resigned
about conditions they find unacceptable. Second, the non-
fatalists tend to blame themselves as well as others for social
failures. They emphasize the possible triumph of justice,
even if only in the distant future, and the possibility of humane and rational behavior, even though many of them
consider such behavior unlikely.

Economic Preoccupations and Political Radicalism

The assembly-line workers are more politically radical
than the other two samples of workers. This manifests itself
in favorable attitudes toward governmental economic controls and antagonisms toward private ownership and the
privileged orders; it is closely related to a strong tendency
among the line workers to emphasize economic problems
and interpretations.

The distribution of attitudes along the liberal-conservative continuum is in the expected direction. The assembly-line workers are the most radical, the skilled workers the least. The patterns for the three groups bears a close resemblance to the scores for skilled, semiskilled manual workers which Richard Centers found in a nationwide sample in the late 1940's.

Symptomatic of their economic preoccupations, two contrasts emerge among the work groups in which the line workers attach a greater emphasis to economic considerations. First, they tend more strongly to view economic problems as the most important ones confronting America today. Fifty-eight percent of the line group ranks economic problems most important, as compared with 36 percent of the repair group and 33 percent of the skilled workers.

The kinds of economic problems mentioned by the different groups were also quite distinct. All of the men in the assembly-line group who mentioned economic problems at all concerned themselves either with unemployment or poor working conditions—both problems very close to home. In contrast, men in the other two groups raised questions about high taxes, foreign aid, welfare excesses, salary differentials and the demise of free enterprise.

Second, the concern with economic difficulties shows itself in response to a question that asks about the nature of the "chains" men feel. The question was phrased: "A man once said, 'Man is born free, but everywhere he is in chains.' Does this mean anything to you?" Eighty-six percent of the line men, 77 percent of the repair workers and only 27 percent of the skilled workers saw Rousseau's "chains" in economic terms. Both the line and repair workers saw these chains as oppressive. Remisik, a repairman, typifies much of the commentary: ". . . has to earn his bread. He is chained to a job of some sort regardless of whether it's here or any other concern . . ." On the other hand, most of those who offer noneconomic interpretations think of the "chains" without the element of oppression. Harris, a maintenance painter, serves as a good example: "Yeah, everybody is born free—but then we acquire chains. It has to be. There's laws, regulations that we have to abide . . ."

Sympathy and Tolerance

None of the questions in the interview schedule was designed to explore dimensions of sympathy or tolerance. Yet several of the questions seemed to elicit punitive responses from some of the men but not from others. All of these questions touched on attitudes toward "out-groups." The questions were: (1) Why are people poor? (2) What should be our policy toward Russia? (3) Do you think it was a good idea to drop atomic bombs on Japan in World War II? (4) How do you feel about capital punishment?

Though the evidence is very skimpy and impressionistic, it appears that the assembly-line group is less sympathetic and tolerant than the others. In all of the four cases, the line workers are slightly more punitive as a group. They tend more strongly to blame the poor themselves for poverty. They were more likely to approve the bombing of Japan without showing any sympathy for the Japanese, and they recommend a policy of toughness toward Russia. Finally, they were somewhat more likely to favor the death penalty.

These findings are worth noting largely because they tend to confirm previous conclusions about authoritarianism and social class. Within this group of workers, punitive attitudes are associated with work frustration and lack of control over work life. These facts point to the possible significance of everyday frustrations in conditioning attitudes toward out-groups. The possibility that such frustrations might play an important role in shaping attitudes is one that psychoanalytic research has left open for the moment.*

IV

In two important areas the three groups show attitudes that are much alike but which are important to describe nonetheless. First, a majority of men in all three groups emphasize the manipulative nature of much of social life. They express concern about the exploiting and unfair practice of their corporation and of big business generally. Moreover, approximately half the men express concern about two-faced, deliberately deceptive tactics of the government and mass media which they see as closely related. Where big business is concerned, these workers see manipulative practices everywhere. A few believe big business or the rich run the United States. Others are not quite so explicit, but believe that big business is free of the restraints that bind ordinary mortals; businesses can initiate wars, bribe judges and representatives and manage to get the government to follow their dictates. In some of these men, hostile attitudes toward big business and especially toward their own corporation attain a frenzied pitch and deep bitterness.

Most of the men feel that the corporation acts as it does because its primary concern is profit-making. Some see businesses caught in a competitive rat race which means do or die. The methods of the rich, as these workers describe them, are not subtle. These men simply affirm the idea that money talks. Very few of them have any praise for big business. Most simply accept it as a fact of life, unable, like the line worker Tencio, to visualize a world without it: "Well, without big business, what could the workingman do? He gotta work for big business."

* S. M. Lipset points out that the unemployed, feeling resentful and alienated, are less tolerant of minority groups than are employed workers, a finding that seems related to the conclusions here about the assembly-line group. See Lipset, *Political Man* (New York: Doubleday, 1960).

It is not particularly surprising to learn that many of these working-class men are critical of big business. But it is very much another thing to find that almost half of the forty-one men are critical of manipulative and deceptive aspects of American government and the mass media. The chief theme of the critics is that the government is immune to popular pressures. The general picture is of a group of men who arrange to keep themselves in power and who don't care about the requests of the common man. The means of governmental manipulation are varied: nepotism, misleading propaganda, suppression of information, bribery, silencing of dissent. The credibility of the media is to some degree tied up with the credibility of the government. Several of the men feel that the radio, papers and television only convey what they are told to. They are tools, willing or unwilling, of the politicians. Five men criticize the media as manipulative in their own right. All who discuss the media do so in terms of their deceptive political content.

Some of the workers who are concerned about manipulations tend in the direction of a conspiracy theory of social control. Yet few of them actually express anything resembling a theory of a hidden oligarchy or oligarchies. At most, seven men give any clear indications of holding to such a picture of American society. In all seven cases, it is the "rich" or "big business" which is said to be the ruling elite.

The remaining two-thirds of the men who criticize various manipulative practices give no indication of adhering to a power-elite theory. They criticize business, government and media for attempting to manipulate the common man, but their criticism is specific and piecemeal. They do not have any clearly formulated picture of social life nor any precise notion about who is to blame for the seamy side of things. They are critical of the excessive power of big business and yet do not believe that big business runs the country. They can believe that people in the government attempt to mislead the public without going sour on government as a whole.

Yet, behind their vagueness and their sense of their own ignorance, most of these men have actually developed an explanation for the practices they criticize. First, they see a society directed toward profit-making. Second, they are aware of wide disparities of power. Out of these elements, these men have constructed a suspicion of human nature. It is human nature and nothing less, they say, which leads to malpractices of business and government. Thus, it is not a particular group of evil men who are to blame but rather the selfishness supposedly inherent in almost all of us.

These workers generally accept the profit motive as a satisfactory explanation of business behavior. But this does not account for governmental behavior. Why these failures, large and small, in the democratic system?

A substantial majority of the men believe that politics, like most other aspects of our society, is basically a business. Three-quarters of the line workers, 57 percent of the repair workers and 60 percent of the maintenance men see politicians as predominately self-seeking. They see elections and platforms designed to fool the public; politicians seeking to perpetuate their own domination; stealing, nepotism, the wasting of public funds, etc. A government composed of such individuals could not possibly be very attentive to the kinds of problems these workers are concerned about. It is not surprising, then, that they see failures in the political system. The selfish nature of politicians springs from their unfortunate and seemingly indelible humanity.

The second important area of similarity among the three groups is political participation. Unexpectedly, all three groups are strikingly alike in regard to voting, discussion of politics and interest in political affairs. The majority of the men in all three groups report talking politics at least sometimes. Only one man indicated he was not interested in Presidential elections.

There were tentative differences among the three work groups in two areas concerning political participation. First, the skilled workers were more likely than the other groups to participate in politics beyond voting. Two-thirds of the skilled group had contributed money, gone to party meetings or actively campaigned in recent years. In the repair group the figure was 43 percent and in the line group, 36 percent.

Second, the quality of commitment varies considerably among the groups. Very crudely, there are two sorts of commitment: positive and negative—being in favor of or being against. Most notably, the line workers phrase their political commitments in terms of their aversion for the Republican Party, as well as their preference for the Democrats. Five of the twelve line workers speak of their ill-feeling for the GOP. This ill-feeling runs the gamut from quiet discontent to raw bitterness.

V

Much of the evidence set out in the preceding sections is impressionistic and statistically insignificant. Yet the weight of the evidence points in a single direction.

It is clear that the two groups of semiskilled auto workers hold different views in various areas of life. First, the men who work on repetitive assembly-line jobs dislike their work more and are more hostile toward and alienated from the union. Second, the assembly-line workers are more fatalistic, less sympathetic with and less tolerant of others. The line workers are also more radical in their political views.

Recent investigations by Arthur Kornhauser tend to confirm these findings. He finds that skill level in manual jobs is clearly related to mental health and also to certain political and social attitudes. He concludes that the higher the skill level of the job, the more likely that men will show high mental health, while mental health is lowest among workers with repetitive conveyor-paced jobs.

Kornhauser's measures of mental health coincide in part with dimensions of attitudes examined in my study. He also found, consistent with the findings here, that workers in lower-skill jobs were higher on economic "liberalism" but lower in liberal attitudes on race relations and international affairs. Kornhauser concludes that the workers at various skill levels differ most sharply in feelings of defeat, pessimism, personal inadequacy, futility and distrust of others.*

Assembly-line workers, as we have seen, do not find their work interesting. They complain bitterly and consistently about monotony. In many respects, automobile assembly-line work reflects the most unhealthy characteristics of industrial work. Line workers have a sense of futility. They are frustrated and at the same time are seeking to undo their sense of inadequacy. Their frustrations are clearly reflected in their alienation, i.e., their feeling of powerlessness and its attendant consequences. Their feeling of helplessness is reflected in their fatalistic acceptance of their lot and of the agonies of the great outside world. Their efforts to restore

---

* Though I have spoken of a causal relationship between jobs and attitudes, I have not really "proven" such a relationship exists. The crucial problem is one of preselection. Perhaps men on assembly-line jobs differ from other semiskilled workers because they were different before they ever took these jobs, rather than because they have been changed by their employment. Perhaps it is only men with a low sense of self-esteem and strong withdrawal tendencies who stay on the assembly line. Kornhauser tries to handle this problem by exploring the life of his interviewees before they took their present jobs. He concludes that there is demonstrable evidence that jobs change attitudes, regardless of what those attitudes were before the job was taken. If so, then personality differences that exist before taking the job do not explain occupational differences in mental health. See Arthur Kornhauser, "Mental Health of Factory Workers," *Human Organization,* XXI, 43–46.

their self-esteem are reflected in their desire for economic improvement.

What are the implications of these findings for our understanding of political life?

First, it seems reasonable to suppose that assembly-line workers and others whose jobs deprive them of control over their physical movements are more likely to sympathize with radical and mass agitations. Assembly-line workers are more isolated and more likely to feel disenfranchised than other industrial workers. Their feelings about politics are likely to be influenced by desires for relatively radical change, even if these feelings are partly suppressed.

Second, it seems clear that the job structure of industry is one factor that needs to be understood in grasping the impact of industrialization. Kornhauser has pointed out that it is not industrialization *per se* but, rather, "discontinuities" in industrial development that have been the basis for antidemocratic movements. Among these discontinuities are excessive rapidity of industrialization or the acute breakdown of the economy. Perhaps along with these factors we should also turn our attention to the job structure of emerging industries, focusing on the proportion of assembly-line-type jobs.

Third, specific job groups may show a clearer relationship to political-party allegiance in countries with multiparty systems than they seem to in America. The great majority of workers in all of the sample groups examined here were Democrats; yet the groups differed in the extent to which they favored liberal economic measures and in the intensity of their antagonism to the Republicans. In a country where a greater variety of political choice is offered, such differences within the strata of manual workers may show up more sharply in party allegiances. And conversely if most of the men in most circumstances voted Democratic anyway, regardless of differences in their feelings, party organizers here may be content to get them to the polls and ignore their findings.

Finally, how widely can these findings be generalized? If recent work in industrial psychology is any indication, a large percentage of manual and white-collar workers are not interested in their work. It seems as yet an open question whether interest in work and control over work increase or decrease with the spread of various forms of automation. At any rate, millions if not tens of millions of Americans in the foreseeable future are likely to be working at uninteresting, repetitive jobs. Perhaps such workers, even if they are not manual workers, will internalize the tensions and dissatisfactions of their work.

I am not attempting to argue that a bored clerk in a department store, a dishwasher in a restaurant, an auto-assembly-line worker and an IBM card puncher are likely to respond to their jobs in the same manner. Their politics and social attitudes are conditioned by the context and status of their jobs and also by the circumstances and expectations they bring with them, as well as other factors. Yet it seems possible that in each status level, those with the most repetitive, least interesting or controllable jobs will be the most dissatisfied, alienated and politically "radical."

VI

Various political analysts have argued that there is a causal connection between industrialization and democracy. Among the most prominent of these probably is S. M. Lipset, who shows correlations between stable democratic systems and various indices which provide ways of measuring the relative modernity of nations. In his view, contradicting Marx, industrialization tends to produce the preconditions for political democracy because the struggle is shaped in moderate directions. Relative wealth and increased education tend to preclude extremism in the lower classes. The absence of deep and stable class differences makes it possible for the rich and privileged to acknowledge the poor as members of the same species.

Robert Lane [see page 119] has recently buttressed Lipset's argument from another direction. His research of the attitudes of a sample of "common men" in an Eastern city reveals that the work situation in which these men find themselves is conducive to the formation of democratic norms. Most of his sample have substantial independence at work, find satisfaction in their jobs, exercise some skill, are in a position to assert their competence and to exchange views with co-workers and superiors. Lane's findings also move in the direction of substantiating Robert Blauner's hypothesis that modern industrial work provides wider opportunities for the exercise of skill than work in previous societies. Lane concludes that the data on industrial work substantiate Lipset's on the relation between democracy and advanced industrial development.

The findings reported here, as well as those of Kornhauser noted before, are not nearly so optimistic. It seems that at some lower skill levels work alienation is considerable and has serious psychological and political consequences, some of which are not very healthy for a democratic polity. On the basis of the very incomplete knowledge we have about the effects of different types of work, skepticism about the overall consequences of industrial work is still in order.

The manual workers in this study are not extremists in the sense of favoring truly radical change, revolution, violence or of lending support to undemocratic political movements. But it is not their jobs, at least in the case of the two groups of semiskilled workers, that have made them supporters of the status quo or taught them very much about the nature of democratic social relationships. If these men are defenders of the political status quo it seems to be largely because of their status as consumers, not because of their work lives. If they have much of a sense of personal adequacy, it is because of the control and judgment they are able to exercise outside their jobs. Though industrial work, for many reasons, may be more conducive to the development of democratic sentiments than the life of the peasant, it is quite another thing to argue that industrial work, at least of the repetitive variety, is generally healthy or enhances an individual's sense of worth.

Lipset's argument concerning the relationship between industrialization and democracy seems to run counter to the analyses of writers such as C. Wright Mills and Erich Fromm. Fromm and Mills emphasize the alienation and apathy characteristic of bureaucratized industrial societies. They argue that democracy is far from being a reality in today's world. As they picture it, many ordinary citizens have become passive and alienated, feel unable to control their fates, and have lost sight of the significant issues of political life. Both Mills and Fromm relate these characteristics of industrial societies to the structure of work. Both argue that alienation and passivity at work breed alienation and passivity elsewhere. If they are right and industrialization creates many kinds of work situations which are not conducive to the development of democratic attitudes, then how can industrialization and democracy be related?

A great part of the difficulty in resolving this antithesis may lie in definitions and points of view. Lipset's definition of democracy is an arbitrary, operational one. He speaks of two characteristics: competitive parties and the absence of strong antidemocratic political groups. Both Fromm and Mills speak of democracy and democratic attitudes in a different sense. Both bring normative judgments to bear on present reality. So it is possible to agree that Lipset's correlation is correct and yet to also agree with Mills and Fromm that present-day democracies are not as democratic as they might be.

Robert Lane has argued that ego strength is a crucial psychological correlate of democracy. Without having experienced an inner sense of mastery as well as a sense of mastery over the environment, men do not develop the requisite ego strength to pursue a consistent long-term course or to effect needed social change. One of the most important, if unproven, implications of my study is that what the workmen do can have important consequences for their ego strength. Here the concerns of Fromm and Mills are significant. Men in a work environment they cannot control may be to some unknown degree damaged in their sense of mastery, and this damage may render them less capable of coping with and altering an environment they find unsatisfactory. To the extent that such damage occurs, men become victims rather than creators. To the extent that work life contributes to such incapacities, it needs to be improved. *Industrial democracy may yet prove to be a prerequisite to political and social democracy.*

A few final *caveats*: first, the severe dissatisfactions found among automobile-assembly-line workers are probably not typical of the attitudes of most modern industrial workers. The nature of the assembly line itself intensifies the problems of a mechanized job. These findings therefore represent only one segment of the working class. Their relevance to men in other types of jobs which are less intensely disliked remains to be seen. Second, the findings presented are based on a rather crude dichotomizing of attitudes appearing in the setting of open-ended interviews. They are, therefore, at best suggestive. Most important, the question of the intensity with which various attitudes are felt must remain moot in many of the areas the article has explored. For example, though many of the men criticize what they consider to be manipulative practices by political figures, most of them are not "alienated" from the political system. How deep their cynicism may go on occasion is a question the study leaves untouched.

LABOR

The Anti-Youth Establishment

---

by Lewis Carliner

Lewis Carliner is currently professor of labor studies at Rutgers University. Previously, he worked for twenty-one years in the education program of the United Auto Workers, where, as a youth, he took part in a "protest movement, the organization of the CIO, which began but failed to complete the job" urged here.

Arthur Hinkle, twenty-eight-year-old white factory worker, and Bradford Jones, twenty-three-year-old black factory worker, are two rank-and-file soldiers in a guerrilla war now being waged in the labor movement. At the moment the war is still sputtering; it hasn't fully broken out. Except for occasional flareups not always recognized as incidents in the war —the Wallace vote in some areas, the rejection of newly negotiated union agreements by the rank and file, the revolutionary unity movement among auto workers in Detroit— the shape of the conflict is only beginning to become visible.

Hinkle and Jones, it needs to be said immediately, are both fighting the old men—in the plant, in the union, in the community and in the society. But because the best indications are that they don't yet know that this is what they are

battling, they are not fighting side by side. Indeed, sometimes they are fighting each other.

Young American workers like Hinkle and Jones are
older than other people we define as young in the United
States and much older than young workers overseas, where
sixteen-year-olds and sometimes fifteen-year-olds go into
factories to work as apprentices. In the United States young
factory workers are generally defined as between twenty-
three and thirty-five. This makes the youngest factory
worker older than the oldest student, except for graduate
students.

This age difference accounts for part of the lack of understanding between young workers and students, although
both have their backs up against the going establishment.
Class differences, resulting in widely opposite cultural and
political attitudes, are another major factor. But even
though they don't realize it, young workers, students and
black youth all have the same basic grievances. What es-
capes them, and affects them all, unequally but powerfully,
is that the economic differences between young and old are
generally more marked than differences between worker
and boss, or black and white. The disparity in the situation
between young and old is heavily weighted to the advantage
of people over thirty-five. Bureaucratic dynamisms have op-
erated to give the older men control over the agencies in the
society which in ordinary circumstances conduct protest activities: unions, political parties, institutionalized reformist
agencies. The slogan "Never trust anyone over thirty,"
which, when it was first raised, seemed to be a joke, is actually based on an empirical understanding of the treatment
accorded by those over thirty to those under.

The under-thirty-five grievances are simple and inescap-
able, once they are looked at squarely. Young workers, like
students, have less money and power than older people, al-

though they often share the same responsibilities. The cries of students for participatory democracy and of blacks for self-determination have been heard across the country, but until recently there had only been mumbles of discontent from young workers. As would be expected, students and black people are far more articulate about what bugs them than are young workers.

But there are other reasons for the lack of understanding about the problems of young workers.

Union newspapers, which represent the views of the union administration, deliberately do not air the grievances of young workers, nor do management publications. Young workers themselves have no organizations, as other dissident groups do, and no means for expressing their views except the traditional methods that workers have always invoked—repudiating their leaders and resorting to wildcat strikes.

There is currently a general belief that there has been a substantial increase in exuberantly violent wildcat strikes led and insisted upon by young workers. The strike at American Motors two years ago is often cited as an example of the kind of strike that is almost, but not quite, an epidemic.

But there is better evidence of disaffection in the rejection of contract terms by the rank and file after they have been negotiated by union officers and staff. Nationally, the number of strike-settlement rejections has been rising steadily since 1964, the earliest year for which data are available.

"A common cause of these rejections," according to the director of the Federal Mediation and Conciliation Service, "is the advent of a young work force. Many young workers who have grown up in a period of relative affluence have never experienced either a real depression or the early history of union struggles. Moreover, they are not very interested in attempts to acquaint them with these hard facts of earlier years. Many have never experienced a strike of any duration. When these facts are coupled with what may be loosely described as the current disillusionment of youth in other areas of activity, negative ratification votes are not surprising."

The implication in these assessments is that young workers are talking back to their elders and betters because they have not experienced the hardships that older union members suffered in earlier struggles. It reflects an attitude that is the object of resentment of young students, workers and blacks throughout the country. The fact is that young people are a minority with the usual minority grievances; they are discriminated against in the matter of rewards and privileges, denied representation in the government of their society and its commercial and educational institutions, and required to be unwilling audiences to traditional declarations by the people in power that the protesters are too young, too inexperienced, too ignorant, too unprepared and, in general, too damned insolent to merit serious consideration.

Against the claim that young workers strike and reject contracts because they have never met a payroll or walked a picket line in the winter of 1938, there is clear evidence in the current work situation and economic data that young workers have serious causes for complaint.

Within the union structure itself, neither the locals nor the national and international unions even begin to give young people the representation on governing boards that, on the basis of their numbers, they are entitled to.

The seniority system and the instinct of people to hang onto their jobs in a bureaucracy account for the fact that the labor movement has become what might be called a gerontocracy. The movement which rejects the view that seniority qualifies superannuated Dixiecrats for chairmanships in the

key Congressional committees has not turned its attention
to its own trade-union arteriosclerosis.

On the job, young workers, especially in their earliest
days in the plant, understandably resent the seniority system
and frequently claim that the local union leadership and
plant management are in league against them in matters of
the distribution of overtime, promotions and desirable
transfers, and are deaf to such grievances connected with
low seniority as having to work the second and third shift.
Granted that the history of the trade-union movement is a
powerful argument for the strongest possible seniority protection, other security provisions and full employment
might still make it possible to give young people clearly defined opportunities to bypass seniority restraints in order to
utilize a particular talent.

One characteristic of today's young workers that mocks
the older worker's claim to know more and be wiser is the
disparity in education between young and older employees.
At present, the majority of new employees are high school
graduates and many have college training; in general they
have better formal educations than those who deny them
representation in the union.

Data compiled by both the unions and the Bureau of
Labor Statistics reveal the importance of demographic facts
to unions and the condition of workers, young and old.
Each year some three million people enter the labor force,
and of these a third of the men and about one-fifth of the
women are employed in factories. In 1960 there were
slightly more than 13 million people in the labor force
under twenty-five, and by 1970 this figure will have increased to almost 20 million. Workers over forty-five will
increase about 18.5 percent in the same period, while workers in the thirty-five-to-forty-four age group will decline.

Thus labor leaders will soon have to deal with a constituency that is relatively old and relatively young, with the young in the majority.

The testimony everywhere in the society—especially in the political sphere, where grievances are the raw materials —is that young workers are being subjected to an intense propaganda attack against pensions and social security. In the plant they are told, very often by foreman but by co-workers as well, that they are being taxed out of wage increases to provide pensions for the older workers.

Outside the plant, management-sponsored organizations and right-wing political groups bombard them with literature that insists that the social security program is a fraud perpetrated against young workers, that if an amount equivalent to what they pay into social security was deposited in a savings bank it would pay them far more than they will ever receive in social security benefits, that the social security fund is bankrupt, and that they are being taxed to pay pensions to the aged today because of this bankruptcy. All these allegations are demonstrably untrue; nevertheless, increases in social security taxes have enraged young workers, especially since their own economic situation is not understood by the labor movement, the government, or even by the young worker himself.

Apart from the poor, no group in the society is under greater economic pressure than young workers. When they are told by their older co-workers in the plant that things have never been so good, wages higher, conditions better, vacations more satisfactory, and that all this is the result of the older workers' sacrifices, their reply is often, "So what? Things aren't all that good now." The truth is that for the younger worker things are *not* very good.

He spends on the average more than he earns and goes into debt each year. At the beginning of the sixties he was going into debt on an average of $100 a year, and he is probably going more deeply into debt now. He sees taxes for pensions and social security as money he could use to pay his bills and keep even.

Wealth and financial well-being among American workers are closely related to the age of the worker and of his wife and children. In part this is because workers under thirty-five are usually married to women whose full-time occupation is raising children. During this period they are under the heaviest economic burden most Americans ever have to bear—buying a home, often paying off the borrowed down payment on the house, buying a car, furniture, appliances, paying for their children.

When their children reach the teens the situation changes. Often their wives return to work and the family income almost doubles; the house is substantially paid for; the installment accounts are paid off; bills are under control. Suddenly, instead of pressure, there is relative affluence.

The changing situation of the young worker as he grows old is revealed in Federal Reserve System statistics.

Families headed by persons under thirty-five had total assets valued at $6,304 in 1963, representing equity in a car, house, investments, insurance and so forth. Scaled down by age, it is obvious that the assets of a family with a twenty-five-year-old head who has one baby and another on the way come to very nearly nothing. Families with heads in the thirty-five-to-forty-four age group are better off, with total average assets of $16,008, of which some $3,541 is invested, and with Liquid Assets of amost $5,000. Things are even better, financially, for the fifty-five-to-sixty-four-year-old group, whose resources averaged $32,527 in 1963 and who had, among other assets, some $12,212 in investments and $6,401 in liquid assets.

The young worker has a two-edged grievance: he is under an impossible financial burden, and part of his burden is due to the fact that he must help provide for the far more well-to-do older worker. Moreover, in recent years this situation has been compounded by inflation. In the case of the younger worker it means that he must pay $3,000 to $5,000 more for a house than he would have had to pay two years ago. In addition, his mortgage exacts a usurious 7½ or 8 percent, as compared with the 4 to 6 percent the older workers are paying off. No wonder it seems to him that the entire society is a seniority swindle designed to victimize him.

Young workers in Sweden, Great Britain, Japan and a number of other countries are not tied in a bind that compels them to resent the pensions paid older workers. They receive housing assistance, grants on marriage, family allowances and a variety of services to help them surmount the mountainous costs of raising a young family.

Unions and political parties responsive to the needs of young constituents should have long ago devised a program to meet these problems. Yet even the student loans offered today become a further burden to the young father who has to repay them. Perhaps there should be very long-term loans for young families with minimal payments in the first fifteen years and higher payments in the last twenty-five years, when inflation and the improved economic position of being an older worker would operate to reduce the required payments to a nominal charge.

Possibly social security could be tied to family-assistance programs for young people, down payments on a house, interest subventions, grants to buy furniture and appliances, and allowances for each child, so that the social security tax and pension deduction would be combined with benefits to the young as well as the old. Better still, loans to young workers could be paid back through a 1 percent surtax on income beginning at age thirty-five.

The unions should explore collective bargaining ventures

aimed at relieving the pressures on young people. But most important, the society and the labor movement should move to admit the young into the government of the community. Otherwise the anti-youth establishment may be confronted from another direction in the society by the cry of "Up against the wall, you old gerontocrats . . ."

THE EXPLOITATION OF WOMEN WORKERS

by Joan Jordan

A resident of San Francisco, Joan Jordan has been exploring and doing research on the economic aspects of women's liberation for a number of years.

The woman question, like the Negro question, is dual and complex. On one side of the duality is direct economic exploitation. On the other are the myriad social forms of discrimination and exploitation, such as those in Southern states that put the flower of Southern womanhood on pedestals so high that they are not permitted to serve on juries since they are "incompetent because of sex."

Economic categories come first. In April 1968, 28.7 million American women sixteen years old and over were employed outside the home. The percentage (48) of women at work has surpassed the peak of 36 percent in the war year of 1945. Today, however, the vast majority of working women are married, and the age level has shifted upward to a forty-year-old median, with 53 percent of the women between forty-five and fifty-four at work. Almost half (49 percent) of the women who are married, living with their husbands, and have children over six are working. One out of every ten families has a female head, and one-fourth of all black families has a female head. About two-fifths (39 percent) of the women who headed families classified as poor in 1966 were in the paid labor force.

Black women workers are the lowest-paid group, followed by white women, black men and white men in ascending order. However, in some categories determined by educational attainment or selected occupation, this order shifts. For instance, median income for white women in two categories—those with some college training and those with four or more years of college—is lower than black women in those two categories, but both groups earn less than white men with one to three years of high school. In 1967 black women were also making more than white women in professional, managerial, clerical and sales occupations in the central city. This suggests that the greater self-assertiveness, independence and militancy of black women is of value and may be a causal factor in their being considered worth more.

One group of women workers seldom included in Labor Department statistics are those who do housework, and bear and rear children. Although some of these workers are within the market economy, most are not. Their unpaid but socially necessary labor is somewhat similar to that of unpaid serfs or peasants in relation to a growing industrializing market economy. The precapitalist formation of the family unit is necessary to the capitalist system in order to provide cheap labor power through the unpaid labor of women in the home. If women were paid equally with men, it would mean a vast redivision of the wealth.

In most cases, housework is the most unproductive work a woman can do. It is arduous, repetitive and monotonous, and its exceptionally petty nature does not provide anything that could promote the development of the woman in any way. According to a monograph by Juliet Mitchell, *"Women, the Longest Revolution"* (1966), it was found that in Sweden women spend 2,340 million hours a year in housework, compared with 1,290 million hours in industry. The Chase Manhattan Bank has estimated that a woman's overall working time in the home averages 99.6 hours per week.

As millions of women have entered the labor market, they have been pushed into the lowest-paying job categories. The median income of women compared with that for men has dropped from 59 percent in 1939 to 30 percent today. In almost every industry and occupation women are paid less than men for doing the same job. Women are massed in the lower-paying major occupations; women are passed over for on-the-job training and upgrading; women are denied advancement. Why? What excuses are given for this discrimination?

Many rationalizations are given for paying women less and keeping them from advancing. Some claim that differences in the performance of men and women on the job justify the differentials. Women, they say, are not as well prepared for jobs as men. They don't have the equivalent formal education and specific training. In addition, women don't make good supervisors; women cost the employer more in fringe benefits; women have a higher turnover rate and more absenteeism than men. Also, woman's place is in the home. Only once in a great while will an employer admit that it's *cheaper* to discriminate.

The case for discrimination against women because of inadequate preparation—with the implication that they lack the ambition to get the preparation—is remarkably similar to that given to justify the treatment of black workers. The vicious circle begins with the refusal of the employer to hire or promote blacks because they aren't "qualified," continues because discrimination on these grounds intensifies discrimination on other more prejudiced grounds, and is completed when the Negro is disinclined to get more preparation be-

cause he knows he will be discriminated against even with
adequate preparation—hence he is unprepared to seize opportunities if they do open up. Women are also caught in
this never-ending cycle.

In addition, the case for discriminating against women
because of their lack of education has not been proved. In
fact, the evidence shows that, except on the highest levels,
women as a whole enter the labor market with more training and education than do men. In 1959 women had completed a median of 12.2 years of schooling, compared with
11.7 years for men. Thirty-eight percent of the women
workers and only 27 percent of the male workers had completed high school.

Consider this in light of Betty Friedan's argument that
women need more education to break out of the trap of the
"feminine mystique." If more education would expose the
political and economic causes of the mystique, she might be
right, but the realities are that even as women are becoming
more and more educated, the proportion of professional
women is shrinking. And even though more and more
women are entering the labor force, they are being restricted to the lower-paying jobs and prevented from advancing.

There is obviously little incentive for a woman to better
her skills if better positions are closed to her. In the unions,
apprentice-training programs are generally restricted to
white males with the rationalization that, after all, a man
has a family to take care of. That this argument is used
against women who are heads of families seems to bother no
one.

Another rationalization for not promoting women is that
they don't make good supervisors, or that both women and
men prefer to work under men. This is a subjective judgment that has not been demonstrated and is open to speculation. It may not be that women do not or could not super-

vise well but rather that men in management (and in
unions, too—perhaps even more) fear that women will succeed too well. The relevant factor here might be the danger
to the male ego. Only a man with a strong, stable core of self
can see a woman as an equal human being and not feel a
threat to his masculinity.

Arguments are also raised about fringe benefits. Employers claim that women cost them more in benefits than men
do, and on that basis justify their use of women as part-time
or temporary full-time workers to avoid giving them such
benefits. Their main complaint is that pregnant women are
required by law to interrupt their work for a number of
months, and in most union contracts the job must be held
open and benefits paid by the employer. In reality, however,
most union health plans exclude maternity benefits with
such rationalizations as "maternity is not sickness but an act
of God."

The results of several studies reported in a Labor Department Women's Bureau pamphlet (*Maternity Benefits Provisions for Employed Women*) reveal that no more than 4
percent of employed women in any one year will become
pregnant. This compares with injury rates among workers at
about 3 percent in 1958, not including sickness. The benefits for pregnancy negotiated in union contracts usually are
no higher than the benefits paid for sickness and disability to
all workers covered by a particular contract, and total
amounts of workers' compensation for injuries are increasing.

By cooperating with employers in their refusal to pay
fringe benefits to women workers, male unionists are in a
weak tactical position when employers try to avoid paying
fringe benefits to men. Plants move to states with "right-to-
work" laws or to nonunionized regions, or they just switch
job classification from men's to women's work, or from permanent to temporary to take advantage of discriminatory

practices, thus turning the lower wage scale into a weapon to be used against male workers too.

The rationalization that turnover rates and absenteeism are higher for women than men usually ignores the fact that women generally work in the worst conditions. The turnover problem also appears to be directly related to the kind and level of work involved. The Women's Bureau of the Labor Department, in a 1950 study titled *Women in Higher Level Positions,* showed that different firms gave different opinions on turnover rates. Almost all firms whose training programs were closed to women gave lack of permanency as the reason. On the other hand, several company representatives in different fields maintained that, although lack of permanency generally was a deterrent to women's advancement, it was not important as far as the higher-level positions were concerned. One large department store had in fact found that there was less turnover among women than men in its promotional department.

There is at present no information on the relative rates of absenteeism of men and women, but one can assume that adequate day-care facilities for children of working mothers would be an important factor. When such facilities were established during World War II, employers testified that they greatly helped to reduce absenteeism and turnover in their plants.

Another rationalization for discriminating against women acts directly to divide the labor movement and pit one section against the other. This is what happens when employers tell skilled male workers, officers or negotiating committees: "We could give you a much higher wage if you just didn't have to drag those unskilled workers along with you." The Teamsters Council of New York published an analysis of marginal workers in New York City, including those in the International Ladies Garment Workers Union, that indicated that women were restricted to the lower-paying jobs controlled by the union. In collusion with the employers, skilled workers would trade off better wages and working conditions of the more numerous unskilled women workers in exchange for greater gains for themselves.

To pull off this kind of a deal it is necessary to intimidate the general workers and nullify any real grievance procedures in their departments. This is done by emphasizing the "role of the woman" and the "male breadwinner" ideologies in order to create an attitude of passive "feminine" acceptance.

The old saw that a woman's place is in the home is used as a rationalization by many employers for paying lower wages and providing worse working conditions for women than men. If these employers really meant what they said, they would not hire women at all, but leave them in the home. Instead they use the feminine mystique to keep women in their place—their place being the reserve labor force.

It is interesting to follow the propaganda used to control women. During World War II idle hands were tools of the devil, Rosie the Riveter was portrayed as a dynamic, patriotic heroine, and articles appeared on the advantages of bottle feeding over breast feeding. Immediately following World War II, women at work were accused of creating juvenile delinquents at home and of competing with men, and surveys showed that eight out of ten infants who die of stomach ailments within the first year of birth were bottle-fed.

However, employers found that the rate of exploitation of men was not so profitable as that of women, so women were allowed to stay in industry—in their place. The middle-class concepts of femininity and its pseudo-psychological twin of passivity are extremely valuable to employers. In addition to providing rationales for discrimination and exploitation, they also serve to give women guilt complexes, making it easier to manipulate them. Women will often compensate by trying to work harder and for less pay. They may do the work of the executive or supervisor without the title or the salary. After all, they don't want to be dominating, aggressive, pushy or *masculine*.

The problems of "human relations in industry" are set up by industrial psychologists employed by the company, and are seen as primarily due to misunderstandings and lack of open communication. The call for more "cooperation" usually means obedience accompanied by talk.

Betty Friedan and other writers have very adequately dealt with the economic value to business of the feminine mystique, particularly in getting women to fulfill their roles as consumers and purchasers of endless commodities. Less has been said about the economic value to business of the mystique in relation to woman as the employee, as the producer of commodities.

It is naïve to believe that women can be fully liberated in an economic system where profit alone—even when it means the waste of the labor power of millions of human beings and millions of working hours—is the chief determinant. It is essential, in solving women's problems, to change society. Women can and will play a key role in this general historical task, but they cannot expect to solve their problems without a struggle. Equality will not be given them as a gift. It must be fought for and won as a human right.

Nevertheless, it is not sufficient to equate the woman question with the struggle of the deprived classes generally. One can no more say to women than to Negroes, "Join us, and when we have socialism your needs will be met." Because the woman question is a dual problem, because women suffer special forms of discrimination and exploitation in addition to those they experience as workers, there is a need for special organizations and special demands to meet their needs.

Economic organizations are a necessity, but most unions have either defaulted in relation to organizing women or used them to protect skilled workers' jobs or as the expendable element in contract negotiations. Although one-third of the present labor force is composed of women, only 15 percent of them are organized into unions.

The current ferment among women may, however, change that. Union leaders know a good thing when they see it. In 1961 and 1962 three-fourths of all new members organized in California were women, and this in spite of the fact that there was a drop in overall union membership in the state at that time. These women came from both government and private jobs. Given the chauvinistic male exploitative attitudes of many union men as well as employers toward women, it is obvious, however, that other organizations are needed too.

Two groups may be of particular interest: the Women's Bureau of the United Auto Workers, and the Negro American Labor Council. The Women's Bureau was organized in 1953, when automation hit Detroit, and women, some with as much as fifteen years' seniority, were laid off. They organized and went to the UAW convention with demands to be included not only in the constitution but in contract demands as well. The critical demand was concerned with job security and promotion in a shrinking labor market. The goal was to prevent women from being used as a reserve labor force and driven back to the home during periods of economic contraction.

The Negro American Labor Council was developed in the late 1950's as an organizaton of black trade unionists fighting to get into unions, to receive apprentice training, upgrading and promotion on the job, and to run candidates

for union office and policy-making bodies. Such an organization as this, based on sex instead of color, would seem
feasible for women. NALC members come from many
unions and exist independently of any one union. In contrast, the Women's Bureau is within one union.

Special economic demands must be made. Three main
trends of sexual discrimination have become more and more
common in this decade.

The first is to lay off women and rehire men in women's
classifications at women's wages; this was used in the 1953
recession in Detroit. However, the men challenged this tactic; there was no feminine mystique to keep *them* passive.

The second trend is to lay off men and use more women
in jobs that have been reclassified from men's to women's at
lower wages. For instance, electrical assembly in California
used to be men's work, and for years the men in the union
felt they could do better and should get more than women.
As the gap in wages and conditions widened, so did the
difference between the number of men and women in the
union and also the number of nonunion women in industry.
In both cases the number of women relative to the number
of men increased as their wages relative to men's decreased.
Electrical-assembly and electronics industries grew rapidly
during and after the war. By that time the work had become
known as women's work "traditionally," and new employees were recruited from among women. The men in the
union complained bitterly about how the women's wages
kept theirs down because women worked so cheaply and
were taking all the jobs, yet this was a result of their original position that they should get more than women.

Naked self-interest should have led the women to (1) organize a women's caucus; (2) raise their demands, with pri-
ority on job security through many methods, but especially
through the sliding scale of hours, such as the thirty-hour

week at forty-hour pay; and (3) develop tactics that would convince their union brothers of the necessity of supporting them, neutralizing those they couldn't convince and actively fighting those in open opposition.

The Civil Rights Bill of 1964 supposedly banned discrimination based on sex. However, the law is simply ignored by many corporations. They claim, as did Fibreboard of California recently, that they are "caught" between the federal law and the state protective laws in such areas as hours, lifting and overtime penalty pay. In reality they are using the protective laws to maintain discrimination and at the same time following a strategy designed to smash these laws. Then in a contracting labor market (i.e., with many idle workers eager to get jobs at any salary) they could extend the working day to ten or twelve hours or more without overtime pay or the right to refuse. In 1969 federal guidelines were established on the basis of the Civil Rights Act which stipulated that preventive laws could not be used as an excuse for discrimination.

Women, Inc., the women's caucus of the Association of Western Pulp and Paper Workers Union, has brought suit in Federal District Court against Fibreboard with job security as a crucial issue. They are challenging sex-segregated hiring lists, promotion lists, layoff lists and labor pools, among other forms of sexual discrimination.

The third trend of economic exploitation is to use more part-time workers and full-time temporary workers to avoid paying fringe benefits. This can be overcome by demands for equal pay to workers of this type, and complete medical coverage beginning immediately and based on the length of time in industry rather than with a given employer; prorated vacations and the scheduling of work over the year to keep on a full-time regular crew; and holiday pay, no matter when the worker joined the company.

.   .   .

Social demands are important too, of course, and must be
made along with demands for economic reform, because economic reforms alone will not solve all the problems facing
both men and women in contemporary American society.
Some of the most pressing are:

—Free public nurseries and child-care centers for all
working mothers.
—Planned-parenthood centers available to any man or
woman.
—Legal abortions in free, well-staffed clinics.
—Summer camps for all children.
—Reorganization of home chores by application of mass-
production methods.
—Equal economic, social and intellectual opportunities.
—Fathers and mothers on four-hour days or shortened
work weeks so that fathers may regain their lost role
and share in the growth experiences of their children,
as suggested by Ashley Montagu.
—Payment of maternity and paternity leaves for three
to five years while parents work two, four or, at most,
six hours daily in child-care centers and nurseries with
their children and also attend classes on child development with specialists.
—Payment of wages to mothers for bearing and raising
children.

This last reform would give social recognition and remunera-
tion for the "job" of motherhood, making it as important as
any other form of labor. It would eliminate both victimiza-
tion due to biological necessity and marriages based on economic necessity. It would recognize that having children is a
part of the socially necessary labor in the reproduction of
life. It would help to eliminate "commodity" relations between people and establish relations based on personality
and emotional needs instead. It would produce strong, self-

confident men and women who do not suffer from the sick-
nesses and neuroses of exploitative relations. Men and
women could then see each other as equal human beings
—as persons instead of things.

RESPECTABLE BIGOTRY

by Michael Lerner

Michael Lerner is a graduate student in political science and psychology at Yale University. He was an editor of The Crimson *at Harvard University and has reported for the Washington* Post *in Washington and in Israel.*

When white Yale students denounce the racist university or racist American society, one has little doubt about what they refer to. One also has little doubt about the political leanings of the speaker. He is a good left-liberal or radical, who is upper-class or schooled in the assumptions of upper-class liberalism.*

Liberal-to-radical students use protest phrases and feel purged of the bigotry and racism of people such as Chicago's Mayor Daley. No one could be further from bigotry, they seem to believe, than they.

But it isn't so. An extraordinary amount of bigotry on the part of elite, liberal students goes unexamined at Yale and elsewhere. Directed at the lower-middle class, it feeds on the unexamined biases of class perspective, the personality pre-

* The terms "radical," "semiradical," "left-liberal" and "liberal-to-radical" are used in reference to "elite," "upper-class" and "upper-middle-class" students, a broad but splintered and diverse group.

dilections of elite radicals and academic disciplines that support their views.

There are certainly exceptions in the liberal-radical university society—people intellectually or actively aware of and opposed to the unexamined prejudice. But their anomalousness and lack of success in making an ostensibly introspective community face its own disease is striking.

In general, the bigotry of a lower-middle-class policeman toward a ghetto black, or of a lower-middle-class mayor toward a rioter, is not viewed in the same perspective as the bigotry of an upper-middle-class peace matron toward a lower-middle-class mayor; or of an upper-class university student toward an Italian, a Pole or a National Guardsman from Cicero, Illinois—that is, if the latter two cases are called bigotry at all. The violence of the ghetto is patronized, as it is "understood" and forgiven; the violence of a Cicero racist convinced that a Martin Luther King threatens his lawn and house and powerboat is detested without being understood. Yet the two bigotries are very similar. For one thing, each is directed toward the class directly below the resident bigot, the class that reflects the dark side of the bigot's life. Just as the upper class recognizes in lower-class lace-curtain morality the veiled up-tightness of upper-middle-class life, so the lower-middle-class bigot sees reflected in the lower class the violence, sexuality and poverty that threaten him. The radical may object that he dislikes the lower-middle class purely because of its racism and its politics. But that is not sufficient explanation: Polish jokes are devoid of political content.

Empirical studies do not show it, but it is my hunch that shortly after Negro jokes became impossible in elite circles the Polish jokes emerged. They enjoy a continuing success in universities even today. It also happens that while Frank Zappa and the Mothers of Invention or Janis Joplin may vie for top position in the hip radical affections, the cellar of their affections—the object of their ample, healthy, appropriate, unneurotic capacities for hatred—is securely in the hands of that happy team of Mayor Daley and the Chicago police. Hip radicals in New Haven are often amused by the Italian Anti-Defamation League bumper sticker: A.I.D.— AMERICANS OF ITALIAN DESCENT. Poles, Italians, Mayor Daley and the police are safe objects for amusement, derision or hatred. They are all safely lower-middle-class.

Part of the vaunted moral development of college activists is their capacity for empathy—their ability to put themselves in the position of the Disadvantaged Other and to see the world from his circumstances. This theoretically leads them to empathize with ghetto blacks and therefore to distrust the authorities who oppress them. Unnoticed goes the fact that the "authorities" who get hated are the lower-middle-class police, the visible representatives of the more abstract and ambivalently regarded "power structure." Other favored targets for confrontation are the National Guard and the military, both bastions of the lower-middle class. It is true that Dow Chemical representatives are attacked and that professors and university administrators are sometimes held captive. It is also true that the police, the National Guard and the Army are the agents of societal racism, student and ghetto repression and the war in Vietnam. But all these things should not blind us to the fact that the people toward whom bigotry, as well as political dislike, is directed by upper-class radicals are all too frequently lower-middle class.

Radicals gloat over the faulty syntax of the lower-middle class with the same predictability that they patronize the ghetto language as "authentic." They delight in Mayor Daley's malapropisms ("Chicago will move on to higher and higher platitudes of achievement") and in the lace-curtain cynicism of his denunciations ("They use language from the bordello, language that would shock any decent person"). Why do they patronize one authenticity and mock another?

These upper-class attitudes are not a narrow phenomenon. *Time, Life* and *Newsweek* print ghetto phrases in reverent spidery italics—surrounded by space to emphasize the authentic simplicity—beneath soulful pictures of the cleansing but terrible, terrible poverty of ghetto blacks or rural poor. They reprint Daley verbatim as the fool.

One of the strongest supports for this upper-class, "respectable" bigotry lies in the academic field of psychology. In much of what practitioners choose to investigate and interpret, the cognitive capacity, moral development and psychodynamic organization of lower-middle-class individuals are described as inferior to radical activities. Lower-middle-class people are more "authoritarian," more likely to have "closed" minds, more likely to rely on "law-and-order morality" rather than the more advanced "moral-principle orientation," and more likely to use "massive" ego-defenses, such as repression, instead of the more refined defenses like intellectualization and isolation. Lower-middle-class people are more likely to get stuck in a stage of "concrete cognitive operations," associated with low capacity for intellectual differentiation, instead of advancing into "formal cognitive operations," with its high capacity for abstract thinking.

When George Wallace said his opponent was the kind of man who couldn't park a bicycle straight, he undoubtedly confirmed for a host of academic observers how concrete and primitive his concept of successful intellectual operations was.

Students in elite universities are described by psychologists as possessing many of the virtues that lower-middle-class authoritarians lack. These scholars frequently find that, among the elite students, radical activists have even greater moral and intellectual virtues than classmates from lower-class or more traditional families. If you examine the incidence of these virtues, they appear, not surprisingly, to cluster. It seems that psychologists are measuring something that has connected cognitive, moral and ego-defensive manifestations. This something is related to class.

The academic yardsticks measure virtues that, as they are defined, appear most frequently in the children of elite psychologists and their classmates—in the children of the upper-middle and upper class.

These virtues do seem to be the consequence of further (although not necessarily higher) development of the virtues of the lower-middle class; that is, one must go through the developmentally prior lower-middle-class virtues to reach the elite virtues. Repression, obedience to law and prompt acceptance of authority are more "primitive" ways of dealing with reality than intellectualized reflection on principles before obeying a law and skepticism toward authority. One psychologist has urged that upper-class virtues are better in a Platonic sense than lower-middle-class virtues. It is revealing that he does not recall that Plato would undoubtedly have restricted the practice of upper-class virtues to the upper class in his city, arguing that in the interest of harmony other virtues must be required of the lower classes.

Should we believe that the psychologists have discovered an empirical basis for distinguishing between more and less developed men? Should we believe that the developed men are superior? We can start with two broad possibilities. Either "further development" is the artifact of class blindness, or upper-class development is merely different from lower-class development. I think the weight of the argument suggests the latter.

If we opt for this possibility, we must then ask whether the further development is an achievement or a degeneration. Since this depends on our social values, further choice is required: We can either compare directly the values of the further developed individual with the formal societal values, or we can ask whether the survival of the formal societal values is enhanced by increasing the number of people whose personal values are similar to the formal values of the society.

This question forces us to be more specific about what we mean by the superiority of elite virtues in comparison with the virtues of the lower-middle class. Recent analysts, lacking Plato's grasp of behavioral data and his rigorous empiricism, have been unrealistically idealistic in considering the consequences of changing a class distribution of virtues. That elite virtues are superior, as Plato saw, does not mean that the society would be better or would even survive if all possessed them.

It may be that the lower-middle-class virtues provide operant support for a society that allows the upper class the luxury of elite virtues, much as Greek democracy was built on slave labor. I stress "operant support for American society" rather than "formal support of democracy" because the lower-middle class is frequently denounced for disregarding formal democratic values, such as regard for due process and for such freedoms as conscience, press, expression and movement.

Those who acclaim the elite radical virtues as superior to the virtues of the lower-middle class would seem, if one admits that lower-class virtues provide operant support for American society, to have three alternatives. They can accept the distribution as necessary and good, in which case they espouse a troublesome elitism that cannot be reconciled with their radical views. Or they can argue that everyone should possess these (elite radical) virtues, in which case they are true radicals and should ask themselves whether they have considered in an unbiased light the implications of this position. Or they can do what I think most people do, which is largely to restrict—without admitting or even being conscious of the restriction—the practice of these superior virtues to the upper class.

The self-serving argument for upper-class hegemony then seems to be that the upper class is more intelligent, more moral and more finely tuned in its ego-defenses than the lower class and that this makes it more fit to govern and to preserve such democratic values as equal access. But in the name of the preservation of these values, elite virtues must be denied to the lower class because their use would be disruptive. To preserve the society that guarantees access to power to those who are virtuous, we must deny the possession of virtue to the lower class and thus deny the access we are theoretically preserving.

Leaving aside the hard choices that a believer in the superiority of radical virtues must make, we can ask in broader perspective what alternative stances one may take if it is true that an upper-class background leads to further moral and intellectual development. They appear to be:

1. In the existing world a "further developed" man may govern worse rather than better. A principled orientation can be disastrous in world politics, as the principled architects of the cold war have shown. An ability to empathize may lead to concessions in negotiations that will be misread by the Other Side as blanket willingness to retreat when faced with force. Capacity to see issues in all their complexity may lead to Hamlet-like paralysis, when any action would be preferable to none.

2. The further development of the upper class might make it best qualified to rule, as its de facto supremacy proves. In a roughly democratic framework there is a chance for the few lower-class individuals who achieve upper-class virtues to rise to the top; that most leaders will be upper-class by birth is necessary and even desirable to preserve social stability and to reduce the anxieties that result from situations of volatile status change.

3. Upper-class individuals are further developed than lower-class individuals, and it is an indictment of our resource-rich society that more people are not brought into these higher stages of development. Analyses claiming that this would destabilize society are too contingent to win credence; the destabilization, moreover, might result in a better society instead of a worse one.

4. This "further development" is development along a path that may lead to the overspecialization and extinction of the human race. It accepts the dubious value of a capitalist Calvinism and conceals assumptions about what constitutes higher development that are disastrous both for the individual and the species (and are rejected by the hippie culture). This building up of surplus repression in ever-higher capacities for intellectualization destroys capacities for feeling, for activity, for love. Elephantiasis of intellect and atrophy of emotion are mirrored in American society, where our intellectual industry, technology, produces the antiballistic missile and the death-dealing gadgetry of Vietnam while our feelings are too atrophied to insist that the logic of our priorities is insane. There is the atrophy of individual sensation inherent in eating Wonder Bread, watching Johnny Carson, and smelling Right Guard.

These are a few of the attitude-policy alternatives that acceptance of the psychologists' findings could lead us to. The third and fourth arguments, which would appeal to liberals and radicals to varying degrees, have in common a disregard for the contributions of the lower-middle-class virtues to what is good as well as what is bad in American society. Let us now ask whether this disregard is based on close analysis of what American society would look like if we all possessed the "superior" elite values, or whether it is the result of an upper-class blindness toward what this might mean.

Operant supports of American society, conservatives and

radicals agree, are very often different from the formal democratic virtues that guarantee the procedures of a democratic policy. In the course of a brilliant denunciation of some mandarinic American political scientists, Noam Chomsky quotes Tocqueville: "I know of no country in which there is so little independence and freedom of mind as in America." Chomsky adds: "Free institutions certainly exist, but a tradition of passivity and conformism restricts their use—a cynic might say this is why they continue to exist."

Although radicals often condemn American society by juxtaposing the "traditional American virtues" of respect for democratic procedure with current breaches of those procedures, it seems probable that historically American justice was at least as pock-marked as it is today and that the lower-middle-class virtues are the real "tradition" supports that Tocqueville observed when he came to see how American democracy functioned.

These virtues—law-and-order morality, acceptance of authority, cognitive processes that present issues in broad terms, ego-defenses that prefer the violence of hockey to the savagery of the seminar table—undoubtedly play a part in whatever orderliness there is in daily American life. They help people accept and carry out decisions that affect them adversely. They help make football a high-salience issue and foreign affairs a low-salience issue, leaving the President, who should be in a better position to decide, a good deal of freedom from mass pressures. In a number of ways, one could argue, they account for what is good as well as bad in American life. Conversely, elite virtues may account for more of the bad aspects of American life than is usually assumed.

Some upper-class radicals, we suggested above, are able to assume that elite virtues are preferable to lower-middle-class virtues across the board because they unconsciously restrict their idea of who should practice these virtues and to what end. Radical students and ghetto blacks, within limits, are the groups from whom these people expect a moral-principle orientation rather than law-and-order morality. Blacks and students are expected to practice skepticism toward authority. If, on the other hand, the colonels, the police, teamsters, longshoremen or garbage collectors practice prolonged skepticism toward constituted authority, or act in accordance with their principles rather than in accordance with law-and-order morality, then the elite semi-radicals have a vague sense that something must be done.

The upper class has reached a plateau of security from which its liberal-radical wing believes that it can mock the politics of the policeman and the butcher and slight their aspirations while still living genteelly in the space between them. I recall a personal example of how these assumptions sometimes work:

A few months ago some black children from the ghetto that is separated from Yale by the old people and students on my street made their biannual pilgrimages to Lake Place to break off all the aerials and windshield wipers on the cars. I was much more enraged the next morning about my car than I was about the distant and understandable riots that are filtered to me through the *New York Times*. I called the police largely, I suspect, because I wanted to be comforted by a typical policeman's observations on what-you-can-expect-from-*those*-kids. In my protected Eastern existence I had never passed through an overtly racist stage. But sometimes I suspect I get satisfaction from the racism of others: they can say what I cannot even think, and since their racism is so vulgar, I get to feel superior to them in the bargain.

The policeman, a likely young Italian, arrived. After surveying the damage, he said: "Mr. Lerner, I know how you feel; but you've got to take into account the kind of environment in which those children were raised. I mean, if you or I lived in the places they have to live in or went through the same experiences, you can imagine . . ." I listened, stunned. Here the man from whom I expected law-and-order morality was dishing out the moral-principled upper-class capacity to imagine oneself in the situation of the other. Like that of the unconsciously hypocritical radicals, my word depended on that kind of behavior being reserved for cocktail parties and seminars at which one comments from a discreet distance on the understandability of the behavior of ghetto blacks.

The hatreds do not go one way: ghetto blacks hate policemen, and policemen hate upper-class radicals. One hates one class up as well as one class down, although the hatred downward is more violent and the hatred upward mixed with aspirations. The natural alliance is between people a class apart who hate people in the middle for different reasons. This suggests why elite intellectuals, for all their analyzed self-awareness, show immediate "understanding" for the ghetto black's hatred of the policeman, yet find police violence directed at a partially upper-class political demonstration a sure sign of incipient fascism.

Examine, on the other hand, the quality of the class-apart empathy radical whites have for ghetto blacks. The radicals are upper-middle-class youth with life histories of intellectual overcontrol. They have reached a point in their lives where, as Erik Erikson suggests, they can experiment with a little controlled regression-in-the-service-of-the-ego.

The response of a permissive upper-class parent, as reflected in the *New York Times,* is, "Society may have a great deal to learn from the hippies." Translated into jargon this might read: "Upper-class psychological controls may be too strict for changing psycho-sexual-social-historical realities. The young people experimenting with controlled regression may be showing the way in politics, drugs and sex to a new synthesis."

From the point of view of the young people *doing* the experimenting, the value is diminished if anyone stresses the "controlled" or even experimental nature of their quest. The regression or the liberation from overcontrol is what matters. To them the lowest class shows—by fact or projective romanticization or both—a life style characterized by open use of the violence, sexuality and drugs that the experimenters find appealing.

The authenticity that the experimenters sense in the ghetto derives from the fact that lower-class violence and sexuality are not a consequence of tentative and strained regression in the service of the ego but represent a normal and stable class pattern deriving from social conditions, tension levels and prevalent primitive ego-defense organizations.

When elite intellectuals urge that authentic black life styles should not be contaminated by bourgeois values, they are asking the blacks not to lose the values whites lost temporarily in the process of becoming elite. In other words, the old path is from lower-class undercontrol to lower-middle-class overcontrol to the upper-class luxury of reducing controls again. Upper-class whites like to think blacks can move from undercontrol to the partial control pattern that *they* find most socially pleasing without the middle step. They do not realize partial control is usually a step taken from the strength of a background of increasingly sophisticated and differentiated overcontrol.

This self-centeredness is reflected in the programs organized for the education of blacks by upper-class whites and by blacks who have assumed university values. These programs usually stress a freedom and lack of controls that is appropriate to the fantasies of their organizers but scarcely appropriate to those who have only had ghetto experience. It is no wonder that programs organized by lower-class blacks without the funding and guidance of whites—such as the Black Muslim program for narcotics addicts, and Black Muslim educational programs in general—stress that ghetto people must learn the capacity for tight control that has characterized Mayor Daley and every other individual and group that have competed successfully in American society.

Since lower-middle-class police are repelled by the uncontrolledness of the lower class from which their families have escaped, they are understandably infuriated by the regression to violence, drugs and sexuality in the class that expects their deference. The radical students and hippies are rejecting the values to which the lower-middle class aspires and by which it is able to repress the behavior that the students are flaunting at it. When a Yippie girl pulls up her skirt in front of a lower-middle-class policeman and tells him that his trouble is that he has not had what she is baring in front of his face, one cannot expect an academically oriented response. And since every cocktail-party psychologist would expect the police to be authoritarian, low in capacity for differentiation and scarcely able to maintain through primitive repression the violence in himself, why is the reaction to the police riot in Chicago so unbelievably ununderstanding? Why do we expect that hippies and radicals and ghetto blacks can experiment with nonrestraint while the police must be models of restraint? Why can so few empathize with the frustrations of lower-middle-class life that have led to Chicago, to George Wallace and ultimately to the Presidency of Richard Nixon? It is because of the really astounding bigotry and narrowness of a class that prides itself on ridding itself of racism and having a broad perspective. There is little broad perspective in the words of the *New York Times* columnist who wrote in shocked tones, "Those were *our* children on the streets of Chicago." That *Times* columnist and the hip radicals did not understand a nation that approved of the police action in Chicago because its children were in the streets of Chicago, too. Its children were the police.

Racism and bigotry toward black people is frighteningly apparent at Yale. But at least the sore has been lanced and lies open. We can be aware of the ugly strains of societal racism still inside ourselves and our institutions, and we can struggle against them.

The hidden, liberal-radical bigotry toward the lower-middle class is stinking and covered. When a right-wing Italian announced for mayor in New York, a brilliant professor in New Haven said, "If Italians aren't actually an inferior race, they do the best imitation of one I've seen." Everyone at the dinner table laughed. He could not have said that about black people if the subject had been Rap Brown.

The consequences of this bigotry are tragic. It would be less serious if it were not the product of an intellectually self-righteous class that is trying to provide functioning, *electable* alternatives to Richard Nixon and George Wallace. Those dissimilar men had the common intelligence and capacity for empathy—or shrewdness—to appeal to a genuinely forgotten and highly abused segment of the American population. It may be that only when radical intellectuals begin to show again, as they did in the 1930's, empathy for the hardships of lower-middle-class life, and begin to integrate the aspirations of that class into their antiwar, antiracism framework, will it be possible to break up the Nixon alliance. Not until the upper-middle class learns to deal with its own hidden bigotry will it be in a position to help destroy lower-middle-class bigotry as well.

PART 4

WHO SPEAKS FOR THE WHITE MAJORITY?

The Politics of Change

THE WALLACE
WHITELASH

---

by Seymour Lipset
and Earl Raab

Seymour Lipset is professor of government and social relations at Harvard. Among his many books are Political Man, The First New Nation *and* Revolution and Counter-Revolution. *Earl Raab is director of the Jewish Community Relations Council of San Francisco. He co-authored* Major Social Problems, *and with Lipset, he wrote* Prejudice and Society. *This essay is part of their most recent collaboration,* The Politics of Unreason: Right-Wing Extremism in the U.S., 1790–1970.

The American Independent Party of George C. Wallace brought together in 1968 almost every right-wing extremist group in the country, and undoubtedly recruited many new activists for the rightist cause. Today many of the state parties organized under this aegis have formal legal status and have announced that they intend to nominate candidates for state and local office during the next few years in an effort to build the party. George Wallace himself has sent out a clear signal that he has plans for the future. He has begun to mail the *George Wallace Newsletter* monthly to a mailing list of over one million names which had been assembled during the election. The old address for Wallace activities was Box 1968, Montgomery, Alabama. It is now Box 1972.

The effort to maintain and build the party, however, faces the perennial problem of ideological extremist movements—splits among its supporters. Even during the 1968 campaign, sharp public divisions over local-versus-national control occurred in a number of states, usually because complete control over the finances and conduct of the party's work was kept in the hands of coordinators directly appointed by Wallace and responsible to the national headquarters in Montgomery. In some states, two separate organizations existed, both of which endorsed the Wallace candidacy but attacked each other as too radical. Since the 1968 election, two competing national organizations have been created and again each is attacking the other as extremist.

The group directly linked to Wallace has had two national conventions. The first, held in Dallas in early February, attracted 250 delegates from forty-four states and set up a group known as The Association of George C. Wallace Voters. The Dallas meeting was attended by a number of top Wallace aides, including Robert Walters, who represents Wallace in California; Tom Turnipseed, a major figure in the Wallace presidential effort since it started; Dan Smoot, the right-wing radio commentator; and Kent Courtney, the editor of the *Conservative Journal*. The same group met again on May 3 and 4 in Cincinnati, and formally established a new national party to be called the American Party. A Virginian, T. Coleman Andrews, long active on the ultraconservative front, was chosen as chairman. Wallace gave his personal blessing to the new party and its officers. One of his Montgomery aides, Taylor Hardin, who maintains a national office with twenty employees in Montgomery, indicated that the party would have a considerable degree of "central control."

The competing national group met in Louisville on February 22, 1969, and established a new national conservative party to be composed largely of autonomous state parties. As if to emphasize the extent to which it fostered local control, this organization called itself The National Committee of the Autonomous State Parties, known as the American Independent Party, American Party, Independent Party, Conservative Party, Constitutional Party. This group, or constellation of groups, was united in its opposition to domination by Wallace and his Montgomery aides. Although the former candidate received compliments at the convention, the delegates were much more concerned with building a movement that was not limited to his supporters in 1968. The national chairman of the new group, William K. Shearer of California, editor of the *California Statesman,* had already broken with Wallace during the campaign on the issue of local autonomy. At the Louisville convention, Shearer said:

> "Governor Wallace has not shown any interest in a national party apart from a personal party. A candidate properly springs from the party and not the party from the candidate. The party should not be candidate-directed. While we have great respect for Mr. Wallace we do not think there should be a candidate-directed situation. We want our party to survive regardless of what Mr. Wallace does."

The Shearer group also appears to be more conservative on economic issues than the Wallace-dominated one. During the convention, Wallace was criticized for being "too liberal" because of his advocacy during the campaign of extended social security and farm parity prices.

The leaders of each faction claim that the other includes

extremists. Robert Walters attacked Shearer's group as composed of "radicals and opportunists" and as having "a pretty high nut content." Shearer, on the other hand, has said that he finds many in the Wallace-dominated party "not too savory."

The publications of the competing groups indicate that each is supported by viable segments of the 1968 party. The Shearer national committee, however, is clearly much weaker financially, since the Wallace national group retained a considerable sum from the 1968 campaign for future activities. It is also unlikely that they can attract many Wallace voters against the opposition of the candidate. The competition for support, however, does give each group an immediate function; and both national organizations appear to be busy holding state and local conventions designed to win over those who were involved in the presidential campaign.

Who *did* support George Wallace in 1968? A detailed answer to that question will perhaps tell us more than anything else about his chances for the future, as well as about the potentiality of right-wing extremism in America.

Election Day results confirmed the basic predictions of the preelection opinion polls. George Wallace secured almost ten million votes, or about 13.5 percent of the total voting electorate. He captured five states with forty-five electoral votes, all of them in the Deep South: Mississippi, Georgia, Alabama, Louisiana and Arkansas. With the exception of Arkansas, which had gone to Johnson in 1964, these were the same states Barry Goldwater won in that year. But Wallace lost two states carried by Goldwater—South Carolina, the home state of Nixon's Southern leader, the 1948 Dixiecrat candidate, Strom Thurmond, and Arizona, Goldwater's home state.

Since the support for Wallace seemingly declined considerably between early October and Election Day, falling from about 21 percent to 13 percent, an analysis of his actual polling strength is obviously important. Fortunately, the Gallup Poll conducted a national survey immediately after the election in which it inquired how respondents voted and whether they had supported another candidate earlier in the campaign. The data of this survey were made available by the Gallup Poll for our analysis. They are particularly useful since it would appear that most voters who had supported Wallace, but shifted to another candidate, did report this fact to Gallup interviewers. Thirteen percent indicated they had voted for Wallace, while another 9 percent stated that they had been for him at an earlier stage in the campaign.

From the national results among whites, it is clear that the data are heavily influenced by the pattern of support in the South. Wallace's voters were most likely to be persons who did not vote in 1964, or who backed Goldwater rather than Johnson. The pattern of an extremist party recruiting heavily from the ranks of nonvoters coincides with the evidence from previous extremist movements both in this country and abroad. Wallace also clearly appealed to those in smaller communities, and his strength was greatest among those with the least education. With respect to income, his backers were more likely to come from the poorer strata than the more well-to-do, although he was slightly weaker among the lowest income class—under $3,000— than among the next highest. He was strongest among those in "service" jobs, a conglomerate which includes police, domestic servants and the military. Of the regular urban occupational classes, his support was highest among the unskilled, followed by the skilled, white-collar workers, those in business and managerial pursuits, and professionals, in that order. The number of farmers voting for Wallace was relatively low, a phenonemon stemming from differences between farmers in the South and in the rest of the country. Among manual workers, Wallace was much weaker with union members than nonunionists.

The voting behavior with respect to other factors also corresponds in general to preelection predictions. Wallace was backed more heavily by men than by women, a pattern characteristically associated with radical movements, whether of the left or right. Suprisingly, young voters were more likely to prefer him than middle-aged and older ones, with the partial exception that voters in the twenty-five-to-twenty-nine-year-old category were a bit more likely to prefer Wallace than the twenty-one-to-twenty-four-year-old age group. Religion also served to differentiate: Wallace received a higher proportion of the votes of Protestants than Catholics—a product of his strength in the predominantly Protestant South.

Viewed nationally, however, the pattern of support for Wallace is a bit deceiving since so much of his support was in the South. He carried five Southern states and received a substantial vote in all the others, plus the border states. To a considerable extent, his movement in the South took on the character of a "preservatist" defense of Southern institutions against the threat from the federal government. In most Southern states, it was a major-party candidacy. In the rest of the country, however, the Wallace movement was a small radical third party, organized around various extreme right-wing groups. While it obviously gave expression to racial concerns, it also included a number of other varieties of the disaffected. One would expect, therefore, differences in the types of voters to whom he appealed in the different sections.

The variations are apparent along a number of dimensions. Northern Wallace voters were more likely to come from the ranks of identified and committed Republicans than were those from the South. Thus in the South, a much larger proportion of people who were identified as Democrats (37 percent) than as Republicans (10 percent) voted for him. Conversely in the North, a slightly larger segment of the Republicans voted for him than did Democrats. This emphasis is reversed, however, with respect to the 1964 vote. In both sections, larger proportions of Goldwater voters opted for Wallace than did Johnson supporters. Relatively, however, he did better among the Southern Goldwater voters. The seeming contradiction may be explained by the fact that Wallace did best among "independents," and that there were proportionately many more independents in the South than in the North. Southern independents presumably are people who have opted out of the Democratic party toward the right, many of whom voted for Goldwater in 1964 and Wallace in 1968. His greatest support, both North and South, of course, came from the ranks of those who did not vote in 1964. Almost half of the Southern nonvoters in the 1964 election who voted in 1968 chose Wallace.

The effect of the social-stratification variables were relatively similar in both parts of the country. In general, the better-educated, the more well-to-do and those in middle-class occupations were less likely to vote for Wallace than voters in the lower echelons.

As far as religion is concerned, nationally, Wallace appeared to secure more support among Protestants than Catholics, but a sectional breakdown points up the fact that this was because of the relatively small Catholic population in the South. Outside of the South, Wallace secured more support from Catholics than from Protestants. The pattern appears to be reversed in the South, but the number of Catholics in the sample is too small to sustain a reliable estimate. What is perhaps more significant than the Catholic-Protestant variation is the difference among the Protestant denominations. Wallace's greatest backing, North and South, came from Baptists, followed by "other," presumably mainly fundamentalist sects which have a history of disproportionately backing right-wing groups. Wallace, after all, became the protector of the "Southern way of life" and the status of those who bear it, not only for Southerners, but for Southern migrants to the North. This, apart from education, is one significance of the disproportionate support of Wallace by Northern Baptists.

As noted earlier, perhaps the most surprising finding of the polls was the consistent report by Gallup, Harris and the Michigan Survey Research Center that youth, whether defined as twenty-one to twenty-four or twenty-one to twenty-nine years old, were more favorable to the third-party candidate than those in older age groups. Two special surveys of youth opinion also pointed in this direction. One was commissioned by *Fortune* and carried out by the Daniel Yankelovich organization among 718 young people aged eighteen to twenty-four in October 1968. It revealed that among employed youth 25 percent were for Wallace, as compared with 23 for Humphrey, 31 for Nixon and 15 without a choice. Among college students, Wallace received 7 percent of the vote. A secondary analysis of this survey indicated that class and educational level differentiated this youth group as well. Thus 31 percent of young manual workers who were the sons of manual workers were for Wallace, as contrasted with but 6 percent among nonmanual workers whose fathers were on the same side of the dividing line. A preelection survey by the Purdue Opinion Poll among a national sample of high school students, reported that Wallace had considerable strength among them as well: 22 percent backing, which came heavily from members of Southern and economically less affluent families.

This "shift to the right" among youth had first been detected among young Southerners. Although various surveys had found a pattern of greater youth support for integration in the South during the forties and fifties, by the 1960's this finding had been inverted, according to two NORC polls reported by Paul Sheatsley and Herbert Hyman. They suggested that Southern youth who grew up amid the tensions produced by the school integration battles reacted more negatively than the preceding generations who had not been exposed to such conflicts during their formative political years. And as the issue of government-enforced integration in the schools and neighborhoods spread to the North, white opinion in central city areas, which are usually inhabited by workers, also took on an increased racist character.

What has happened is that increasing numbers of white young people in the South and in many working-class districts of the North have been exposed in recent years to repeated discussions of the supposed threats to their schools and communities posed by integration. They have been reared in homes and neighborhoods where anti-Negro sentiments became increasingly common. Hence, while the upper-middle-class scions of liberal parents were being radicalized to the left by civil rights and Vietnam war issues, a sizable segment of Southern and Northern working-class youth were being radicalized to the right. The consequence of such polarizations can be seen in the very different behavior of the two groups in the 1968 election campaign.

The indications that the Wallace movement drew heavily among youth are congruent with the evidence from various studies of youth and student politics that suggests young people are disposed to support the more extreme or idealistic version of the politics dominant within their social strata. In Europe, extremist movements both of the right and left have been more likely to secure the support of the young than the democratic parties of the center. Being less committed to existing institutions and parties than older people, and being less inured to the need to compromise in order to attain political objectives, youth are disproportionately attracted to leaders and movements which promise to resolve basic problems quickly and in an absolute fashion.

So much for those who actually voted for Wallace. Equally significant are those who supported Wallace in the campaign but didn't vote for him. Presumably many who shifted from Wallace did so because they thought he could not win, not because they would not have liked to see him as President. This is the uneasiness of the "lost vote." There is also the "expressive" factor, the votes in polls which do not count. Casting a straw vote for Wallace was clearly one method of striking a generalized note of dissatisfaction in certain directions. But since total considerations take over in the voting booth, the nature of the defections becomes one way to measure these dissatisfactions in various quarters. On another level, there is the factor of the social reinforcements that may or may not exist in the voter's milieu and are important for the ability of a third-party candidate to hold his base of support under attack.

In general, Wallace lost most heavily among groups and in areas where he was weak to begin with. Individuals in these groups would find less support for their opinions among their acquaintances, and also would be more likely to feel that a Wallace vote was wasted. In the South, however, almost four-fifths of all those who ever considered voting for Wallace did in fact vote for him. In the North, he lost over half of his initial support: only 43 percent of his original supporters cast a ballot for him. Similarly, Baptists and the small "other" Protestant sects were more likely to remain in the Wallace camp than less pro-Wallace religious groups.

There were certain significant differences in the pattern

of defections with respect to social stratification. In the South, middle-class supporters of Wallace were much more likely to move away from him as the campaign progressed. He wound up with 90 percent of his preelection support among Southern manual workers, and 61 percent among those in nonmanual occupations. In the North, however, Wallace retained a larger proportion of his middle-class backers (52 percent) than of his working-class followers (42 percent).

The data from the Gallup survey suggest, then, that the very extensive campaign of trade-union leaders to reduce Wallace support among their membership actually had an effect in the North. Almost two-thirds (64 percent) of Northern trade-union members who had backed Wallace initially *did not* vote for him on Election Day. A similar pattern occurred with respect to the two other measures of stratification, education and income. Wallace retained more backing among the better-educated and more affluent of his Northern supporters, while in the South these groups were much more likely to have defected by Election Day than the less educated and less privileged.

The variations in the class background of the defectors in the different sections of the country may be a function of varying exposures to reinforcing and cross-pressure stimuli in their respective environments. On the whole we would guess that middle-class Wallace supporters in the North came disproportionately from the group of persons previously committed to extreme rightist ideology and affiliations. Wallace's support among the Northern middle-class corresponds in size to that given to the John Birch Society in opinion polls. If we assume that most people who were pro-Birch were pro-Wallace, then presumably Wallace did not break out of this relatively small group. And this group, which was heavily involved in a reinforcing environment, could have been expected to stick with him. In the South, on the other hand, he began with considerable middle-class support gained from people who had been behind the effort to create a conservative Republican Party in that section. The majority of them had backed Barry Goldwater in 1964. This large group of affluent Southern Wallace-ites encompassed many who had not been involved in extremist activities. And it would seem that the efforts of the Southern conservative Republicans (headed by Strom Thurmond) to convince them that a vote for Wallace would help Humphrey were effective. Conversely, among Northern manual workers an inclination to vote for Wallace placed men outside the dominant pattern within their class.

Which of the other two candidates the Wallace defectors voted for clearly depended on background. Three-fifths of those who shifted away from Wallace during the campaign ended up voting for Nixon. But those Wallace backers who decided to vote for one of the major-party candidates almost invariably reverted to their traditional party affiliation. The pattern is even clearer when Southern Democrats are eliminated. Among the twenty-nine Northern Democrats in our sample who defected from Wallace, 90 percent voted for Hubert Humphrey. Humphrey recruited from among the less educated and poorer Wallace voters, Nixon from the more affluent and better-educated.

The pattern of shifting among the Wallace voters points up our assumption that Wallace appealed to two very different groups: economic conservatives concerned with repudiating the welfare state, and less affluent supporters of the welfare state who were affected by issues of racial integration and "law and order." As some individuals in each of these groups felt motivated to change their vote, they opted for the candidate who presumably stood closer to their basic economic concerns. The data also point up the difficulty of building a new movement encompassing people with highly disparate sentiments and interests.

After specifying what kinds of groups voted for whom, the most interesting question still remains, especially with respect to deviant and extremist political movements such as Wallace's: What creates the differentials within each of these groups? Why, in other words, do some members of a group vote for a particular candidate, but not others? Quite clearly, members of the same heuristic group or class may vary greatly in their perception of the world, and will therefore differ as to political choice. Since candidates do differ in their ideology and position on particular issues, we should expect that the values of the electorate should help determine which segments of a particular stratum end up voting one way or another.

Data collected by the Louis Harris Poll permit us to analyze the connection between political attitudes and voter choice in 1968. The Harris data are derived from a special reanalysis of the results of a number of surveys conducted during the campaign that were prepared by the Harris organization for the American Jewish Committee. Based on 16,915 interviews, it points up consistent variations. The question that best indicated differing political attitudes among those voting for a given candidate was one in the Harris survey that asked, "Which groups are responsible for trouble in the country?" Choices ranged from the federal government to Communists, students, professors, Jews and others.

The findings of the Harris organization clearly differentiate the supporters of the different candidates in 1968 and 1964. On most items, the rank order of opinions goes consistently from right to left, from Wallace to Goldwater to Nixon to Johnson to Humphrey. That is, the Wallace supporters show the most right-wing opinions, while the Humphrey ones are the most left. As a group those who voted for Goldwater in 1964 are somewhat more "preservatist" than the Nixon supporters in 1968. There is, of course, a considerable overlap. Since none of these items bear on attitudes toward the welfare state, what they attest to is the disdain which rightists feel toward groups identified with social changes they dislike.

The Wallace supporters differ most from the population as a whole with respect to their feelings toward the federal government, Negroes, the Ku Klux Klan and, most surprisingly, "ministers and priests." Although Wallace himself did not devote much attention to attacking the liberal clergy, his followers were seemingly more bothered by their activities than by those of professors. Although the electorate as a whole was inclined to see "students" as a major source of trouble, Wallace backers hardly differed from the supporters of the two other candidates in their feelings. As far as we can judge from these results, they confirm the impression that Wallace appealed strongly to people who identified their distress with changes in race relations, with federal interference, and with changes in religious morality. It is of interest that the Wallace supporters in the South and those in the non-South project essentially the same pattern. The Southern differential is very slight with respect to blaming Negroes, still slight but higher in blaming clergymen, and higher yet in blaming the federal government.

Fears that Wallace would convert his following into an extraparliamentary influence on the government and terrorize opponents by taking to the streets—fears based on statements that Wallace himself made during the campaign —have thus far proved unwarranted. Wallace seems largely concerned with maintaining his electoral base for a possible presidential campaign in 1972. The effort to continue control of the party from Montgomery seems to be dedicated to this end.

. . .

The existence of local electoral parties, even those willing to follow Wallace's lead completely, clearly poses a great problem for him. Wallace's electoral following is evidently much greater than can be mobilized behind the local unknown candidates of the American Party. To maintain the party organizations, they must nominate men for various offices. Yet should such people continue to secure tiny votes, as is likely in most parts of the country, Wallace may find his image as a mass leader severely injured. He seems to recognize this, and though concerned with keeping control over the party organization, he has also stressed the difference between the "movement" and the "party," describing the two as "separate entities" which agree on "purposes and aims." Wallace is emphatic about this: "The *movement* will be here in 1972. The *movement* is solvent and it will be active." Speaking at the Virginia convention of the American Party in mid-July of 1969, he said, "A new party ought to go very slow. It ought to crawl before it walks. It ought to nominate a candidate only if he has a chance to be elected." In Tulsa, he again warned his followers to move slowly, if at all, in nominating Congressional and local candidates. He argued that if he was elected President in the future he "wouldn't have any trouble getting support from Congress, because most of its [major party] members were for the things [I'm] for."

One aspect of the nonparty "movement" may be the reported expansion of the Citizens Council of America, whose national headquarters is in Jackson, Mississippi. Its administrator, William J. Simmons, helped direct Wallace's presidential campaign in Mississippi, where he received 65 percent of the vote. In June 1969, Simmons said, "There has been no erosion in Wallace strength. Wallace articulates the hopes and views of over 99 per cent of our members. This state is not enchanted with Nixon, and Wallace sentiment is very strong indeed." He also reported that the

Council, mainly concerned with the maintenance of segregation in the schools, had expanded "as a result of backlash generated by campus riots and better grassroots organizational work." The impetus of the Wallace campaign remains one reservoir of future organization strength for Wallace.

Moreover, Wallace has attempted to maintain his ties to other groups whose members had backed him in 1968. The Birch Society's principal campaign during 1969 has been against sex education and pornography; Wallace devoted a considerable part of his talks during the year to the subject. In addition, he publicly embraced for the first time the ultraconservative "Christian Crusade" of Billy James Hargis by attending its annual convention.

In his speeches and *Newsletter* Wallace has retained the same combination of "preservatist" moralism and populist economic issues that characterized his presidential campaign. On the one hand, he continues to emphasize the issues of "law and order," "campus radicalism," "military failures in Vietnam," and "the need for local control of schools." On the other hand, speaking in Tulsa, one of the principal centers of the oil industry, he called for tax reform that would benefit the little man, adding that "the 27½ percent oil depletion allowance ought to be looked into." He argued that we must "shift the [tax] burden to the upper-class millionaires, billionaires and tax-exempt foundations." Since this kind of rhetoric flies in the face of the deep-dyed economic conservatives among his supporters, such as the Birchers, it is clear that Wallace's grab bag of appeals still suffers from the same sort of contradictions that characterized it in 1968—contradictions, it might be added, which have characterized most other right-wing extremist movements in American history.

Another problem that Wallace faces comes from supporters who want to build an extremist movement rather than an electoral organization for one man's candidacy. This can be seen in the activities of an autonomous youth organization, the National Youth Alliance, formed by those active in Youth for Wallace. As of September 1969, the NYA claimed 3,000 dues-paying members recruited from the 15,000-person mailing list of the Youth for Wallace student organizations. The group has a more absolutist and militant character than either adult party, and it is much more unashamedly racist. Members wear an "inequality button" emblazoned with the mathematical symbol of inequality. Among other things, the Alliance advocates "White studies" curricula in colleges and universities. According to its national organizer, Louis T. Byers, "The purpose of these will be to demonstrate the nature of mankind. The equality myth will be exploded forever." In an article describing its objectives the then-national vice-president, Dennis C. McMahon, stated that NYA "is an organization with the determination to liquidate the enemies of the American people on the campus and in the community." The tone of this pro-Wallace youth group sounds closer to that of classic fascism than any statements previously made by Wallace's associates. As McMahon wrote,

> The National Youth Alliance is an organization that intends to bury the red front once and for all . . . The NYA is made up of dedicated, self-sacrificing young people who are ready to fight, and die if necessary, for the sacred cause. . . .
>
> Now is the time for the Right Front terror to descend on the wretched liberals. In short, the terror of the Left will be met with the greater terror of the Right . . . Tar and feathers will be our answer to the pot pusher and these animals will no longer be allowed to prowl and hunt for the minds of American students. . . .
>
> A bright future full of conquest lies ahead of us . . .

Soon the NYA will become a household word and the Left will be forced to cower in the sewers underground as they hear the marching steps of the NYA above them.

The racism of NYA leaders includes approval, if not advocacy, of virulent anti-Semitism. Its national headquarters in Washington distributes literature by Francis Parker Yockey, including his book *Imperium*, which defines Jews, Negroes, Indians and other minorities as "parasites" in the Western world. The five members of its adult advisory board have all been involved in anti-Semitic activities. Two of them, Rivilo P. Oliver and Richard B. Cotten, were forced out of the Birch Society because of their overt racist and anti-Semitic views. A third, retired Rear Admiral John Crommelein, ran for President on the anti-Semitic National States Rights Party ticket in 1960; while a fourth, retired Marine Lieutenant General Pedro A. Del Valle, is an officer of the Christian Educational Association, which publishes the overtly anti-Semitic paper *Common Sense*. The fifth member of the board, Austin J. App, former English professor at LaSalle College, is a contributing editor to the anti-Semitic magazine *American Mercury*.

Perhaps most interesting of all the problems that Wallace will have to deal with is the fact that the national chairman of his American Party, T. Coleman Andrews, has publicly advocated the Birch Society's version of that hoary international conspiracy, the historic plot of the Illuminati. The Illuminati, which was an organization of Enlightenment intellectuals formed in Bavaria in 1776, and dissolved, according to historical record, in 1785, has figured in the conspiratorial theories of assorted American right-wing movements as the insiders behind every effort for religious, economic and social reform since the 1790's. In recent times both Father Coughlin, the former right-wing extremist of the 1930's, and Robert Welch, the head of the Birch

Society, have explained various threats to "the American Way"—from the French Revolution to the Communist movement—as well as the behavior of most key officials of the government, as reflecting the power of this secret cabal of satanically clever plotters. In a newspaper interview following the establishment of the American Party in May, Andrews bluntly announced:

> I believe in the conspiratorial theory of History . . .
> [The Birch Society has been] responsible, respectable. . . .
> Recently, the Birch Society has begun to prosper. People
> are beginning to see that its original theories were right
> . . . There is an international conspiracy.

Though George Wallace himself has never publicly stated a belief in the conspiracy of the Illuminati (he prefers to talk about the role of Communists, pseudo-intellectuals and the Council on Foreign Relations), the formal organization of his personally controlled national party is headed by a man who has no such hesitation. On May 26, 1969, Wallace formally sanctioned the American Party as the political arm of the movement and said that if he ran for President again it would be under the American Party's banners.

However, while the pulls toward the conspiracy theory and toward ideological racism are evident in the background, the logic of the Wallace-ite movement and its future as a mass movement obviously rests on other foundations. S. M. Miller points out that many had been shocked by "the attraction of George Wallace as a presidential candidate to a large number of union members . . . racism appeared to be rampant in the working class. When the vote came, however, racism seemed to have receded before economic concerns." Their disaffection remains, nevertheless. As Miller writes, "About half of American families are above the poverty line but below the adequacy level. This group, neither poor nor affluent, composed not only of blue-collar workers

but also of many white-collar workers, is hurting and neglected." It is the members of this group that the Wallace-ite
movement must grow on if it is to grow, not so much out of
their ideological racism as out of their general sense of neglected decline.

Whether the Wallace movement itself will have returned
to full or fuller electoral vigor by 1972 depends on a number of factors which emerge from an examination of America's right-wing extremist past. Determinative—not just for
the Wallace movement but for any extremist movement—
will be the larger historical circumstances. The disaffection
of the white working class and lower-middle class has been
noted; if that disaffection grows, and *at the same time* the
pressures of an increasingly disaffected black population increase, the soil will of course be fertile for a George Wallace
kind of movement. It is the pressure of the emergent black
population that provides an essentially preservatist thrust to
the social and economic strains of the vulnerable whites.
Whether the major political parties can absorb these con-
comitant pressures in some pragmatic fashion as they have
in the past is another conditional factor, which is also partly
dependent on historical development.

Wallace, however, is clearly preparing to use another issue in 1972—the responsibility for American defeat in Vietnam. Like others on the right, he has repeatedly argued
that if the U.S. government really wanted to win the war, it
could do so easily, given America's enormous superiority in
resources and weapons technology. Consequently, the only
reason we have not won is political: those who have controlled our strategy consciously do not want to win. But, he
argued recently, if it "should be that Washington has committed itself to a policy of American withdrawal, irrespec-
tive of reciprocal action on the part of the enemy, in effect
acknowledging defeat for our forces, which is inconceiv-
able, we feel that such withdrawal should be swiftly accom-

plished so that casualty losses may be held to a minimum." And in late 1969 he left for a three-week tour of Vietnam and Southeast Asia, announcing that he would run in 1972 if Vietnam was turned over to the Communists "in effect or in substance." Clearly Wallace hopes to run in 1972 on the issue that American boys have died needlessly, that they were stabbed in the back by Lyndon Johnson and Richard Nixon.

In order to do so, however, Wallace must keep his movement alive. As he well recognizes, it is subject to the traditional organizational hazards of such a movement, notably fragmentation, and the ascendancy of overt extremist tendencies that will alienate the more respectable leadership and support. During the year following the 1968 election, he performed as though he understood these hazards well. He has attempted to keep his organization formally separated from the fringe groups and the more rabid extremists, even those who were in open support of him. In a letter sent to key Wallace lieutenants around the country, asking about the local leadership that might be involved in the next Wallace campaign, James T. Hardin, administrative assistant to Wallace, carefully emphasized that "perhaps of greatest importance, we would like your opinion as to those who demonstrated neither ability nor capability to work with others and who were, in fact, a detriment to the campaign . . ."

Whether Wallace can succeed in avoiding the organizational hazards of which he seems aware, and whether historical circumstances will be favorable, is of course problematical. But whether his particular movement survives or not, George Wallace has put together and further revealed the nature of those basic elements which must comprise an effective right-wing extremist movement in America.

WORKERS
AND LIBERALS
Closing the Gap

by Brendan Sexton

A veteran American trade unionist since the founding of industrial unionism, Brendan Sexton is now Director of Education Activities for the United Automobile Workers.

Much of my life has been split between two worlds: blue-collar unions and the intellectual-academic arena—a sort of long-haired working stiff, or at least an uncommon marginal man.

Born in a tough Irish working-class neighborhood and reared on Catholicism, Irish rebellion and, later, socialism, I fell into the life of an organizer during the great depression and the early days of the CIO. As a reader of everything in reach, I have followed with great regret the growing schism between organized labor and middle-class liberals during the past decade. Like others, I was stunned to see the old liberal coalition finally fragment during the 1968 Presidential election under the separate discontents of workers (out of sight and mind to most observers, but not, alas, to George Wallace) and the middle-class liberal antagonists of LBJ.

What the consequences of the fragmentation will be only Nixon and Agnew may know.

Yet I continue to believe, in my old-fashioned, radical-populist way, that a broad alliance between these two groups at their center remains the best hope for reconstructing our society along democratic-humanist lines.

Many issues need clarifying if we are to halt a national move to the right. I wish to explore only one here: the assumption that blue-collar workers are "middle-class" and sitting pretty. I'd also like to suggest some of the political consequences of both the assumption and the reality of workers' lives.

In September of 1969 the "average production worker" with three dependents took home $102.44 for a full week's work. Measured against the previous year, his dollar income rose about $5.14 a week. In fact, however, his actual purchasing power *declined about 39¢ per week*. He was worse off in 1969 than in 1968, and probably even more so in 1970.

Now, $102.44 take-home is not "middle-class," especially if you are an "average" family head with three dependents. If such a man puts aside $25 a week for house or rent payments (a modest enough sum), he's left with a little less than $78 a week to pay for food, clothing, medicines, school supplies, etc., for two adults and two children. That comes to roughly $2.79 per day per person, for a family of four— about the amount a big-city newspaper reporter (or any of us in the real middle class) is likely to spend for lunch. These figures are distorted a bit by the inclusion of Southern, and largely unorganized, workers. But in 1968, *manufacturing* workers (most of whom are organized) with three dependents averaged only $106.75 in take-home pay. As against the previous years, they also experienced a slight

increase in real income and purchasing power (1965—
$88.06; 1966—$87.93; 1967—$87.07; 1968—$88.08).

In New York, the locale of many observers who write so
expertly about "middle-class" workers, manufacturing
workers average a gross income of $121.48. Only in Michi-
gan, among all continental states, where the weekly gross
was $164.15, could an average manufacturing worker come
close to the national family median (about $8,600) with a
full year of work.

At the other end of the scale, retail workers averaged just
slightly less than $75 per week during 1968. The retail
worker, if he worked a full year, earned a gross income high
enough to lift him barely above the "poverty line" of
$3,000, but low enough to leave him with less than half the
national family median income. This is the extreme example. Still, there are more than 9 million workers in retail
trade. Even when they wear white collars, they can't, at this
rate, be factored into the middle class.

Skilled workers are the aristocrats of labor; yet the median earnings of male craftsmen who were employed full-
time in 1968 was only $7,978.* Of course, a good many of
the elite and highly organized urban craftsmen—electricians, typographers, lithographers, etc.—earn up to and
above $10,000 a year. For a blue-collar worker, this is
really "making it." For the new college professor, fresh out
of graduate school, it's just so-so.

Where affluence begins and ends no one knows, but it
must be above the levels cited. In the spring of 1967, the
U.S. Department of Labor said that an income of $9,076
would enable a city family of four to maintain "a moderate
standard of living." Only about one-third of *all* American
families reach that now-dated standard. Certainly, the typical production worker is much better off than a Mississippi-

---

* Gaps of a year or more sometimes occur in government statistics. In all
cases, I have used the most recent annual reports available.

farm tractor driver or a city mother living on welfare, but he hardly lives opulently. He treads water, financially and psychically.

The myth of the "middle-class" worker is kin to the Negro of folklore who "lives in the slums but drives a big new Cadillac." He's there, all right, but his numbers are grossly exaggerated.

Workers with small families and two or more paychecks coming in each week may be able to make it. Among all American families with incomes of $10,000, the multi-incomes are twice as numerous as the single income. Still, millions of families combine two or even three paychecks and yet earn less than $5,000 a year.

The young worker is hardest hit and hence most discontented. He often holds down the lower-paid and more onerous jobs. He is somewhat less likely to work overtime at premium rates and more likely to be caught in temporary layoffs, though in some union contracts he is now protected against loss from the latter.

No less than others of his generation, the young worker expects more. Why not? He belongs to a generation with rapidly rising expectations. As long as he's single, his first paychecks may give him more money than he's ever seen before. He dresses well, owns a new car, and generally lives it up.

But once married, his problems multiply. He furnishes a home, perhaps buys it. He does it "on time." He pays more for furniture and appliances than anyone ever did before. The house that cost his father $12,000, with mortgage at 5 percent, now may sell for twice that and be financed at 8 percent. The young married worker aged twenty-five or thirty will probably carry twice the burden of debt as the worker aged forty or forty-five. When children come, the wife of the young worker will probably drop out of the labor market, leaving him as sole support for perhaps fifteen or twenty years. In these years, his financial needs increase with the size of his family, but his paycheck does not respond to need.

These economic realities confront workers with a long list of harrowing problems. How, for example, do they provide equal opportunity for their children? How do they shelter them against the draft for four years when the cost of sending a son to the state university now averages nearly $2,000 a year? *Perhaps less than a quarter of all high school graduates who are children of factory workers enter college.* (The myth that something like half of all young Americans go to college is very nearly unshatterable. Actually, 47.6 percent of the eighteen- and nineteen-year-olds but only 22 percent in the age group of twenty to twenty-four are "in school." U.S. Office of Education reports are so unclear here that I suspect the agency of misleading us regarding the accessibility of college opportunities.)

Children of workers are overrepresented in the mass of those excluded from college. Working-class kids make their trips abroad as members of the armed forces, while some middle-class youths, student deferments in hand, spend a junior year at European universities. While the college boy steps on an escalator that moves rapidly upward, the worker's son may step on his father's assembly line and into a job without much promise.

Relatively few colleges, social agencies, schools, or other public institutions mount programs to meet special needs of workers. In many places, even the services provided by "Red Feather" agencies seem more closely geared to middle-class than working-class needs.

Inevitably, many workers come to feel they are being dunned and taxed for the benefit of others. Considering the notorious imbalance of our tax structure, they have a point. *In general, the rate of taxation declines as income rises.* This is most obviously true of the state sales tax. It is almost as true of the federal income tax, under which, in the most extreme cases, some individuals and corporations pay little or no tax at all, though their incomes may exceed $5 million annually. Estimates of total tax loans indicate that 33 percent of the income of those earning $3,000 to $5,000 goes to taxes, and only 28 percent of those earning $15,000 or more.

So we have the case of the "invisible" and aggrieved worker. Many of his breed are even found among Mike Harrington's invisible poor. In fact, about one-third of all heads of impoverished families hold down full-time jobs. They are generally not organized, but they are workers. While millions of workers live in poverty, millions more barely escape it. Most are in income brackets between $3,000 and $10,000 (which includes some 50 percent of all American families), with probably more workers near the bottom than the top.

Reporters often talk about the sweeper who "makes more than a teacher." True, a sweeper in an auto plant in Michigan or New Jersey probably earns more than a teacher in a backwoods school in Mississippi, but his pay is hardly a pot of gold. The sweeper seems to fit a set of hidden assumptions according to which the society is divided, at a magical line, between rich and poor. The premise of this stereotype is that our class structure is a dualism—rich and poor. In this simplified pseudo-Marxian schema, organized workers are seen as part of the richer half, along with bankers, businessmen, professionals. They are, it is assumed, well fed, well cared for, up to their hips in "things," and all-around partners in an open and affluent society. According to this hidden assumption, all or nearly all the poor are black. They are mostly mothers of large families living on welfare in big city ghettos. The rest (except for a few Appalachian whites) are young blacks who can't find jobs because they are school dropouts or because they are excluded from unions by corpulent and corrupt union bosses. So goes this version of things, especially popular in some college circles. But, in fact, about 80 percent of the poor are white, and a startling proportion of them work full-time.

In real life the typical worker has lived on a treadmill, except where union contracts have protected him from rises in the cost of living. Everyone else—including the poor and the militant blacks (at least their image was cast by the media)—*seemed* to be moving forward, while *they* only stood still, waiting in a twilight zone somewhere between hunger and plenty. Some comforts came to them through expanded consumer credit, but the credit exacted high costs in tension, insecurity, and interest rates. They gave increasing taxes to the government, their sons to the army. They seemed to get little in return: only conflict, and sometimes mortal combat with the emerging black poor over jobs, neighborhoods, and schools.

Here is fertile soil for the growth of resentment. For a time it grew like a weed under the cultivation of George Wallace. A turning point in the presidential campaign may have come when Hubert Humphrey began to see something Wallace always understood: that while many "experts" said "old issues" were dead, millions of American workers angrily disagreed and wanted a better life. Many workers were ready, in short, for a campaign resembling Harry Truman's historical effort of 1948, a hell-raising campaign about the "old" economic issues (social injustice, more and better jobs, more opportunity, good schools, health care, etc.).

The trap almost sprung by Wallace was set by those "opinion-makers" who dismissed all Wallace supporters as red-necked bigots and opponents of Negro aspirations. Fortunately, they were mistaken. While many workers have no doubt been shaken up quite a bit by the black revolt, they have been even more shaken by their own failure to get on in life. Being far wiser than we think, they knew this was not the fault of the blacks.

Sadly, some of the Wallace-ite resentment was, of course, turned against the poor and the black. Yet it is possible that Wallace's exposed bigotry finally did him in among Northern workers. Industrial workers generally have closer relations with Negroes than any other class, and the big factories in steel, auto, rubber, glass, etc., are probably the most integrated work places in the society. Most workers who were drawn to Wallace because he spoke their economic language must have had problems of conscience about blacks with whom they worked and had friendly relations. As Wallace's campaign became more violent in tone, many of them probably grew uneasy and fell away from his camp.

When "opinion-makers" bothered to talk with workers, they found to their surprise that not all were racists. After talking with Wallace supporters in Flint, Michigan (said to be a hotbed of Wallace sentiment), Mike Hubbard, a student editor of the University of Michigan *Daily,* wrote:

> Certainly these Americans do not identify with red-necked racism . . . No one ever taught them Negro History, but they grew up with blacks . . . They don't dislike blacks, they just feel black men shouldn't be given a bigger break than anyone else. The white UAW members as a whole do not believe Wallace is a racist. All they know is what he told them, and he never said he hated blacks. Even the most militant Negro workers I talked to didn't feel there was large-scale prejudice in the Union. They dislike Wallace, but not the men who are voting for him.

Others found many Wallace supporters who would have preferred Robert Kennedy, and some even Eugene McCarthy. *Time* found many such in its 150 interviews across the country, and Haynes Johnson of the Washington *Star* reported this comment from a leader of the Wallace movement in Duluth, Minnesota: "The reason I got into this actually was when Robert Kennedy was shot . . . That assassination—plus that of Martin Luther King—pointed up for me just how sick it was in this country, and I decided to do something for my country."

The "new issues"—the war on poverty and bureaucracy, the struggles for racial justice and world peace—can be lost unless they are paralleled by campaigns on issues that are important to those millions who are often ignored except by demagogues.

The mythology that obscures the realities of working-class life derives in large part from the success story of unions and what various observers have made of that story. Unions have made great gains in wages, working conditions, fringe benefits, politics; but they started from very far back, and they are still very far from the millennium. Since our society has been late and miserly in providing social insurance, unions have had to push hard in collective bargaining for benefits that don't show up in paychecks. Their focus on such goals has had some negative side effects. Fringe benefits mean more to older than to younger workers—and it is the young who are drawn to men like George Wallace.

Unless unions were to act irresponsibly toward the aging (one of the most impoverished and helpless groups among us), pensions had to be won. Pensions cost money, and that money was subtracted from the wage package won at the bargaining table. Also, older workers need and make more use of hospitalization, medical, and sickness insurance. These too came out of the total package, leaving less for wages. It was humane to help the older worker, and it helped him retire and make way for younger workers. But it was costly. *In the UAW alone, more than 250,000 members have retired and received pension benefits of over $1.5 billion.* Unions sometimes may have overresponded to the older workers, as in seniority and vacation benefits, etc., but one can hardly look at the life of the aging worker and say he has too much.

Unions need to make a new beginning, paying more attention to the needs of the young. An aging and sometimes feeble union leadership needs to refresh itself with activists and new leadership recruited among younger generations. Unless the young become partners in the union movement, they may end up wrecking it. The dramatic rise in the rate of rank-and-file rejection of union-contract settlements is a clear signal of distress among workers. Usually, veteran unionists report, the increased rejections result from organized opposition among young workers.

Unions need to do a lot of things, far more than I can mention in this brief piece. I come from a union that has split from the AFL over some of these issues, including foreign policy, interest in the poor and minorities, and general militancy. I have opposed the Vietnam war, and I think labor should have. I have been involved in the war on poverty, along with many other unionists—though it is remote from many others. Still, one observer says, "If the labor movement in this country moves to the right, it's not least the fault of those, like Sexton, who will not say a word of criticism of its policies." I leave nothing to the imagination of readers, for we are all deeply aware of the shortcomings of unions. I do not dwell on these flaws for another reason: Whatever their blemishes, unions have given workers the only support and attention they have had—and they needed a lot.

Unions are, however, limited in what they can do for members. They are limited by their own willingness and that of their members to go into battle, to strike. They are limited by the public's willingness to accept strikes. The middle-class liberal himself is often offended, sometimes outraged, by strikers. He may say, "They're selfish and out for themselves." When the desperately poor hospital worker strikes, the liberal will see only the patient as victim; but he will offer no clues as to how else the hospital worker can win a measure of justice. When subway and sanitation workers in New York strike for a modest $3.50 or so an hour (to perform some of the most disagreeable jobs known to man), many middle-class liberals complain bitterly, without also noting that New York's affluent can afford to pay men decent wages to do hard, often dangerous, always unpleasant work.

Many liberals dismiss as unimportant, if not irrelevant, every claim workers make for their attention and support. In few cases do they distinguish workers from union leaders, for some of whom their contempt may be warranted. It is not surprising, considering their mentors, that so much of the young New Left seems to despise the working class.

Not since the early and dramatic days of the CIO have liberals and intellectuals (with some honorable exceptions) shown much sympathetic interest in workers or unions. Now workers come sharply to their view only when they threaten to make life inconvenient or dangerous. A subway strike, shutdown at the *New York Times,* or a large vote for Wallace may do the trick—momentarily.

I believe that liberals and moderate leftists—in whose circle opinion-makers are heavily represented—are out of touch with the reality of American working-class life. Many of them live at rarefied levels where everyone's income is at least $15,000 a year. *Less than 15 percent of the nation's families earn that much;* still, they form a mass of between 23 and 28 million people. Those who live within that income can easily come to think that all Americans, except the poor, are living just about as they and their colleagues and neighbors do. Having little contact outside their own circles, and having heard so much about the great gains of unions, they may naturally assume that workers have made it too.

Many of these opinion-makers are men of my generation
or near it. Forgetting the ravages of inflation, they may
think of $6,000 a year as a fairly substantial income. They
may remember maintaining a modest existence on even
less. I recall that I was thirty-five years old when I first
earned $5,000 a year as president of the nation's second
largest local union. Now when I hear that auto workers
gross more than $8,000, I too sometimes forget the dollar's
decline and assume they've got it made. Relative to most
other workers, they have; but they are still far from well-off.
These opinion-makers greatly influence what appears in
periodicals and dailies, and what is said on TV and radio.
They often draft political platforms and write candidates'
speeches. When they don't, their readers do. They think of
themselves as open-minded and sensitive, and sometimes
they are. But too often their policies are introspective—concentrated only on issues that touch them, plus a now-
fashionable interest in the poor.

Their political attitudes are sometimes expressed in the
kind of thin-lipped and vinegary liberalism that found its
ultimate expression in Senator McCarthy's endorsement of
Hubert Humphrey. To the dismay of at least one early sup-
porter—me—McCarthy urged in that endorsement that
the rights of honest draft dissenters be protected, but he
said nothing about the draft's discrimination against Negroes, the poor, and the working class, and made no significant comments about other social and economic issues. The
senator's failure to ignite fires outside the middle class can
easily be understood in the light of that arid statement. In
the primary campaign his speeches (at least in the printed
text) were often unexceptionable; but, notoriously, he
often left unsaid what decent liberals and radicals on his
staff wrote into those speeches. Later in the campaign, and
in the Senate leadership fight, the warts on that handsome
façade grew larger.

Senator McCarthy, like some who supported him, had to subdue his conscience before endorsing Hubert Humphrey, yet he has always seemed comfortable with Senator William Fulbright, a man whose record on civil rights almost duplicates George Wallace's except for greater gentility of expression.* (A friend explained to me that he could support Fulbright because the senator had "style," a matter of overriding merit to many liberals.)

The chemistry of the Kennedys has been different. The contrast is highlighted in Senator Edward Kennedy's appeal to supporters of his two slain brothers to reject the "dark" and "extremist" movement of George Wallace.

> Most of these people [Kennedy said of Wallace supporters] are not motivated by racial hostility or prejudice. They feel that their needs and their problems have been passed over by the tide of recent events. They bear the burden of the unfair system of Selective Service. They lose out because higher education costs so much. They are the ones who feel most threatened at the security of their jobs, the safety of their families, the value of their property and the burden of their taxes. They feel the established system has not been sympathetic to them in their problems of everyday life and in a large measure they are right.

If a meaningful New Politics is to work in this country it must be based on the kind of empathy expressed in these words.

Too few liberals realize that millions of workers and voters fit Ted Kennedy's description. Young workers outnumber all college students, and there are perhaps fifteen or twenty of them for every disaffected youth upon whom various advocates of a New Politics are counting. The big three in

* I don't wish to downgrade Senator Fulbright's obvious courage. We are all in his debt. Some young Americans may owe him their lives. I do wish to point out that liberal and radical intellectuals of principle are also capable of compromise, though their evaluation of issues may differ from the trade unionists or even the black militants.

auto alone employ about 250,000 workers who are thirty or under. Total UAW membership of that age group may reach 600,000 with perhaps half of these under twenty-five. Among organized workers, possibly 5 million are young people under thirty.

Young workers seem to be tougher and to have more staying power than students. Their stake in social change may turn out to be greater and more compelling. Most will never experience the softening effects of well-paid, high-status jobs in the professional, academic, artistic, or business world—jobs to which most student rebels are on their way. Knowing they're unlikely to escape individually, workers can grow desperate when denied political hope.

One pollster puts many workers in the "no-change" coalition. He misunderstands. Workers simply oppose changes that benefit or seem to benefit others while increasing their own burdens.

The auto industry's average wage of $3.80 per hour, though the highest in manufacturing, still does not mean affluence. The UAW (like many other unions) has won comprehensive medical protection, including coverage for psychiatric care, for a million members. Its contracts now provide tuition-remission plans for members who wish to take classes that may help them escape from dead-end factory jobs. In December of 1968, the hourly wage system came close to ending for perhaps a million UAW members; thus, in one industry, workers have almost scaled an important barrier between them and the middle class—they will be salaried rather than hourly workers. UAW contracts have moved toward the guaranteed annual income and retirement with decent security. Gains have been made, yes; but even auto workers still have far to go.

One friend tells me, "Intellectuals still cling to a hopeful and perhaps incorrect view, idealizing the union members as an instrument of class struggle." What members and their unions try to do, at best, is not class struggle in any classic sense. Their conscious antagonists are the employer and the conservative legislator, not the "capitalist system." Yet their efforts have profoundly influenced American life. And unionists have tasted enough of victory so that they generally do not believe in the "final conflict" for which the "prisoners of starvation" must arise.

Those publicists who seek such an apocalypse will not find unionists mounting the barricades with the swiftness and pleasure of student rebels or black militants. Unionists have learned a hard lesson after almost a century of fierce bloodletting on the picket line: *Combat is the last, not the first, resort.* Unionists have possibly been too moderate in this respect, for open conflict sometimes is the only way to rally people and get what you want. But they have learned many other good ways to get on with it. They will not be found burning down their own neighborhoods to prove a point, or otherwise sacrificing their own ranks in unproductive, self-destructive conflict. In this respect, interestingly, some black militants seem to be taking a rather active interest in labor studies. Most militants, coming from poor families, are interested in the "old issues" (opportunity, jobs, etc.) and in ways of organizing people for effective action. A similar interest in unions has not come to the campus, thanks to the myth of the middle-class worker and other academic folklore. (My wife and I taught a graduate sociology course, Labor and Society, at New York University in 1968. So far as I know—outside the narrow limits of labor-and-industrial programs—it is the *only* such course taught in the country.)

Workers and their unions have many problems and they need lots of help. On the other side, the middle-class left may find itself isolated if it accepts the standard mythology about workers. If they are to create a New Society, liberals and radicals need to become aware of socially excluded workers and find avenues of communication with them, as well as with Negroes, Latin Americans, and the oppressed poor generally.

CAN THE AMERICAN WORKER BE RADICALIZED?

by Kim Moody

Kim Moody is a graduate student in political science at the New School in New York and is a member of the International Socialists.

For twenty years the American working class has been silent—a sleeping giant lulled to sleep by its own victories and the ability of American capitalism to expand and provide a gradually rising standard of living. The working class has had to struggle to realize these gains, but this struggle has been contained within the limits and rules established by the system.

Furthermore, the struggles of the 1950's and early 1960's were essentially parochial in nature, limited to particular industries, shops or unions, virtually never taking on an overall class political character. Able to win real gains, the working class became fragmented and local in outlook. This fragmentation of working-class consciousness reinforced the political conservatism of the class and, therefore, the willingness of some workers to turn to reactionary and racist solutions to their problems.

The only institutions of working-class struggle in America, the trade unions, have followed and exacerbated this fragmentation by becoming bureaucratically ossified, politically reactionary, and institutionally integrated with the administration of industry. Once genuine if limited instruments of class struggle, the unions and their leaders have become parochial "interest groups," not only incapable of inspiring their members but often restricting struggle.

This conservatizing process rested on the ability of American capitalism to provide discernible improvements in the living standards of the majority of the working class. Since the mid-1960's, however, these conditions have been eroded, and the system has been unable to raise real wages for the majority of workers or to prevent a drop in the living standards of black, Spanish-speaking, and poor white workers.

The mechanisms that have sustained the stability of the system, notably the permanent arms economy, have begun to backfire, even to the point of enhancing the contradictions they once served to suppress. The reemergence of these contradictions, in somewhat new forms, has brought an accompanying growth in intensity of working-class struggle. Whereas, ten years ago, workers struggled to gain improvements in their living and working standards, today workers must struggle even more militantly just to hold the line. Furthermore, the interpenetration of industry and the state that was required by the arms economy and the subsequent stratification of the economy tend to give a more national and political focus to what were previously viewed as local issues. The enemies of the working class are more centralized and visible.

At the same time, recent changes in the structure of the working class have combined to produce an extreme unevenness of consciousness. Lacking any readily adaptable institutions of struggle, this unevenness of consciousness poses serious problems for the growth of class-conscious struggle in response to the instability of the system. It would be misleading to simply discuss the class as a whole until we understand and the roots and nature of the fragmentation, stratification, and differentiation within the class.

In the Marxian definition, the working class is composed of all those people who, divorced from the ownership or control of the means of production and forced to rely on the sale of their labor power (ability to work) for their livelihood, produce the great bulk of the total wealth of the nation.

Numbering 60 million or more in the active labor force, these workers and their families make up the vast majority of the population, perhaps 180 million people. This common condition is defined by their subordinate relationship to the means of production, i.e., by their subordination to capital and its social personification, the capitalist class.

Just as the definition of the class as a whole derives from its position in production, so is the structure of the class defined by the structure of industry. Since the technique, products, and circulation mechanisms of the capitalist mode of production are always in flux, the structure of the working class must always change accordingly. Both the perimeter and the internal lines of division of the working class are always in a state of transition. In the past twenty-five years, in particular, the structure of the American working class has gone through important changes.

The best known of these changes is the growth of white-collar occupations in proportion to the traditional blue-collar, industrial proletariat. The absolute size of the industrial proletariat has increased somewhat since 1950, but this is due largely to the growth of arms production in general and to the Vietnam war in particular; the arms economy as a whole employs about 10 percent of the labor force. The greatest increases in white-collar employment have been among professional, technical, and clerical workers. Service jobs have grown as well, but not so rapidly as white-collar jobs.

The traditional social distance between white-collar and blue-collar workers has contributed to the failure of white-collar workers to respond to their changing situation through collective action. White-collar unionism is as weak today as it was a decade ago. As a percent of total union membership or of white-collar employment, union membership among white-collar workers has remained stable—about 14 percent. It has not grown significantly in numerical terms.

The few gains that have been made were mostly in government employment and that is numerically rather small. The American Federation of Teachers has grown rapidly since the mid-1950's, but still has only about 125,000 members. Strike activity among government workers is minuscule. In the most active year before 1965, workers on strike as a percentage of all government workers was only 38 percent. In qualitative terms, government professional employees have conducted some very militant union struggles. In general, however, the hopes held by some a couple of years ago that the AFT and the independent welfare workers' unions would spark a revival of militant unionism have collapsed.

The AFT nationally has been content to rest on the liberal positions it developed in the early 1960's, while the situation has passed them by, and has even come to the point of discussing a merger with its old rival, the National Education Association. Virtually all of the independent welfare unions have been defeated and isolated. Most of them have merged with more conservative AFL-CIO unions, in some cases the same ones they split from in the first place.

Perhaps even more significant is the fact that in many areas and cities both the teachers and welfare workers' unions have come into conflict with the black community.

In all cases, the radical notion of forging an alliance with recipient or parent groups has faded from all, but for the rhetoric. In New York, the United Federation of Teachers has conducted a strike directed against the black community. The facile ability of various city governments to direct the struggles of certain professional workers against other sections of the working class, particularly blacks, points to a peculiarity in the consciousness of many professional workers (this is not to deny the importance of racism in such a situation).

Thus it seems unlikely, given the state of the unions and the general consciousness of white-collar workers, that unionization will play much of a role in the development of consciousness among white-collar workers—either as a cause or a reflection. Given the diversity and range of jobs and the lag in consciousness that still exist, it seems more likely that any major breakthrough among white-collar workers will only occur in the context of a general upheaval in industry. That is, the consciousness of white-collar workers is more likely to develop in response to overall social crisis than to the specifics of the job around which unions are often built. This portends a leap in consciousness rather than its gradual development.

The conditions that might stimulate such a leap are in formation. Some of them are part of the process of proletarianization already discussed—these are but the necessary conditions. Perhaps the sufficient conditions lie in the growing crisis of capitalism that is affecting the working class as a whole. Taxes and inflation, endemic to the crisis, affect all sections of the working class. Furthermore, although white-collar workers have been receiving continuous wage increases, they do not have any organized way of fighting to keep these increases at least to the level of inflation. It is significant that the wage increases of industrial workers under union contracts have been greater in recent years than those of professionals, thus narrowing the differentials. As inflation continues, what is more, the second family income becomes more important.

All of this must be seen in the context of advancing technology. Even assuming a fall in the rate of innovation, many clerical jobs will be displaced. Both the possibilities for second incomes and job prospects for young workers will narrow. The "macro-economic" nature of these problems means a great tendency toward unification of class consciousness, that is, a reversal of the general fragmentation that has existed for the past twenty years and an overcoming of much that has separated white-collar from industrial workers.

The increased attack on the living standards of the entire working class has spurred a significant and growing intensification of the class struggle. By every measure, strikes have risen to massive proportions since 1965. Major national strikes in auto, copper, electrical, East Coast longshore, communications (for the first time since 1947) and airlines were long and large. Furthermore, the years 1967 to 1969 have seen a significant rise in local and wildcat strikes.

There are also some indications of the decomposition of the apolitical consciousness of the past ten to fifteen years. For the first time in decades, groups of workers have shown a willingness to accept or even request the aid of radical students. The first and best-known incident of this kind was the 1969 strike by Local 1-561 of the Oil, Chemical and Atomic Workers at the Richmond, California, Chevron works. The oil workers voted to accept student help and even to endorse the demands of the Third World Students at San Francisco State. In the case of the Buffalo railroad wildcat, in 1969, one of the leaders of the strike actually called the University of Buffalo and asked to speak to any radical student leader. The willingness of workers to accept student, i.e., radical, support doesn't mean that the workers accept the politics of the students. It does, however, point to a significant change in the attitudes of struggling workers toward alliances with other struggling groups.

That workers are increasingly viewing their problems as political in nature was strongly indicated by the size of the support received by George Wallace. The Wallace phenomenon is a sign of the dangers of this period as well as its hopes. A number of radical writers have pointed out that Wallace support cannot be viewed *simply* as a matter of racist backlash among workers. In fact, the bulk of Wallace's support was not working-class, but petty bourgeois and middle-class. The working-class support that Wallace did get, however, was largely concentrated in heavy industry. Roughly it was of two types: those skilled workers from the traditional ethnic groups associated with auto and steel (Polish, Italian, etc.) who feel threatened primarily in terms of their communities, e.g., towns such as Dearborn, Michigan; and young white production workers, many of whom have been ardent rank-and-file rebels, largely from the South.

Both groups have been hard hit by inflation and taxes. The young production workers have also experienced vicious speed-up in the past few years. Discussions with both types of workers by various union and radical organizers show that, while for the skilled workers the "law and order" element of Wallace's appeal was dominant, the young production workers viewed the Wallace movement as a rebellion against union and management. More than one young auto worker commented that if "Reuther was for Wallace, we'd be for Humphrey." In the past few years, young workers in auto and other industries have generally ignored politics altogether. Wallace, as a volatile anti-Establishment (though not anticapitalist) crusader appealed to their sense of rebellion. For both the older and younger (Southern) workers, the racist form of rebellion was consistent with their cultural backgrounds (though in different ways). Thus, the legacy of the Wallace phenomenon is ambiguous. On the one hand, it was, at least for the volatile young workers, a form of political rebellion against the deteriorating conditions of their lives, in an election in which there was no other real alternative to Humphrey and Nixon. On the other hand, it represents the possibility that the growth of industrial militancy may assert itself, at least in some sections of the working class, on the basis of old (racist) cultural assumptions deeply rooted in American society. One hopeful sign that this alternative will not become dominant is the difficulty that Wallace's American Independent Party has encountered in organizing a permanent base in Detroit. Another is the fact that very few of the wildcat movements that have sprung up since Wallace have been marred by overt racism.

The problem of racism and the division of the working class that results from it is one of the most difficult ones facing the working class. It is clear that there are no pat "techniques" or tactics at hand to solve the problem. Only the barest outlines of a strategy can be deduced from the history and present direction of working-class struggle. In general, it is clear that black workers must be in a position to command the respect of white workers and that, at the same time, the class consciousness and activity of white workers must be at a relatively high level. Indeed, those instances in the history of the working class, and other oppressed classes, in which racism was subordinated have been periods of intense class struggle—the Knights of Labor in the 1870's and 1880's, Populism, the IWW, and the CIO.

Even the history of these movements would indicate, at least in a negative way, that the self-confidence of black workers, itself a prerequisite of respect by white workers for the needs of black workers, requires some degree of independent black organization—autonomous but within the context of the struggle of the class as a whole. Nor is it possible or even desirable for black workers to kowtow to the current level of consciousness of white workers. In the context of class struggle, groups within the class do not "wait" for other groups to move; rather, they tend to pull these other groups into the struggle. Remember that the fights waged by the CIO workers brought forth an enormous upsurge among AFL workers, even though the AFL bureaucracy went to great lengths to convince their members that CIO efforts were a threat to them.

At the same time, the growth of struggle among white workers means that they are feeling the pressures of capitalist decay and instability more strongly than in the past and are responding to attacks on their living standards. Periods of intense class struggle usually begin by actions directed at the defense or improvement of living standards. In the present situation this means a struggle against conditions at work as well as at home.

The development of more radical forms of struggle depends on, and preexists in, this current "economic" struggle. The primary task at this moment is to push and encourage this struggle in such a way that it further exposes the political and systematic roots of the attack on living standards. The demands of the state that workers make sacrifices for the sake of the economy and "national interest" should be, and for the most part have been, met with a cold shrug of the shoulders.

Radicals can play an important role by exposing the class nature of such state demands. In short, for the struggle to develop and the consciousness of white workers to grow, white workers will have to struggle for their own immediate class interests, i.e., those which are common to all workers. The various "radical" demands for sacrifices by white workers (or all workers), such as the demand that white workers renounce their consumer practices or their "white-skin privileges," are based on an abstract moral approach to politics more akin to liberalism than Marxism. In the heat of class struggle, workers have proven themselves capable of enormous self-sacrifice and idealism (in the conventional sense of the word). In such a context black workers, by their own action, can smash racist barriers in oppressive institutions within the class as well as without, but this situation flows from the dynamics of struggle and not from abstract moralizing. It must be remembered that intense class struggle shakes loose the foundations of even the strongest institutions of oppression. It is for this reason that Marx spoke of the proletariat as the leader of all oppressed classes. The institutions of racism, oppression, and cooptation that seem so immovable today can be severely weakened even before the struggle reaches revolutionary proportions.

The working class, located in the central institution of society—production—is the only class that has the power to weaken and ultimately destroy these institutions. The struggle of black people is in a dynamic relationship with this overall struggle. Struggle in one's immediate self-interest, by both blacks and whites, is a necessary step in unfolding this dynamic. It is the step in which self-confidence and class identification develop. Insofar as racist attitudes are reinforced by insecurity, privatization, and fragmentation, this step is crucial to the destruction of racism within the working class. Insofar as white workers view blacks as an enemy because they are an easier target than the ruling class, black organization is a necessity, both to make blacks a less vulnerable "enemy" and to expose management, the union bureaucracy, and the state as the real enemy.

As we have noted, the interpenetration of the state and the corporation, and the contradictions exacerbated by the arms economy, in the form of taxes and inflation in particular, are simultaneously sparking new struggles and giving them a more national and political character. These phenomena tend to lead to still further attacks on the working class by the state, such as through wage control or, at the very least, increased federal intervention in strikes. In short, the ruling class itself is exposing the class nature and national scope of its attack on living standards. At the same time, the nature of this attack means that it affects all sections of the working class simultaneously, though not to the same degree. This fact is an enormous counterpressure to the previous fragmentation of the working class. To one degree or another, all industrial, occupational, and income groups (and the infinite mixture of these) are victims of a common attack by a common enemy. Thus, the basis for overcoming fragmentation has been laid.

It is clear, however, that not all groups within the class are affected to the same degree, or that all are equally capable of responding at the same time or in the same way. The degree of organization, previous traditions of struggle, concentration in the work place, etc., are all conditions which determine what sections of the class will move first. In general, the events from 1965 on show that it has been the industrial proletariat, rather than white-collar or service workers, who have moved first and with the greatest force. By all the criteria mentioned above, and for other reasons, industrial workers are better equipped to raise the level of struggle. Unlike any other section of the working class, the industrial proletariat is fairly well organized and has a long, and continuous, tradition of struggle. Many of the other groups and strata within the working class that were discussed earlier are either relatively new groups (having no tradition of struggle), or are not highly concentrated or organized in their place of work. Many of these conditions are reflections of the structural and strategic fact that mass-production industry is still the heart of the capitalist system, and within industry the proletariat is still the heart of production.

The strategic position of the proletariat and the fact that it is this section of the class which is moving first point to its centrality in any overall strategy. Furthermore, this national-political attack on the workers occurs at a time when the struggle over working conditions is itself more intense. This is not merely a coincidence of issues but a synthesis. The attempt to increase surplus value through inflation and taxes, or through wage restraints, puts the significance of deteriorating working conditions in their real context. The arguments, and the real reasons as well, used to justify price increases and taxes are the same as, or closely related to, those used to impose speed-up or measured-day-work. The local appearance of working conditions fades as the attack becomes total. On the other side of the coin, the impulsion toward workers' control inherent in fights over working conditions takes on a more political and class character in the context of this overall attack. The necessity, and therefore the possibility, of a total program around which to fight can transform the fight for better working conditions into the struggle for control over these conditions. Such a qualitative leap, however, is by no means automatic or "inevitable."

In the past ten or more years, the struggle over working conditions and the wildcat strikes have been led by informal shop-floor groups with little or no official standing in the union. The basic problem with these groups has been their isolation. The only unifying factor has been the intention of these groups and their choice of enemies. Most of these struggles have been directed against the union bureaucracy and the contract as well as management. Within an industry with one union, this can be the basis of an industry-wide movement. Outside of auto, steel, and rubber, however, this is not an adequate basis even for this.

Furthermore, this phenomenon offers little hope at all for cutting across industry lines. The shop groups and their rebellion are, nonetheless, the basis for expanded struggle. A strategy that didn't begin at this point would be by-passing the real struggles of the working class. (Alvin Gouldner, in his book *Wildcat Strike,* quotes one corporate executive as saying that the workers seem to "have a strong desire to run the plants.") The linking of these shop-floor groups is possible on the basis of the programmatic synthesis of national economic issues and working conditions. This is to say, linkages require politics. In general, alliances with other groups in industry, or the class, can be formed around such a program and the groups unified through a common struggle against the state as well as against management and the union bureaucracy. The Wallace campaign showed that an attack on the major bourgeois parties (those that administer the state) based on issues of real concern to workers can attract working-class support. The West Virginia miners' strike showed that workers' activity directed at the state, the bosses, and the union leadership can do the same thing, whether or not electoral action is used as a matter of tactics. The point is that the state is a focal point for struggle by groups of workers whose specific demands do not immediately appear related on the industrial level. The relationship, real enough in the economy, has to be made in a way that cuts across industrial and union (or nonunion) lines, without shunting aside the specific demands. Political action, direct, industrial or electoral, offers a way to do this in the concrete realm of action.

It is clear, because of bureaucratism, the managerial nature of contract administration, and the web of state controls, that the unions cannot be the vehicle for this transitional development. Yet, it must be recognized that rank-and-file rebellion, while unable to gain direct sources of power, has had an effect on the unions. The bureaucratic monolith that was the AFL-CIO has been broken with the formation of the Alliance for Labor Action by the UAW and the Teamsters in July 1968. While there is no reason to believe that these unions will change their internal practices significantly, or abandon their commitments to the Democratic Party and liberal politics, the mere fact of a break of this sort changes the political atmosphere and legitimizes new kinds of movements. In some cases, rank-and-file militancy has actually won some concessions within the unions. The most notable recent rank-and-file victory was the withdrawal of the United Steelworkers from the industry's "Human Relations Committee," the joint labor-management committee through which the way for automation was paved. The unions and their leaders are bound to change to some extent, if only as a way of attempting to coopt rank-and-file rebellion. Yet, it seems unlikely that the structure of most unions or the interrelationship with management and the state can be sufficiently modified to actually transform the unions into adequate forms of struggle.

At the same time, the union is a natural focus for political action within the industry. Political campaigns within the union can be, in some circumstances, a means for politicizing shop struggles. In this context, and unlike most union election campaigns in the past, the union becomes more an arena for action than the goal of the campaign. Clearly, however, the emerging movement, and the political movement that has the potential to emerge, is distinct from the union, a synthesis of shop economic and political organization and struggle.

Capitalism's instability and growing crisis affect every aspect of life. Beginning with students and black people, the decay of American society pulls one section of society after another into turmoil. Just as the industrial proletariat has begun to intensify, and in some cases deepen, its struggle, so in coming years other sections of the working class can be drawn into the struggle. As new sections of the class enter the struggle—e.g., the unorganized—the struggle may be transformed or pushed to a new level. Similarly, what is now primarily an economic struggle may turn into a political struggle tomorrow, as with the miners' strike. Rosa Luxemburg observed that there is a dynamic interrelationship between economic and political struggle. Commenting on the events leading up to the Russian upheaval of 1905, she said:

> In a word, the economic struggle is the factor that advances the movement from one political focal point to another. The political struggle periodically fertilizes the ground for the economic struggle. Cause and effect interchange every second. Thus, we find that the two elements, the economic and political, do not incline to separate themselves from one another during the period of the mass strikes in Russia, not to speak of negating one another . . .

The economic struggle of American workers has, indeed, advanced to a new political focal point. What remains is for the economic struggle to become explicitly political. Rosa Luxemburg also commented on the prerequisites for mass political action:

> In order that the working class may participate *en masse* in any direct political action, it must first organize itself, which above all means that it must obliterate the boundaries between factories and workshops, mines and foundries, it must overcome the split between workshops which the daily yoke of capitalism condemns it to.

In the United States, with its lack of working-class political traditions, the elimination of such boundaries may require political action in the first instance. Whether it is through political action or through the unification of strike movements, the strategy of alliances within the class must be pushed to its utmost.

The vehicle for unity in struggle is program. A program that can really accomplish such an ambitious task must speak to the real needs of the working class as its members see these issues. Insofar as the radical movement can contribute to the development of such a program, and that is surely its main task at this point, it must avoid the most ancient pitfall of the left, the inability to provide a transition from the reformist demands of workers today to revolutionary program and organization. The dilemma was clearest with the pre-World War I Social Democracy, which presented itself as a revolutionary movement. There was a minimum (reformist) and a maximum (revolutionary) program. The minimum program was the one upon which action was based, the maximum being the program that was articulated at May Day celebrations. In a period when revolution is not imminent, but in which growing class action is possible, revolutionary rhetoric counts for nothing, while reformist practice serves as a roadblock. To go from a period of economic activity to one of revolutionary consciousness, a transitional program is needed. In Trotsky's words, a transitional program is a "bridge" which should lead "from today's consciousness of wide layers of the working class . . . to one final conclusion: the conquest of power by the proletariat." Today we are at the reformist end of this bridge. The barriers in consciousness and in the system are massive. Nonetheless, the beginnings have been made, by the system, on the one hand, and the working class, on the other. Revolutionary struggle does not emerge instantaneously. Even the French mass strike of May 1968 was preceded by more than two years of intense economic strike activity. Transitional demands, such as those relating to taxes, inflation, and workers' control of production standards, which expose the nature of the crisis, must be counterposed to reformist demands or programs (Edward Kennedy and the "left-wing" of the Democratic Party) or demagoguery (Wallace and racism combined with pseudo-independent political action). If they are not, the ever-present trap of the Democratic Party, or an aggressive racist alternative, will deflect the struggle as it has in the past. Every rank-and-file struggle of large proportions comes under pressures from the ruling class. The West Virginia miners were heavily courted by various liberal politicians, or liberals with political ambitions. In such a situation revolutionary rhetoric is no counterbalance.

The development of a revolutionary movement of the working class is a long and difficult task. The new generation of workers who are entering the shops now may prove to be the spark that makes such a movement a reality. This is a not a question of any particular life style, but rather of the fact that youth is generally the first section of any class to interpret the experience of the entire class in a new way. Already being reached, to some extent, by the radical movement in the high schools, community colleges, armed forces, etc., this coming generation of workers can translate the radical ideas it is being exposed to into a program and struggle in the shops and in the society as a whole. The effect of these radicalized young workers on the rest of the class depends on the extent to which they are reached by today's, largely middle-class, movement and by the reality and quality of the ideas and analysis with which they are reached. Virtually all sections of the radical movement have made a rhetorical commitment to the working class. The crucial task for radicals and revolutionaries, now, is to translate the rhetoric into concrete analysis, program, and action that speak to the real needs of the working class.

IS THERE A NEW
REPUBLICAN MAJORITY?

by Andrew Hacker

Andrew Hacker is professor of government at Cornell. He has written widely on Republican and Presidential politics.

It is not easy to argue that Richard Nixon's election marks a revival of Republican fortunes. While he need not apologize for entering the White House with less than a popular majority—after all, Abraham Lincoln, Harry Truman and John Kennedy shared that distinction—his is nevertheless the smallest plurality any candidate has mustered since 1912. Moreover, he failed to carry a Republican Congress on his coattails; and his campaign showed no success at all in inducing dissident Democrats to change their registrations. A recent Gallup survey could only find 30 percent of the electorate willing to call themselves Republican, hardly a popular base for a party entering a new era.

As a participant-observer of Republican persuasion—I confess to having voted for Nixon four times—I pay more attention than most to plans and prescriptions for improving my party's performance. However, just recently, and for the first time in almost twenty years of GOP-gazing, I have seen an analysis which rises above wishful thinking. Kevin Phillips, currently a young assistant to the incumbent at-

torney general, believes that our country now possesses an
"emerging Republican majority." His book (*The Emerging
Republican Majority*, Arlington House) may or may not be
mistitled, but his argument deserves serious attention, if
only because its major premises may guide future Republican campaigns.

At the same time, Phillips's proposals should be seen as
the end-product of a generation-old dialectic within the
GOP. The Republicans' problem has been their propensity
for second place in most elections most of the time over the
past thirty-nine years. For the great Sisyphean rock remains
the Democratic registration roll, which has held its majority
ranking for more than a generation. In every election, the
GOP's candidates must start their seductions from scratch:
Democratic defections simply do not carry over from one
contest to another. Hence the perennial quest for one or another bloc of voters who can be uprooted from the Democratic weedbed and transplanted in Republican loam.

If nothing else, the Republican malaise has been of benefit to the publishing industry: in politics, as elsewhere, there
is something about a loser which appeals to authors; and
my five-foot shelf of party books has at least four volumes
on the GOP for every one about the Democrats. Louis Harris started the ball rolling a decade and a half ago by spending 231 pages asking, *Is There a Republican Majority?*
Eisenhower had just received 55 percent of the vote, and
was to do even better on his second time around. Yet he
made no Republican converts. "The key elements in the
Eisenhower majority are by and large a new breed of political independents," Harris wrote. The swing-voters Harris
had in mind were sensible suburban types, grown too sophisticated to settle for Main Street maxims or Prairie
pieties of the Robert Taft variety. Harris therefore suggested
a "moderate, middle-of-the-road" course as the best way
for the GOP to woo marginal voters who give candidates

their eventual majorities. The Harris theory has worked in Senate and gubernatorial races, especially on the two coasts where Thomas Kuchel, Clifford Case, Hugh Scott, Mark Hatfield, Edward Brooke, and a dozen or so other liberal-leaning Republicans adopted postures having independent appeal. But it didn't work for Richard Nixon in 1960.

Nixon's 1960 campaign was not at all Neanderthal. (Indeed his major domestic difference with John Kennedy was that he favored spending federal funds on school construction, whereas Kennedy wanted money for teachers' salaries as well as buildings.) While it has been customary to point out that Nixon came within two-tenths of a percentage point of the Presidency that year, my own view is that he was lucky to have done as well as he did. The real trouble is that "moderation" can end up as "me-too-ism"; and, as Wendell Willkie and Thomas Dewey learned, voters tend to prefer the real article. If Nixon's defeat consigned Harris's handbook to the remainder counters, it spurred Republican printing presses into two directions.

Barry Goldwater's *The Conscience of a Conservative* and Phyllis Schlafly's *A Choice, Not an Echo* were more than exercises in economic orthodoxy and anti-Communist ideology; they also proposed a novel strategy for Republican revival. A third of all adult Americans never bestir themselves to go to the polls, an apathy social scientists have usually attributed to the inability of lower-class citizens to see elections as relevant to their lives. The Goldwater forces took a different view, and not simply because they suspected anything social scientists said. To their eyes, most of the stay-at-homes were true-blue conservatives unwilling to waste their time choosing between Tweedledee and another egg. Give them a real choice—an opportunity to vote for a principled conservative—and they would flock to the polls, bringing Republican strength well over the majority mark. If evidence were needed, one had only to look at Arizona,

where Goldwater himself won successive victories by un-
covering hitherto hidden sentiments. In 1964 Goldwater
carried Arizona again. And Alabama and Georgia and Louisiana and South Carolina and Mississippi. And that was
all. The theory was wrong.

So to Nixon's nomination in 1968, and his less-than-
auspicious showing against a decimated and dispirited
Democratic Party. And hence the earlier-than-usual appearance of new programs for Republican resuscitation.
Predictably enough, some are suggesting that moderate Republicanism be given another chance. The most active
moderate publicity-mill is the Ripon Society, whose offices
off Harvard Square have, over the last several years, issued
a steady stream of position papers on subjects ranging from
Ronald Reagan and Cuban refugees to Selective Service and
the military-industrial complex. All are intelligently written, handsomely produced, and largely unread by the Republican rank and file. Though the Society sends its releases
to a large mailing list, it seems to carry on without meetings
or members. I have reason to believe that Nelson Rockefeller
mails them a five-figure check every so often, an amount
sufficient for his and their purposes.

The Lessons of Victory, put together by seventeen young
men on the Ripon payroll, argues that Nixon's victory was
nothing to boast about. In many parts of the country the
party fared worse than in 1960, and anyone unconnected
with the Johnson-Humphrey record would probably have
won. The authors are pretty well persuaded that Nixon is
still the same old Nixon, reminding us that even in last
year's campaign he "assured his audiences that Johnson and
Humphrey were not traitors on so many occasions that he
created the impression that he expected people to think
they were." Yet what really annoys the Ripon authors is
their party's paranoia about anything new: "At many rallies, including Nixon's climactic appearance at Madison

Square Garden on Halloween night, anyone wearing a beard was systematically turned away." Hence their proposal that the GOP should make a pitch not only to enlightened suburbanites (especially those who "admired Eugene McCarthy's integrity") but also to black voters and union members. They are upset that Nixon attracted only 750,000 black votes and that only one union delegate (the Glass Blowers' president) was at Miami.

This approach *has* succeeded—on the state level. In addition to the old stand-bys—Javits, Case, Percy, et al.— those of the Ripon persuasion can point to new senatorial entrants, such as Charles Mathias, William Saxbe, and Robert Packwood, who ran ahead of Nixon in Maryland, Ohio, and Oregon in 1968. The real difficulty is that moderate Republicanism has not been able to make much headway when the party foregathers to nominate its national candidates. The treatment accorded Nelson Rockefeller and George Romney at recent GOP conventions shows clearly that the sorts of people chosen as Republican delegates simply will not settle for a candidate to the left of Nixon. Nor can it be claimed that the last several conventions have been unrepresentative of rank-and-file Republican opinion—as an insider I will attest that recent proceedings have mirrored grassroots GOP sentiment as perfectly as any gathering can.

About midway through *The Lessons of Victory* the authors ask, "What accounted for Richard Milhous Nixon's plurality in 1968?" "The reason," they tell us, "is quite simple: the middle class got bigger." This is true. The American middle class has been expanding, and from its attitudes and aspirations may be deduced a good deal of the nation's political future. However, I am not at all persuaded that the Ripon writers know as much as they should about the character and composition of this social stratum. It is true they are well acquainted with the suburbs that sported

McCarthy bumper-stickers, but middle-class America also
extends into precincts seldom visited by moderate Republicans. Kevin Phillips understands this terrain far better than
the Ripon Society ever will, and therein lies the force of his
appeal for a far different kind of Republican reconstruc-
tion.

Though a graduate of Harvard Law School, Phillips
writes less as a Harvard man and more as a boy from the
Bronx. But it is the upper, semisuburban reaches of that
borough: the Bronx of Mario Procaccino and Paul Fino—
homeowning, churchgoing, and uneasy over its association
with the larger city. If most Harvard graduates never go
home again—after all, their law degree is a ticket to new
ambitions and eminences—Phillips returned to the Bronx,
where he spent four years as assistant to Fino, the borough's only Republican Congressman. He caught John
Mitchell's eye early in Nixon's 1968 campaign, largely because of his shrewdness with statistics and his aptitude for
electoral analysis, both of which are fully evident in *The
Emerging Republican Majority*. If, like others before him,
he attempts to show how the GOP can recruit new adher-
ents, he relies less on casual observations and more on the
two hundred maps and tables he deploys in the course of
his countrywide canvass. It is an impressive exercise and a
plain-spoken application of social science to a real political
problem.

The Phillips thesis may be simply stated. The Republicans, he writes, now have an "opportunity to fashion a majority among the 57 percent of the American electorate
which voted to eject the Democratic party from national
power." Of this 57 percent, about 43.5 percent came from
Republicans, while the remaining 13.5 percent were supporters of the American Independent Party. Thus, the GOP
should make a serious and strenuous bid for the 9,906,473
citizens who cast their ballots for George Corley Wallace.

Courting a bloc of this magnitude is a legitimate political
pursuit. (Between now and 1972 the Democrats will try to
make inroads of their own into the Wallace constituency.)
The only question at issue is what kind of appeal one makes
to citizens who once succumbed to the charms of an Alabama governor.

As I read him, Phillips proposes that the GOP approach
Wallace's supporters on their own terms: not to persuade
them out of their prejudices, but rather to produce a Republican record paralleling that promised by the Wallace
party. But this is not simply a replay of the "Southern strategy" advanced by Goldwater's staff in 1964 and reactivated
by Strom Thurmond in 1968. For only half of Wallace's
votes came from the South; the attraction he held for
Northern voters emerges as a fact of far greater significance.

At the same time, Phillips's comments on the South carry
more than regional implications. It is in the Republicans'
interest, he suggests, to encourage black voting in the
former Confederate states. "Maintenance of Negro voting
rights is essential to the GOP," Phillips points out, although
not out of affection for the Fourteenth Amendment, for only
if Southern blacks become more dominant in Democratic
politics will Southern whites flee to a Republican haven.
"Unless Negroes continue to displace white Democratic
organizations, the latter may remain viable spokesmen for
Deep Southern conservatism." Phillips has nothing against
Deep Southern conservatism: he just wants it enlisted in Republican service, in state and local elections as well as at the
Presidential level. (Right now Republicans hold only 13
percent of the seats in Southern legislatures.) He has no
objections whatever to the Democrats' becoming an all-
black party—in fact, the more Julian Bonds and Charles
Everses the better. Such a party would soon descend to minority status, winning only a few rural counties and a hand-

ful of ghetto precincts and leaving all the white refugees to the GOP.

This tactic clearly has relevance to the North, where the Wallace vote ran to 10 percent in Kansas and Michigan, and 12 percent in Ohio and Indiana. (Indeed, even in New York City, almost one voter in ten pulled the Wallace lever in Bronx, Brooklyn, and Queens neighborhoods like Parkchester, Greenpoint, and South Ozone Park.) Most of these voters were Democrats indulging their periodic penchant for punishing their own party: the sort of thing many of them did when they voted for William Buckley or against Carl Stokes and Richard Hatcher for mayor. But their grievances against liberal legislation and litigation may have grown to the point where their loyalties are, in Phillips's words, "in motion between a Democratic past and a Republican future."

The trick, then, is to steal Wallace's thunder without repelling bedrock Republican voters. And the way to achieve this is not by imitating his method but rather by co-opting his message. One of the reasons Wallace got only five million votes in the North was that he was just a bit too square. Consequently, the issues he raised, treated with just a shade more sophistication, could well be turned to a Republican advantage.

Restyling itself as a party of "populist conservatism"— Phillips's term—the GOP should, he says, appeal to the apprehensions of wage-earning homeowners and white-collared taxpayers. And in the North, as in the South, this would be a white party, welcoming Americans of every region who find themselves disquieted over black behavior— whether criminal or constitutional. This posture would probably produce some losses among groups put off by so scapegoat a strategy. Yet even when aggregated, these elements add up to less than meets the eye. For example, young people. Phillips's slide rule reveals that the average voter is aged forty-seven and those under twenty-five cast less than 8 percent of the ballots. (Moreover, within the group we call "youth" many more work as secretaries or garage mechanics than attend elite universities.) The Ripon-Rockefeller notion that the GOP can gain black votes emerges as political science-fiction—even when the party could find a James Farmer to run under its banner, he got only 27 percent of the vote in Bedford-Stuyvesant. In fact, the task of fashioning a Republican majority may actually be speeded up by refusing to court liberal-leaning elements in the electorate. In any populist program it is wisest to to write off opinionated minorities who demand basic programmatic changes in return for their votes. A good case in point is the current governor of California, who won his million-vote margin largely by implying that he had no wish for the support of blacks, intellectuals, or the poor. ("One of the few suburbs that Reagan lost," Phillips writes with apparent approval, "was rich, theatrical, and quite Jewish Beverly Hills.")

Phillips also shows a shrewd statistical eye for the nation's growth patterns. Parts of the country still under the "Yankee sphere of influence" tend to be areas of decline: not only central cities like New York, Providence, and Philadelphia, but also out-dated factory towns such as Scranton, Fall River, and Duluth. Even if they persist in their Democratic habits, their electoral weight diminishes with every passing year. The real population explosion is occurring in the "Sun-Belt Conservative Cities"—Anaheim, Tulsa, Shreveport, Orlando, Albuquerque—where patriotism and piety commingle with split-level housing and aerospace employment. The Republicans have already begun to make inroads here; but they have yet to plumb the anxieties of these sun-loving citizens. A populist posture is well suited to this constituency, and for its platform Phillips suggests—somewhat more diplomatically than Wallace—

the politics of "ethnic polarization." Implicit in Phillips's
state-by-state tabulations is the message that a "large national majority" of voting Americans can be mobilized by
approaching them in terms of their lowest common denom-
inator: white fear of the black presence. (To be sure, white
radicals—particularly privileged undergraduates who cut
classes to disrupt campuses or party conventions—can also
be used as an issue. But such confrontations are not really a
principal concern of the people Phillips wants to win over;
they are certainly secondary to race.)

Ethnic polarization is already enmeshed in our politics,
although mainly at the local level. If many of these racial
antipathies are based on stereotypes, the anxieties infect-
ing white Americans still have good statistical foundation.
Disproportionate numbers of addicts and criminals are
black, and strange black faces in one's neighborhood do in
fact signal greater probability of theft or violence than unknown white visitors. (Any white person who claims that he
can pass a group of black youths on a dark street as equably
as a group of whites is an out-and-out liar.) The widespread approval of measures like preventive detention as-
sumes that the detained defendants will not only be black
but also presumptively dangerous; and popular opposition
to putting civilians on police review boards has been
spurred by the desire to give the police greater freedom in
arresting black criminals. Whether or not "racist," these
fears are not unreasoned. The stumbling block, properly
emphasized by civil libertarians, is that any wholehearted
attempt to round up black criminals will—as does any
roundup—inevitably lead to the conviction of at least some
innocent black citizens. (And any white person who believes
that the conviction of an innocent black is "less important"
than the conviction of an innocent white, is a racist.) Furthermore, the air of arrogance worn by many blacks and
the disdainful demonstrations of the Panthers and Afro-

American societies on campuses have converted not a few erstwhile liberals to the law-and-order campaign.

None of this needs to be said, of course. But if the issue comes to the surface, it is possible to argue that tensions of this sort simply continue an old political tradition. "Ethnic polarization," Phillips writes, "is a longstanding hallmark of American politics, not an unprecedented and menacing development of 1968." Perhaps he really believes that an explicit white-black stand-off in our day will be analogous, say, to Boston's Back Bay–Irish animosities of an earlier time. Others might conclude that the race-based populism of an all-white party could bring repression less akin to Boston's and more like that of the Black-and-Tans.

But any talk of populist politics remains largely theoretical until such a movement is mustered and mobilized, indeed brought into being by politicians willing to rouse such sentiments to the surface. This is what William Jennings Bryan, Joseph McCarthy, and George Wallace all tried in turn; and all failed because their personal styles were not attuned to a variety of regions and classes. Indeed, in the past, populist success has depended on an appealing personality—an ingredient Phillips hardly mentions—and charismatic men are rare commodities in Republican circles. About the only Republican I can think of who might fill this bill on a national scale would be Ronald Reagan: his smooth, suburban appearance appealed to Californians in every part of that prototypical state; and my own guess is that had his party nominated him last year he might even have won. However, Reagan will be well into his sixties by 1976, and there is no one else remotely like him on the Republican horizon.

As an alternative, the GOP may try to speed the polarizing process by administrative means. And at this point the moving spirit seems to be our very un-charismatic attorney general, to whom *The Emerging Republican Majority* is partially dedicated (Richard Nixon shares this honor). It may well be that a mixture of action and inaction on John Mitchell's part will have the desired effect: conveying to Wallace-ites and other dissident Democrats that the Republicans can be relied upon to keep the blacks in their proper place. But I am not sure that voters of this sort can be counted on to get the message: postponement of desegregation suits, the arrest and indictment of activists, and similar Justice Department initiatives may fail to come across as a coherent program. Still and all, this is the best the party can do with the personnel it now has: populism via bureaucratic procedures rather than soul-stirring rallies or pulsating television performances.

But Phillips also has plans for reforming his party from the inside, and here he may encounter his greatest obstacle. If he finds the GOP "much too establishmentarian," this does not mean that the Republicans are an aristocratic or a patrician preserve. Indeed, John Lindsay, Ogden Reid, and the two Rockefellers just about exhaust the list of upper-class offspring willing to stand up on platforms and appeal for votes. (In fact, scions of old families who get the political urge usually choose the Democrats, who always reserve some room for pedigreed candidates.) Thus, while the well-to-do may write occasional checks for the GOP, they have left the running of the party to people rather different from themselves.

The Republican Establishment consists largely of small-town lawyers backstopped by the merchants and businessmen based in medium-sized cities. This is America's true bourgeoisie: self-employed, self-reliant, and not a little pleased over their own success and superiority. If not always of Yankee antecedents—Spiro Agnew cannot claim Anglo-Saxon bloodlines—most are still apt to invoke puritan precepts when confronted with conditions they do not understand. At the same time, the segment of the middle class these men symbolize has lost much of its influence and importance, and therein lies much of the Republican problem. For GOP committees continue to look like local business clubs, frightening off less prepossessing citizens whose newly acquired conservatism ought to be attracting Republican interest. In the past, the Republican rank and file was remarkably quiescent, deferring to the bankers and merchants who made policy and selected candidates. Phillips's proposal is that these worthies make room for the clerks and salesmen who have hitherto stood outside the GOP threshold. In addition, he faces up to the religious implications inherent in any Republican expansion program. For a broadened GOP base would necessarily involve giving power and preferment to Catholics, something this essentially Protestant party has always been slow to do.

Therefore, much of Phillips's message is ecumenical, and he chides his party for failing to enlist Catholics in the Republican fold. His own experience in the northern Bronx showed him that Irish and Italian voters could be turned into enthusiastic Republicans when given a candidate with whom they could identify. Many Catholics now have lower-middle-class incomes but retain remnants of their working-class past, and one way for the GOP to win them over is by giving more of its nominations to men with names like Edward Derwinski, Martin McKneally, and Paul Fino.

Curiously, Phillips hardly mentions New York's Conservative Party, which has done exceptionally well with Catholic voters in recent elections. The Conservative Senatorial candidate, James Buckley, got over 17 percent of the statewide vote in 1968; and in sixteen of the state's forty-one districts Conservative votes ran from 20 to 29 percent. Indeed, what Phillips would like is a Republican-Conservative coalition in all parts of the country, welding white Protestants and Catholics together in an equitable admixture of candidates and compatible issues. Moreover, while the

official ideology of the Conservative Party runs parallel to
the position of the *National Review,* it has confined its campaigns to closer-to-home questions, such as preserving
neighborhood schools, crime in the streets, and keeping the
blacks at bay. What is also instructive is that the great majority of Buckley supporters voted for Nixon rather than
Wallace. Still, all too many of these Buckley-Nixon voters
continue to register—and regard themselves—as Democrats.
Only if they are weaned away from the party of their parents
and grandparents can they be counted upon—as upstate
New York Republicans can—to pull GOP levers as a
matter of reflex.

And in this regard the Conservatives provide another
clue. Irish and Italians wearing Robert Hall suits have been
made to feel at home at Conservative rallies in Syracuse,
Sunnyside, and Suffolk County. The Conservatives have
come across as a truly lower-middle-class party, carrying
none of the snobbish connotations associated with GOP
county committees. Hence the big problem for the Republican Party, in New York and elsewhere, is in its internal arrangements. If I may paraphrase an unlikely authority, the
specter which will haunt the Grand Old Party is a class
struggle between its upper-middle establishment and the
lower-middle arrivals it hopes to attract. Future dinners
may have to be held in American Legion halls rather than
at the local Sheraton Inn, with GOP burghers forgoing their
martinis in favor of beer. Phillips seems willing to have the
catering done by Kentucky Fried Chicken, but I am not
sure how many other Republicans have an appetite for paper cups and plastic plates.

Though the "large national majority" that Phillips hopes
to attract to the GOP consists of relatively prosperous citizens—homeowners and taxpayers who now have something
to lose—it would be a mistake to assume that they oppose

federal spending and government subsidies. Phillips commits this error when he opines that "Wallace's vote would probably have dipped much lower had Richard Nixon chosen to rally aberrant multitudes of 1964 Goldwater backers by sounding the anti-Great Society clarion . . ." Nonsense of this sort weakens much of Phillips's case. In the first place, Goldwater himself was never supported by "multitudes": if he got 27 million votes, at least 20 million of these came from Republican regulars like my Anglo-Saxon in-laws who come to the aid of their party no matter who is nominated. But more important, a large majority of voters do in fact favor Great Society-type programs—or at least those which assist the middle class: Medicare, aid to education, tax reform, consumer protection. They may complain about taxes, civil-rights enforcement, and welfare for people less upstanding than themselves. But they hardly favor dismantling Social Security or turning TVA over to Tennessee Edison. In fact, most of the Wallace voters Phillips wishes to attract have enjoyed federal subsidies and services for most of their lives. Wallace himself sensed this and hence emphasized the racial issue throughout his campaign.

What this means is that if the GOP is to win over lower-middle-class clerks in Queens, steelworkers in Youngstown, and retired police lieutenants in San Diego, it will have to embrace the tradition of Tory democracy. That is, it will have to deliver at least those public programs which provide amenities for Americans in the $7000–$15,000 income range. Such services can be supplied even while other measures freeze welfare payments and public housing, repress racial and radical protest, and adjust the Constitution to facilitate criminal convictions. We know from recent experience that punishing unpopular minorities can win local elections; nevertheless, in the long run the lower-middle class will want its share of subventions, whether in the form of

parochial school aid for their children, nursing-home subsidies for their grandparents, or new commuter trains for
themselves. Outlays such as these—which the Democrats
are always willing to promise—can be expensive. At the
moment, it remains to be seen how many Republican regulars would accept expenditures of this magnitude.

While hardly a Benjamin Disraeli, Richard Nixon probably sensed the scope of his party's problem even before
Kevin Phillips put pen to paper. For if John Mitchell sat at
his right hand, he at first made a secure place for Robert
Finch on his left. While the one adviser's indifference to
civil rights and civil liberties could raise Republican popu-
larity in many precincts, the other's sympathy for public
spending and activist assistants could fill a less flamboyant
but nonetheless necessary role. If Nixon would give simul-
taneous attention to these twin approaches, I predict his
easy reelection. And if GOP candidates at lesser levels can
bestir themselves to support such a double-edged strategy,
the party may well begin to chalk up majorities as it has not
since the days of Calvin Coolidge.

Merging the Wallace constituency with the Republican
rank and file, though not an appealing prospect, stands out
as a real possibility. By coalescing the class Alexis de
Tocqueville once called the "eager and apprehensive men of
small property" and making use of anxieties that more gen-
tlemanly generations thought best to ignore, the line between majority rule and majority tyranny could easily be
crossed. The losers would be those Americans the Republicans will have written off. And their reaction to repression
and repudiation—which is not my topic at this time—would
have an impact of its own on the character and quality of
this country's political life.

SHARING THE
BURDEN OF CHANGE

by S. M. Miller

Professor of education and sociology at New York University, S. M. Miller is co-author, with Frank Riessman, of Social Class and Social Policy *and, with Pamela Roby, of* The Future of Inequality.

The obvious, continually rediscovered, never fails to amaze. We are surprised to learn of the poor in America and plan programs to help. Then the revelation of the working poor emerges and changes the way we think about welfare policy. And now we detect that one can be working and not poor, and still be excluded from the affluent society. A white working class and lower-middle class comes to public attention and we find that many are in fact struggling to make a decent living.

To be over the poverty line does not necessarily mean economic and social well-being. Indeed, recent calculations suggest that a decent standard of living now costs over $10,000 for a family of four. About half of American families are above the poverty line but below the adequacy level. This group, neither poor nor affluent, composed not only of blue-collar workers but also of many white-collar workers is hurting and neglected. They are, in Herbert Gans' phrase, "sub-affluent." *

It is time to recognize that workers, both blue- and white-collar, are victims at least as much as villains. There are objective economic and social reasons for their discontent. Even if, as many believe, they harbor authoritarian attitudes (which I am sure is not the case in any simple way), changes in their conditions and prospects are needed to reduce the resentments that fuel racist behavior.

Social policy can be oriented either to reducing the salience of anti-Negro attitudes and behavior among whites under the $10,000-income level or to aiding them as a neglected group with great needs. Whichever the choice, many similar courses would be followed. But if the nonpoor non-affluent are regarded as an important target of policy, needing aid in their own right, the measures would probably be more appropriate and effective. The issue is: Is the objective only to abate some of the flames of anti-black anger or to improve the position of a group which is nibbling at the edges of affluence? I favor the latter view.

The effort to improve the position of the poor and the blacks, as Martin Rein and I contended at the very beginning of the war on poverty, was aimed at remaking the social-stratification contours of this nation. If effective, it would inevitably implicate other groups and many institutions and practices. The emergence of the nonpoor non-affluent as a group deserving of and requiring public attention and aid is major evidence that, although we may try piecemeal attempts at change, its effects will reverberate throughout the society.

Within the category of "subaffluent" I think there are

---

* Obviously a large number of blacks are sub-affluent—almost half. But we will be neglecting them in this paper as they contend they are neglected in society.

three subgroups involved in current discussions. The first is the hard-core prejudiced and discriminatory. People in this category have long been prejudiced and are not particularly influenced by their current situation. Consequently economic and social actions would little relieve their animosity toward blacks and toward social change. But that does not mean that nothing affects their attitudes and behavior. In the early and mid-sixties, when national elites were accentuating the importance of black progress, the hard-core subaffluents did not resist very hard. They seemed rather surprised and overwhelmed by the favorable attitudes toward blacks and held their tongues and their peace. It was when national elites became more critical of blacks and when the Ciceros felt very directly threatened that open aggressive action flourished.

It is commonly believed that all of the subaffluents fall into the category of the hard-core prejudiced. My guess—admittedly only a guess at this time—is that most don't. There is also the backlash subgroup made up of those who were not previously unfavorable to black advance, but who were increasingly angered by the turbulence of the sixties. And finally there is a third subgroup who resent their own lack of improvement in the sixties, but do not reject the importance of black advance and social reform.

My estimate is that these two latter groups are the bulk of the subaffluents. While the hard core certainly exists, its members are probably not the majority. More important, they are strongest when counter-values are not strongly asserted by national elites and when there is a slowdown in the improvement of conditions of life of the subaffluents.

What seems to me crucially important and widely neglected in understanding American attitudes and political life is the fluidity of attitudes. (I sometimes feel that survey experts and pollsters should report in their findings the conditions under which attitudes would change rather than just giving us straight reporting of what attitudes are at a particular moment.) Immediate circumstances, the reduction or piling up of resentments, the discovery of new facts—all deeply affect the moods of public opinion. Therefore, I do not take as foreclosed the attitudes at this moment on race, Vietnam, President Nixon, or economic issues.

In one sense, pollsters know this because they are acutely aware that the way a question is phrased deeply affects the responses to it. Consequently, one must be doubtful of a Louis Harris poll at the end of 1969 which reported that 53 percent of the population favored open-housing legislation, 72 percent the location of housing and jobs for low-income families in suburbs, 90 percent expanded job-training programs for disadvantaged groups. I do not take the figures as gospel, but rather as indicating that not only do attitudes shift but that many of the subaffluent probably go along with significant economic and social change—if they do not feel hurt by it.

I do not believe that economic action will dissolve all resistance and negative feelings toward blacks. But I do fear that without economic improvement and reduction in the burdens borne by the subaffluents little will change. And I do believe that they are deserving of attention and aid.

I see seven major strategies to improve the conditions and prospects of the marginal population suspended precariously above poverty and submerged below affluence: expanding the economic pie; reducing economic insecurities; lessening inequalities; sharing the burden of integration; universalizing services; promoting educational and job mobility; and increasing participation and power.

Spurring Growth

An enlarged economic pie is the basic condition for social change without anger and negative reaction. As the pie expands, more can be given to everybody while even more is given to the poor and the black. Redistribution has the best chance of occurring as a calculated policy in a situation of general economic improvement.

We have to learn therefore how to overcome the stop-go character of American economic policy: expansion followed by price rises and then government policies to rein the price increases—policies that result in unemployment and retarded growth in real incomes. American policymakers and economists have to be more creative and open-minded in moving to a continuous high-employment, high-growth program than they have been. Expansion is needed to make politically possible the kind of redistribution required today to improve the lot of both the poor and the subaffluent.

Reducing Economic Insecurity

The so-called "hard-core" unemployed (read black, poorly educated males) who were hired by companies in the economic expansion of 1968 through the government-subsidized JOBS program (Jobs in the Business Sector) were threatened by layoffs in 1969 and 1970. There is the prospect of serious competition between blacks and white workers with greater seniority. Some companies have been considering reducing the work week for all instead of following the traditional practice of laying off low-seniority workers and maintaining the normal work week. If this were done, white workers would be sacrificing part of their income to provide employment for the new black workers.

In the construction trades, the Philadelphia Plan to assure jobs for blacks should be coupled with programs to guarantee employment for those already in the unions. While the threat of the loss of jobs is not the only important issue for union members (William Simon has suggested to me that the loss of status in no longer being able to open the door to the union for a relative may be more important than job security), it *is* significant. Making it easy to accept change by removing economic threats has psychological advantages: current workers would be paid or rewarded for accepting what they see as a loss or deprivation. They would not be "patsys," for they would not be giving up something without recompense. They would be paid for their agreement, as is the usual situation in our society.

Lessening Inequalities

If we divide white families into five groups ranked by income, we see that in the decade between 1956 and 1966 the bottom fifth slightly increased its share of the total income of white families, rising from 5.4 percent to 5.7 percent. But the second fifth declined in that period from 12.8 percent to 12.6 percent (recovering from the low of 12.3 percent in 1964), and the third or middle fifth also declined slightly in these years, from 17.9 percent to 17.7 percent. If we take the second and third fifths as the groups with which we are mainly concerned when dealing with the nonpoor marginal whites, there has actually been a small decline in their relative position. If spendable income—that is, after-tax income —were the variable rather than gross income, the decline would be sharper.

More effective redistribution policies are needed. Our regressive taxation system imposes a heavier burden on these income groups than those better off and needs to be changed. Local and state taxes should become less important and the federal income tax should become the mainstay for meeting public needs. In turn, the income tax should become increasingly progressive.

A sizable part of the gains won by unions in collective bargaining has been given over to fringe benefits, improved pensions, and medical insurance. The improvement of federal systems of social security and health care would make it possible for more union advances to be received as straight income, a major need of young families.

It is difficult to see how the income of marginal workers can be augmented at the source—wages and salaries. Unionization would help many, especially white-collar workers. A high-employment economy encourages a redistribution of income toward blue- and white-collar workers, especially if inflation is checked. But it is hard to manage a sizable shift in the proportion of income going to the second and third fifths without more controls over private enterprise than are politically possible today. One way might be to try to affect the distribution of income after its initial distribution by the utilization of income transfer systems. For example, a family allowance for all households with children or a negative income tax with a high maximum income for eligibility would make it possible to supplement the income of the disadvantaged nonpoor by providing cash supplements.

Sharing the Burden of Integration

It is the presumed national objective to have open housing and integrated schools. Aside from enforcing punitive measures, which is difficult, there are really no policies to achieve these objectives.

Instead, there is little effort to make even the small steps that are taken toward integration effective or attractive. The result is that subaffluent whites bear the brunt of integration

and social change. It is their neighborhoods that are filled
with new black residents; their schools that become over-
crowded with new black students and more difficult to operate as new populations are added to the old; and it is their
homes that run the danger of losing value in the real estate
market. It is not the affluent who are threatened by change
but the marginal whites.

One typical reaction of the more affluent whites and the
blacks is to rail against the subaffluent whites who appear to
be unwilling to absorb the shocks of social change. A more
sensible reaction would be to have the costs of social change
and integration borne by the nation as a whole rather than
by vulnerable individuals whose recalcitrance and anger reflect the risk and costs they have to bear as individuals un-
supported by any overall program.

How can we federalize or make national the expenses and
travails of integration? Frank Riessman and I, in *Social
Class and Social Policy*, outlined the general lines of the
strategy.

First, integration efforts should be rewarded by providing
advantages for integrating rather than ineffectively depending on penalties for not doing so. The neighborhoods im-
pacted by social change should be provided with more
money for their schools, which now have a more challenging task than before. Garbage pickups should be increased,
recreational facilities expanded, police protection improved.
If the nation wants to achieve greater measures of integration it must reward those who are moving willy-nilly in that
direction rather than curse them because they object to being alone in absorbing the burdens of change.

Second, the questions of real estate values should not be
ignored. True, studies show that in most situations changing
neighborhoods do not suffer losses in values. But some
neighborhoods do, especially in the short run, and many of
the nonaffluent are very frightened by this prospect, even if

their anxiety is unrealistic. It should be remembered that one of the prices of not being well-off is endemic anxiety about well-being.

I suggest that insurance for homes be extended to cover any depreciation in value due to the changing characteristics of the residents of an area. This policy has at least one drawback—it would probably reduce the rate at which housing prices might come down. But a policy of this kind is needed to lessen the threat of loss of equity that is now completely borne by individual homeowners in a changing neighborhood. I am sure that some plans could be developed to lighten the risks for those most vulnerable.

It could be argued that white resisters to residential integration would not be mollified by having a guarantee against loss of their equity because they simply do not want to live close to blacks. I am sure this is true of some of the white resisters. But others—how many I am not sure—would be less unwilling if they did not think their neighborhoods would deteriorate and their equity be reduced.

Universalizing Services

Many of the subaffluent feel left out of the sixties. The concentration has been upon the poor and blacks. New services have been inaugurated that benefit the poor: day-care centers for working AFDC (Aid to Families with Dependent Children) mothers, legal-aid services, Medicare, Headstart. The nonpoor nonaffluent are not getting these services, which they, too, could use. Many blue- and white-collar wives work and have makeshift arrangements for caring for their children; a day-care service for all would help them. Their children could profit from a good Headstart program or from the pocket money and experience of the Neighborhood Youth Corps. Their medical bills are high and a national health service would benefit them as well.

And so it goes. The services initiated to help the poor are not meeting needs unique to the poor, although perhaps they are more acute among them. These services are also needed by other groups in society, especially the marginals.

Promoting Educational and Job Mobility

Many young blue- and white-collar workers feel caught. Their chances of getting onto the fast-moving, high-paying white-collar and technical escalator are limited by their lack of educational credentials. We need to increase promotion possibilities within their present job structures, with more rapid and more frequent movement into technical jobs. An even more important objective is to make it possible for young or young-minded workers to get into new and better-paying jobs in quite different fields.

For some, this would mean scholarships so that they could get formal educational credentials by returning to school. At present, scholarships are most often awarded to single persons, young families with few children, or two-member families where the wife works, and the scholarship is essentially a wage supplement during the beginning years of apprenticeship in a professional career. What is needed is a scholarship system that is not aimed at the very young but at men with established families who wish to move into new careers. Such scholarships would provide a living income, rather than merely a supplement, which may be adequate for a new family with young children and fixed obligations that cannot be postponed.

But being able to afford college or technical school is only part of the struggle. A true second-chance program would help older students get through this advanced education by making their courses more relevant to their future occupations, shortening the time of study, and providing other aids tailored to their needs. Educational programs must be changed if they are to help the blue-collar or marginal white-collar worker who wants to make a big occupational shift.

While I think a better scholarship program and a second-chance university approach are very much needed, I do not think they will help great numbers of workers. The waiting period to get to new jobs is too long. Basically, we need to remove the credentials barrier so that people without diplomas can get into apprenticeship slots and then be trained and upgraded in new careers. In some cases they might take part in residential educational programs for several months. Part of their recompensed work time could be spent in educational upgrading and other activities, as is now the case for many executives in large companies. New styles of recruiting, work, and training for the growth jobs are needed if many of the marginals are to cross over to these occupations.

I have emphasized the marginal adult, but the occupational potential of his children is also blunted since low income and lack of education of parents are often associated with limited academic success and college attendance. The schools that children of the marginal whites attend have been neglected in the sixties. They are poor schools. The reliance on property taxes in local areas has resulted in non-affluent residents' voting down increases in school expenditures because they already feel overburdened. Greater federal support for education is needed. Perhaps there should be a graded index of need so that localities with the poorest populations would get the most aid, those with marginal-income populations less, and those with higher-income populations proportionately much less. Unfortunately, the issue is not only the amount of money expended and the relative share but the effectiveness with which it is spent. The experience with the Elementary and Secondary Education Act does not encourage optimism.

Junior and community colleges seem to be the most likely places for the children of the nonaffluent to continue their formal education. At present these schools are the higher-educational backwaters, with unclear or conflicting mandates and missions. A major reappraisal of their function is needed. My feeling is that the federal government should spend much more on them, including student stipends, and that these institutions should have more connections with better jobs than they now do.

So far I have suggested how to increase the educational chances of the marginals, but I think improved opportunities are not enough. I am more and more convinced that if the poor and the marginals are to get a fairer share of the good jobs the educational requirements for entrance into these jobs will have to be changed. I fear we have missed an opportunity for profound change in credentialism; the recent high-employment situation has made many aware of the irrationality of the credentialing and certifying processes. Unfortunately, structural changes, except for New Careers programs in public services, have been few. With the rising unemployment that will accompany the effort to dampen inflationary forces in the economy, my guess is that anti-credentialism will lose its force. But there may again soon be a rising employment situation. If there is, those groups favoring deep change in our society's approach to the recruitment and development of people for better jobs should be prepared to concentrate—as has not yet been done—on this fertile ground for structural transformations: testing, credentializing, licensing, hiring, and upgrading.

I hasten to add that we should not stop trying now, but we should not be disappointed if our efforts in the next months are not very successful—their effects will become more visible in a rising employment period.

Increasing Participation and Power

The subaffluent frequently feel not only neglected but powerless. The problem is complicated because gains in their areas of control and participation may be possible only at the cost of black emergence. Hopefully, perhaps very hopefully, if blacks and marginal whites can develop joint interests rather than competing claims and divisive interests, they may not fight each other. I have offered a small example of this mutuality of concern in recommending that changing neighborhoods should receive more aid for services and facilities than before. I think there are other possibilities—if the funds available for these two groups are increased markedly. A tight-money situation because of low growth and/or constrained federal budgets will worsen all situations.

Let me also indicate what I see as the issue of participation. Marginal whites in big cities frequently feel that they have little say in what takes place. Like many other Americans—rich as well as poor, white as well as black—they see bureaucracy, public or private, as unresponsive and insensitive to their needs—indeed, as out of control, at least their control. At the lowest level, various forms of grievance procedures, whether in the form of ombudsmen or review boards, are needed to facilitate responsiveness to aggrieved citizens. But the nonaffluent also want greater participation in decision-making. They have yet to make these feelings known, but I expect that as demands of blacks for increased power grow, similar concerns will be voiced by subaffluent whites, who also feel shut out. New mechanisms for citizen participation are needed in the city and nation, and not only in selected poverty or Model City neighborhoods.

And we should not act as though the work world can't be a possible arena for participation—a commonly held belief among many trade-union and labor-oriented social scientists. I agree that there will be little movement among workers toward more participation in plant or company decision-making as long as the union is seen only as protection against management arbitrariness. But I am impressed with the beginning of a regrowth of concern with worker participation in Great Britain and its strong vitality in Yugoslavia. I don't argue that worker participation is inevitably the wave of the future but I think the concept has a good chance of gaining strength.

Two economic situations are occurring simultaneously that I think may promote workers' interest in broader participation in decision-making at the plant level. The first is that the government is operating more and more as the guarantor of company profits (e.g., manipulation of tax policies and monetary and fiscal policies) and of employment, not only with broad economic policies to raise production and profits but also through retraining programs. Cash subsidies to workers, a negative income tax, or a family-allowance program would extend the emphasis on manpower programs, as would the hoped-for policy of the government functioning as an employer of last resort (which it already is for youth in the Neighborhood Youth Corps, although the role is officially disguised as training). The second is that we are likely to continue as a stop-go economy, with economic expansion leading to price rises that result in pressure to contract the economy by inducing unemployment. The security attached to the first change (toward guaranteed employment) and the insecurity attached to the second (a stop-go economy) mean that companies have arbitrary power in deciding which of its plants operate and under what conditions, and who gets retrained.

I am suggesting that the kind of economy we are evolving will make new types of participation more important. Coupled with the unrest within unions about the low level of democracy and dissatisfactions with many decisions and collective-bargaining contracts, the new style will not only broaden areas of negotiation but deepen the involvement of workers.

In conclusion, I look upon the new concern with subaffluent whites as a move that broadens the concern with the poor and the black to a commitment to improve the situation of those in the bottom half of the income scale in the United States. It is an effort to reduce the inequalities that exist in our society. It is an effort to improve not only the economic but the social, political, and psychological conditions of the disadvantaged, who are disadvantaged not by the old standards but by the new standards of well-being in our society.

Changing the economic circumstances of the subaffluent will not automatically change their sentiments, but it is a prerequisite. Improvement of the scope needed will require some structural changes. The efforts to attain them could provide—in the long run if not at present—the basis for a political movement of the disadvantaged half of society in cooperation with those of the advantaged who also seek a better world.

AFTERWORD

by Louise Kapp Howe

The ignored man of the sixties is the star of the seventies. His face gleams on the covers of national magazines like *Time* and *Newsweek,* his views are aired respectfully and faithfully by David, Walter and Frank and, more to the point, his political opinions are scrutinized microscopically by all the major politicians.

Ideologists of all stripes, from Wallaceites to Weathermen, have gone to the factories and offices and schools to woo him with pamphlets and promises and plans of better days. Republicans and Democrats alike are terming themselves neo-populists—whatever that precisely means—to prove they are each the friend of the little man. And if in the process we hear very little any more about the continuing stigma of American poverty and racism, we do not need a Presidential adviser to explain to us the politics of neglect.

The articles in this book have sought to describe the men and women of the white majority—who they are, how they are, and what they may become. We have also looked at a number of approaches now being suggested to encourage the political direction to the right and to the left. That Richard Nixon will be following, with only slight modifications, the famous Southern strategy is now the one thing that he has indeed made perfectly clear. The trick, as Andrew Hacker writes, "is to steal Wallace's thunder without repelling bedrock Republican voters, and the way to achieve this is not by imitating his method but rather by co-opting his message."

The problem, then, for all those trying to stave off the continued push to the right is how to appeal to the people of the white majority without retreating from the prior and still-priority commitment to the blacks and the poor. The belief that it can't be done rests on the assumption that race is the issue that concerns the majority of white Americans the most. But it is the opinion of almost all the contributors to this book that other issues are striking far closer to home: the estrangement of working-class youth from the affluent mainstream; the exploitation of women both in the factories and at home; the inadequacy of education and almost all the public services; the discontents of work; the feeling of powerlessness; and, most of all, the very real economic hardships faced by anyone living today between the boundaries of poverty and affluence.

If Nixon and friends are so ready to appeal to the worst instincts of the white majority, it is not an uninteresting experiment to see what can happen when you appeal to the best—appeal, however, in practical terms showing the advantage of change to both white and black (such as through measures suggested by Joan Jordan, S. M. Miller, Brendan Sexton and others), not, as in the past through abstract preachments calling for the working class to be the first to sacrifice for the sake of humanitarian America. It could in fact be the most critical experiment of our lives. For if the error of the sixties was that the people of the white majority were never given a concrete personal reason for social advance, the clear and present danger of the seventies is that they won't be warned in time against the threat of social repression being waged in their name.

Suggested Readings

For those who may wish to read more about the men and women living between poverty and affluence today, here are some of the books I found of particular interest. It is a personal, selected list, and is far from being a complete bibliography.

Berger, Bennett M. *Working-Class Suburb*. Berkeley: University of California Press, 1960. A study of auto workers and their families in suburbia.

Binzen, Peter. *Whitetown USA*. New York: Random House, 1970. Explores the problems of working-class whites and the schools their children attend.

Fuchs, Lawrence H., ed. *American Ethnic Politics*. New York: Harper Torchbooks, 1968. Thirteen essays by political scientists and sociologists on the intricacies of ethnic voting.

Gans, Herbert J. *The Levittowners*. New York: Pantheon, 1967. Ways of life and politics in a new suburban community.

Gordon, Milton M. *Assimilation in American Life*. New York: Oxford University Press, 1964. The role of race, religion and national origins.

Hoggart, Richard. *The Uses of Literacy*. London: Chatto & Windus, 1956. A fascinating and eloquent discussion of changes in working-class culture in England during the past forty years, with much of relevance to U.S. life as well.

Kohen, Melvin L. *Class and Conformity*. Homewood, Ill.: Dorsey Press, 1969. A study of the relationship of social class to human values.

Komarovsky, Mirra. *Blue-Collar Marriage*. New York: Random House, 1962. A comprehensive and sensitive study of almost every aspect of married life among a small group of working-class families.

Kornhauser, Arthur. *Mental Health of the Industrial Worker: A*

Detroit Study. New York: Wiley, 1965. Analyzes the differences in attitudes between the skilled and unskilled, factory and non-factory worker.

Leggett, John. *Class, Race and Labor*. New York: Oxford University Press, 1968. A study of working-class consciousness in Detroit.

Lipset, S. M., and Reinhard Bendix. *Social Mobility in Industrial Society*. Berkeley: University of California Press, 1950. The classic study shattering the illusion that America is the most fluid society in the world.

Rosen, B. C., H. J. Crockett and C. Z. Nunn, eds. *Achievement in American Society*. Cambridge, Mass.: Schenkman Publishing Co., 1969. The impact of class, race and ethnicity on occupational achievement.

Shostak, Arthur B. *Blue-Collar Life*. New York: Random House, 1969. A wide-ranging analysis, from child-rearing patterns to political preferences, of the American blue-collar worker.

Shostak, Arthur, and William Gomberg, eds. *Blue-Collar World*. Englewood Cliffs, N.J.: Prentice-Hall, 1964. Sixty-one essays about the style of life of the American blue-collar workers.

Terkel, Studs. *Division Street*. New York: Pantheon Books, 1967. Revealing interviews, bitter and sweet, with young and old, rich and poor, and in between, in Chicago, USA.

The Reacting Americans. American Jewish Committee pamphlet, 1968. Highlights of a national consultation on ethnic America held by the committee in June 1968.

INDEX

About the Author

Until this summer, LOUISE KAPP HOWE has been editor of *New Generation*. She is now a free-lance writer and editor and lives in San Francisco. At present she is working on a forthcoming book on youth.